Socialism and Self-Reliance in Tanzania

Socialism and Self-Reliance in Tanzania

Kimse A.B. Okoko

KPI
London and New York
In association with the University of Port Harcourt Press

First Published in 1987 by KPI Limited
11 New Fetter Lane, London EC4P 4EE

Distributed by
Routledge & Kegan Paul, Associated Book
Publishers (UK) Ltd.
11 New Fetter lane, London EC4P 4EE

Methuen Inc., Routledge & Kegan Paul
29 West 35th Street
New York, NY 10001, USA
and
J.M. Dent Pty Limited
112 Lewis Road
Knoxfield 3180
Victoria, Australia

Produced by Worts-Power Associates

Set in Times
by Alan Sutton Publishing Ltd
30 Brunswick Road
Gloucester GL1 1JJ
and Printed in Great Britain by
Dotesios Printers Ltd
Bradford-on-Avon, Wiltshire

ISBN 07103 0269-X

To Dad,
for his inspiration.

To Franebi,
who encouraged and took charge of the family
responsibilities in my absence.

To Eriye, Deniye and Keniebi
who were denied their fatherly care and love for
a whole year.

Contents

List of Tables

Chapter 5

Chapter 6

List of Abbreviations

AID:	Agency for International Development
BRALUP:	Bureau of Resource Assessment and Land Use Planning.
DAC:	Development Assistance Committee.
ECA:	Economic Commission for Africa.
ECLA:	Economic Commission for Latin America.
ERB:	Economic Research Bureau.
FAO:	Food and Agricultural Organization.
GDP:	Gross Domestic Product
GNP:	Gross National Product.
IBRD:	International Bank for Reconstruction and Development.
ILO:	International Labour Organization.
NDC:	National Development Corporation.
NUTA:	National Union of Tanganyika Workers.
OECD:	Organization for Economic Co-operation and Development.
OSAS:	Overseas Service Aid Scheme.
PRC:	Peoples Republic of China.
TANU:	Tanganyika African National Union.
TYL:	TANU Youth League.
UDI:	Unilateral Declaration of Independence.
UNCTAD:	United Nations Commission on Trade and Development.
UNDP:	United Nations Development Programme.
UNICEF:	United Nations International Children's Emergency Fund.
UNIDO:	United Nations Industrial Development Organization.
UNRISD:	United Nations Research Institute for Social Development.

UWT: Umoja Wa Wanawake Wa Tanzania.
VDC: Village Development Committee.

Acknowledgements

I wish to express my sincere appreciation to my colleagues at Carleton University, especially A.R. Cadribo, Gordon Dohle, John Idode, Martin W. Mason and Stewart Hyson whose incisive criticisms and suggestions proved invaluable in helping me complete this study. Special thanks are due to Eme N. Ekekwe who undertook the unenviable task of painstakingly going through the entire manuscript, making very astute criticisms and suggestions.

I am particularly grateful to Professors R. Bedeski, Steve Langdon, V.S. Wilson and Paul Rosen for their rich comments which helped greatly to clarify my ideas and above all for the guidance given me throughout the preparation of the draft manuscript.

Several institutions have helped me to write this study. The Ontario Government, through its Graduate Scholarship Programme, provided, in part, the funds which made it possible for me to complete the research in Tanzania, and I thank them. I am also very thankful to the University of Port Harcourt for their financial assistance and, perhaps more importantly, for their understanding and patience.

I wish to acknowledge my indebtedness to the various institutes attached to the University of Dar es Salaam for making available to me most of the relevant data for my study. Special thanks are due to the staff of the East Africana Collection of the Library of the University of Dar es Salaam, Professor M. Mbilinyi of the Institute of Education, Ndugu Mlawa of the Institute of Development Studies, Professors Mushi, Goran Hyden and Claude Ake (who was at the time with the University of Dar es Salaam) of the Department of Political Science, and several others who have contributed to this study whom I cannot thank individually here. As a collectivity, my obligation to them all is nevertheless very great. Scholarship is indeed a collective endeavour and I do not mean this in the formal sense. I should also like to thank Mrs.

Dulcie O'Neill for very skilfully typing the manuscript. She made the production of the final draft a lot less painful.

While I remain greatly indebted to them all, I accept full responsibility for whatever errors in judgement or interpretation that exist in this study.

Chapter 1

Introduction

This study develops from a keen interest in the politics of contemporary Africa, especially in regard to the seemingly intractable problem of political dependence with its economic correlate of underdevelopment.[1] The most interesting contemporary work on African political economy explores the link between economic underdevelopment and political dependence.[2] Development and independence are seen as moving in the same direction in the long run, even if in the short run there appear to be inherent contradictions in their immediate needs in a concrete situation.

For our purposes, the focus will, however, be manifestly different. We will emphasize the 'internal contradictions' (such as exist between the bureaucracy and the political leadership) within Tanzania rather than the external linkages. Thus the thesis of this study will be that: the absence of a systematic and coherent theoretical basis or the appropriate ideological framework for practical programmes of action, *inter alia*, is largely responsible for the failure to fundamentally transform most of the developing states in Africa along desired goals – which for many of them is 'socialism' – albeit, in various assortments.[3] We suggest (no novelty is claimed) that theory – ideological framework – in turn guides practice. As Cabral writes:

> To those who see in it a theoretical character we would
> recall that every practice produces a theory, and that if it
> is true that a Revolution can fail even though it is based
> on perfectly conceived theories, nobody has yet made a

successful revolution without a revolutionary theory.[4]

What we regard as the appropriate ideological framework is itself explained by our approach, which is socialist. Our preference for the socialist economic theory approach is based on the dismal failure of neo-classic economic theory (given its ahistoricism and its preoccupation with the techniques of keeping capitalism 'prosperous and crisis free') in explaining underdevelopment* and dependence.** Most of the theoretical and empirical analysis on the political economy of contemporary Africa clearly demonstrates, contrary to the earlier neo-classic economic theories of development,*** that the adoption of capitalism (euphemistically dubbed 'mixed economy') by the poor countries of Africa is likely to perpetuate underdevelopment in several important respects:

1   the increasing integration of the world capitalist system will tend to heighten the economic, political and cultural subordination of the countries of Africa to the rich metropolitan countries;

---

* In the interest of clarity and togetherness we shall refer to 'underdevelopment,' within the context of the developing states, as the: 'present peculiar mix of productive forces and production relations among the 'have-not' countries, which at the prevailing levels of human technological development constitutes the objective basis of their poverty and of the growing inequalities of income and wealth which the world system of production and exchange naturally produces.' See Clive Thomas, *Dependence and Transformation* (New York: Monthly Review Press, 1974), p. 25.

** We shall refer to 'dependence', to paraphrase Thomas, as the extent to which the economic structure of the economies of the developing states is predominantly shaped by foreign trade, foreign aid, payments, capital, technology, and decision-making to generate domestic economic processes. *Ibid.*, p. 30.

***By 'development' we shall mean: 'a change process characterized by increased productivity, equalization in the distribution of the social product, and the emergence of indigenous institutions whose relations with the outside world, and particularly with the developed centres of international economy, are characterized by equality rather than dependence and subordination.' See E.A. Brett, *Colonialism and Underdevelopment in East Africa: The Politics of Economic Change 1919–1939* (New York: NOK Publishers, Ltd., 1973), p. 18.

2   that capitalist institutions within African countries aggravate rather than diminish inequalities in the distribution of income and power; and

3   that capitalism in these countries will be unable to promote development sufficiently rapid to provide benefits to the whole population, let alone reduce the income gap between the poor and the rich countries.

As a science which deals with the 'laws of development,' socialist economic theory has always stood for a methodologically integrated treatment of philosophy, political economy and the methods of socialist construction. Our task is how, on the basis of a planned socialist transformation, we can overcome under-development and poverty, raise the levels of development of the productive forces, improve the quality and standard of living of the broad mass of the population, eliminate exploitation of man by man, and achieve equality in the distribution of income and wealth. We shall argue in this study that the political leadership of Tanzania is committed to the socialist approach to achieve these objectives.[5] Our aim therefore is to show whether the policies and programmes in the key areas of education, Ujamaa Vijijini, industrialization and foreign aid, were designed to reflect and achieve these objectives based on their ideological framework.

It should be clear, by now, that basic to our choice is an underlying assumption that there are only two viable alternatives to development in the context of our definition.* And since we have rejected 'capitalism' as being inappropriate, 'socialism' becomes the only logical viable alternative for us.

Our decision to focus on the interplay between the appropriate ideological framework and practical programmes of action stems from the fact that much of the most important analysis of dependence in contemporary Africa has tended to focus on external linkages as the decisive link in the 'causal' chain – hence

---

* What we are saying in effect is that in the context of the modern world there are two basic systems of economic and social organization – capitalism and socialism – with several variations, of course, within these broad classifications (e.g., democratic socialism, 'humanistic socialism,' welfare capitalism). The broad distinctions between the two systems to a very large extent however remain valid.

the key notion of 'disengagement'. Consequently, many of the internal contradictions which forestall efforts to mitigate the effects of underdevelopment and dependence in the transition phase to socialism have been largely subsumed under or subordinated to the analysis of the relationship between international capitalism and underdevelopment. Both Frank and Shivji, for example, represent this school. Thus Shivji writes in the context of Tanzania:

> . . . the fundamental contradictions in the Tanzanian society are not to be found in the rural peasantry (including the big farmers) but in the content and nature of the relationship of Tanzania's economy with international capitalism.[6]

We intend in this study to highlight the importance of the external linkages but our major focus of analysis is the internal contradictions. We will argue that these reflect, to a large degree, the non-congruence between the appropriate ideological framework and the practical programmes of action initiated in post-Arusha Tanzania.

The starting point of our analysis must therefore be the theoretical underpinnings of the elaborated version of Ujamaa* – socialism and self-reliance – which forms the basis for practical programmes of action in Tanzania. A word of caution must be made. For any given country one is bound to find lines of causation** that do not fit easily into more general theories. Conversely, too strong a devotion to theory always carries with it the danger that one may over-emphasize facts that fit a theory

---

* Walter Rodney describes the word Ujamaa as having been already popularized in two contexts: firstly, as referring to the extended family of African communalism; secondly, with reference to the creation of agricultural collectives known as Ujamaa villages; and we will add a third, with reference to self-reliance.

** We do not necessarily intend to posit a monocausal model. But we recognize that at the heart of the problem of the kind of intelligibility aimed at by the student of politics is the problem of whether causal explanations of human actions are appropriate. See David Hume, *A Treatise of Human nature*, ed. by L.A. Selby-Bigge (Oxford: The Clarendon Press, 1888), p. 170.

beyond their importance in the history of individual countries. Now, the thesis that the absence of a theoretical basis or the appropriate ideological framework for practical programmes of action is the underlying cause of the failure of the developing states of Africa to fundamentally transform their societies (this implies a congruence between theory and practice), has in essence been posited by Ake. He argues that the failure of African leaders to initiate any fundamental transformations in the new states of Africa is largely a result of 'congruence of current political ideologies (which are in themselves a legacy of the colonial past), and political economies'.[7] Paradoxically, congruency also carries with it the seeds of its own negation through what Ake calls 'defensive radicalism'.[8] Indeed, as Carr wrote earlier:

> The facts of History are indeed facts about individuals, but not about actions of individuals performed in isolation and not about the motives real or imaginary, from which individuals suppose themselves to have acted. They are facts about the relations of individuals to one another in society and about the social forces which produce from the actions of individuals results often at variance with, and sometimes opposite to, the results which they themselves intended.[9]

We basically agree with Ake that the salient features of the post-independence ideology of the nationalist leaders in Africa are the same features which have dominated all ideologies associated with the establishment and consolidation of the 'dictatorship of the bourgeoisie'* (based on his thesis of the congruence of ideologies and political economies). But we would, as a point of departure, argue that the post-independence ideology of the leadership in Tanzania is significantly different from that of most of the other African leaders. The post-Arusha leadership in Tanzania has accepted 'socialism' as the 'national ethic' and has consciously directed its energies on how Tanzania can most effectively achieve

---

* It is the 'dictatorship of the bourgeoisie' to the extent that we see the governments of these countries coming to power through bourgeois revolutions.

a transition to a socialist society. It has not been impelled by 'defensive radicalism' to the brink of socialism.[10] We will further postulate that in general there has emerged in post-Arusha Tanzania policies and programmes which are based on a clearer definition of, and a growing commitment to, socialist solutions for Tanzania's development problems. Such problems as we shall examine include:

1 The relationship between a policy of socialism and self-reliance with that of continued aid from both socialist and capitalist countries, with the capitalist ones following very different development strategies. Is there a contradiction between receiving aid and self-reliance? In this regard, has the Chinese experience (1950–60) with the Soviet Union anything to offer?
2 Similarly, on the industrial front, how do we reconcile the apparent acceptance by the National Development Corporation (NDC) and other parastatals of the need to depend on foreign consultants and partnerships in the industrial sector, with the policy of socialism and self-reliance?
3 As regards the policy of establishing Ujamaa villages, is a policy of persuasion realistic or in fact possible in a society where the benefits of such a policy are not fully appreciated, not only among the rural population but even among those charged with its implementation? Does the transformation of the otherwise scattered homesteads to Ujamaa villages require a standard format throughout the country? Are the primary goals of the Ujamaa Vijijini scheme, control and management of the rural population or maximum production and self-sufficiency?
4 What are the educational and therefore the socialization imperatives of planning for socialism and self-reliance in order not to obscure the importance of ideological considerations and political choices at every stage of the process?

This study is therefore in large part an analysis and a critical evaluation of the practical programmes of action of post-Arusha Tanzania relevant to the task of socialist construction and transformation under a socialist-oriented national leadership. We would, of course, in our analysis remind ourselves of Saul's observation that for a realistic discussion of policy:

> . . . an abstract evaluation of the content of policy in
> particular sectors of the economy and the society which is
> carried out without reference to a parallel exploration of
> the context within which such a policy is generated very
> quickly becomes meaningless. For seeming inconsistencies
> in policy actually may reflect social and political realities
> and diverse pressures as much or more than they evidence
> mere lack of intellectual clarity! And the ability both to
> articulate and to implement particular kinds of policies will
> be vitally dependent upon the nature of existing institu-
> tions and the character of the men who influence and staff
> them.[11]

It now remains for us to delineate the plan of the study. In
scope, the study is limited to a description and an analysis of
certain key areas of policy, programmes and practices in the
political, social and economic realms relevant to the difficult phase
of social, political and economic transformation to socialism in
post-Arusha Tanzania. It is a case study concerned with the
working relationship between the living institutions of the government and party and the political, economic and social goals
towards which the leadership aspired.

Structurally, the study has been divided into seven chapters.
Chapter 1, the introduction, states the basic hypotheses and the
problems. In Chapter 2 we undertake a broad theoretical overview
of socialism and self-reliance with reference to the developing
states of Africa, and in particular Tanzania, with the view of
establishing a basis on which to premise our later analysis of the
programmes of action. In Chapters 3 through 6, our analysis will
focus critically on the role of four key areas of policy and practical
programmes of action designed to aid the process of transition to
socialism in Tanzania. We will enquire as to whether these policies
and programmes are in fact complementary to the desired national
goal of socialism and self-reliance; whether they are congruent
with the theoretical basis or the appropriate ideological framework
upon which they are claimed to be predicated. More specifically,
in Chapter 3 we examine the role of education and
political socialization in implementing the policy of socialism and
self-reliance. In Chapter 4 we examine the policy and implementation of Ujamaa Vijijini in rural Tanzania. The role of the NDC

in building a socialist and self-reliant Tanzania is examined in Chapter 5, and in Chapter 6 we take a close look at the international dimension of the policy of socialism and self-reliance in the context of foreign aid.

Finally, we shall attempt in the concluding chapter to not only pull all these strands together but also to evaluate the possibilities that lie ahead for Tanzania, based on our analysis, in her attempt to break away from the dependency cord in the light of her own theoretical formulations.

Chapter 1 Introduction

1. We do not intend to further explore the link between dependence and underdevelopment here since this has been done by able scholars in that field of specialization.

2. It is perhaps significant that much of the most important material on the political economy of Africa and the Third World in general has been produced by scholars who are Marxists, Marxist oriented, or have used Marxist methodology in their analysis. For a general guide to some of the most significant publications in the field see: S. Amin, *Accumulation on a World Scale* (London: Monthly Review Press, 1974); G. Arrighi and J.S. Saul, *Essays on the Political Economy of Africa* (New York: Monthly Review Press, 1973); P. Baran, *The Political Economy of Growth* (New York: Modern Reader Paperbacks, 1968); L. Cliffe and J.S. Saul, eds., *Socialism in Tanzania* (2 vols.) (Nairobi: East African Publishing House, 1972); J. Cockcroft and G. Frank et al., *Dependence and Underdevelopment* (New York: Doubleday and Co., 1972); G. Frank, *Capitalism and Underdevelopment in Latin America* (New York: Monthly Review Press, 1967); P. Gutkind and Waterman, eds., *African Social Studies: A Radical Reader* (London: Heinemann, 1975); P. Gutkind and I. Wallerstein, eds., *The Political Economy of Contemporary Africa* (Beverly Hills: Sage Publications, 1976); C. Leys, *Underdevelopment in Kenya* (London: Heinemann, 1975); Oxaal et al., *Beyond The Sociology of Development* (London: Cass, 1975); W. Rodney, *How Europe Underdeveloped Africa* (Dar es Salaam: Tanzania Publishing House, 1972); J. Rweyemamu, *Underdevelopment and Industrialization in Tanzania* (Nairobi: Oxford University Press, 1973); A. Seidman, *Comparative Development Strategies in East Africa* (Nairobi: East African Publishing House, 1972); I. Shivji, *The Silent Class Struggle* (Dar es Salaam: Tanzania Publishing House,

1973); T. Szentes, *The Political Economy of Underdevelopment* (Budapest: Akademiai Kiado, 1971); C. Thomas, *Dependence and Transformation* (New York: Monthly Review Press, 1974) and M. Yaffey, *Balance of Payments Problems of a Developing Country: Tanzania* (Munich: Weltforum Verlag, 1970).

3. We find the various assortments of 'socialism' in such writings as: Senghor's African Socialism, Kaunda's Humanism, Tom Mboya's African Socialism, etc. For a general work on the various assortments of 'African Socialism' see: Friedland and Rosberg, eds., *African Socialism* (Stanford: University of Stanford Press, 1964).

4. A. Cabral, *Revolution in Guinea* (London: Stage 1, 1969), p. 12.

5. We recognize that our position is diametrically opposed to those of Shivji, Forster-Carter and perhaps Ake. Shivji, for example, argues in his *Class Struggles in Tanzania* that the progressive initiatives of Nyerere and his supporters (post-Arusha) are essentially deceptions, exercises in ideological manipulation in the narrow class interest of the 'bureaucratic bourgeoisie' or, at best, as reluctant concessions to popular forces. This essentially is the view of Forster-Carter and perhaps Ake. On the other hand, both Raikes, Pratt and Green, for example, do not think that Ujamaa policy serves the interest of the 'petty-bourgeoisie.' Indeed, Raikes thinks that a view such as Shivji's is 'oversimplified and invalid.' See P.L. Raikes, 'Ujamaa and Socialism,' *Review of African Political Economy*, No. 3 (1975), 39.

6. *I. Shivji, 'Tanzania: The Silent Class Struggle' in Cliffe and Saul, eds., Socialism in Tanzania (Vol. 2) Policies* (Nairobi: East African Publishing House, 1973), p. 304.

7. Claude Ake, 'The Congruence of Political Economies and Ideolgies in Africa' in Gutkind and Wallerstein, eds., *The Political Economy of Contemporary Africa* (Beverly Hills: Sage Publications, 1976), p. 206.

8. Ake describes 'defensive radicalism' as a delay tactic by African political leaders in order to hang on to power in spite of the 'revolutionary pressures' from a 'brutally exploited' mass of the population who have become conscious of their extreme poverty and the injustice of economic inequality. The tactics involve making concessions or rather to be seen to make concessions to the demands for economic equality, for example from the exploited masses. It also includes making pious statements about the need to improve the lot of the common man. But it remains essentially a progressive force in the sense that as the political leadership buys time with 'defensive radicalism,' it also fosters the development of consciousness among the masses and hence 'class struggle' as the latter become aware of the contradictions of the social order to which they belong. Hence 'defensive radicalism' carries with it the germs of its own negation.

9. E.H. Carr, *What is history?* (London: Penguin Books, 1964), p. 52.

10. While it is true that the Arusha Declaration reflects, among other
     things, the sad experiences of the country following the unexpec-
     ted withdrawal of aid by Britain and West Germany, as well as
     the army mutiny and the student riots, we suggest that it did not
     reflect a dissatisfaction of the masses with the country's leader-
     ship. Quite the contrary; the President enjoyed the support of the
     masses even in those difficult times. Thus, to describe the Arusha
     Declaration as a symbolic act of 'defensive radicalism' appears to
     us as an exaggeration. More importantly, while many of Nyerere's
     counterparts in Africa do not contemplate initiating real changes
     in the socio-economic structure of their countries, as they play the
     game of 'defensive radicalism', we would argue (unlike Shivji)
     that the post-Arusha policies in Tanzania on foreign aid, educ-
     ation and the villagization scheme, for example, were genuine
     attempts by the political leadership to 'improve the lot of the mass
     of the population.'
11. Cliffe and Saul, eds., *Socialism in Tanzania (Vol. 2), Policies*
     (Nairobi: East African Publishing House, 1973), Introduction,
     p. 4.

Chapter 2

Socialism and Self-Reliance in Tanzania: A Theoretical Overview

. . . the deeper I enter into the cultures and the
political circles the surer I am that the great
danger that threatens Africa is the absence of
ideology.

Frantz Fanon

While the historic importance of the October 1917 revolution in
Russia and the subsequent institutionalization of socialism in that
country are generally acknowledged, the origins of socialism as well
as the meaning of the term itself are still subject to intense debate
amongst scholars. And although it is not necessary for the purpose
of this study to trace the genesis of socialism[1] (much has already
been written in the field), it cannot be overemphasized that the
theoretical content of socialism as an ideology or as a set of
institutions and structures cannot be divorced from the
circumstances of its birth, as though it were a timely protest
against inequality or injustice which accidentally took on flesh at
one particular moment. In essence therefore, socialism came into
being as a result of dislocations following the modern bourgeois
economic and political revolutions, partly to develop and partly to
oppose the forces unleashed in this period.[2] It is necessary to point
out the saliency of this historical development because, as we shall
see later, it informs Nyerere's understanding of the development
of modern socialism and therefore it affects the institutionalization
of socialism in Tanzania. In a clear if over-simplified statement on
the development of modern socialism Nyerere writes:

11

> European Socialism was born of the Agrarian Revolution
> and the Industrial Revolution which followed it. The
> former created the 'landed' and the 'landless' classes in
> society; the latter produced the modern capitalist and the
> Industrial proletariat. These two revolutions planted the
> seeds of conflict within society, and not only was European
> Socialism born of that conflict, but its apostles sanctified
> the conflict itself into a philosophy. The European
> Socialist cannot think of his Socialism without its father –
> capitalism![3]

So far we are agreed that the various renderings or interpretations of the term socialism are at best problematic. The question then is how do these compare with the conceptualization of the term by the socialist theoreticians who are themselves almost invariably the political leaders of the developing states of Africa and in particular Tanzania? Have they improved upon the clarity of the term or created even a bigger jungle (no pun intended)?

In the preceding discussion we argued that the theoretical content of socialism cannot be divorced from the circumstances of its birth. Thus socialism or 'African socialism', in its most popularized form, was born of the post-colonial crises of economic development and national identity.[4] In this sense, like the classical varieties of socialism, African socialism also underscores the primacy of the economic element in socialism. It is therefore not surprising that the overriding theme in the literature on African socialism (since it came to vogue in the 1960's) has consistently been economic. Thus in their introduction to *African Socialism* Friedland and Rosberg conclude: 'One of the most significant features of African socialism is its identification with economic development.'[5] In much the same vein Mohan writes: 'And when they talk of "socialism" the African leaders mean economic development; many of them use "development" and "socialism" interchangeably. That there is a "capitalist" as well as a "socialist" way of development receives but little recognition in their rhetoric; most African leaders appear to acknowledge only the "socialist" way.'[6] More concretely, Nkrumah, for example, argued that the presuppositions of capitalism were contrary to those of African society and that 'with little or no investment capital of our own, with a very small core of technical men, we have to point out

12

to our people that the fastest rate of development accompanied with a humane distribution of the largess of progress could be achieved only by following the socialist path of development.'[7] President Dacko, of the Central African Republic, echoed the same sentiments when he commented: 'There is no African capitalism. . . . Thus, by the very force of things, we are proceeding toward a socialist economy, with the state more and more forced to intervene.'[8]

But behind the façade of consensus in the economic primacy of African socialism lies a seemingly gaping divide in the interpretations or renderings of the term itself. In their various formulations the adherents of African socialism stress the existence in African societies of an organic relationship between the individual and community. Thus, an organic relationship, *inter alia*, is then acclaimed as the traditional foundation of African socialism. Nyerere asserts:

> In primitive African society, this question of the limits of
> responsibility as between the individual and society in
> which he lives was not very clearly defined. The traditional
> African community was a small one, and the African could
> not think of himself apart from that community in which
> he lived. He was an individual; he had his wife – or wives
> – and children so he belonged to a family. But the family
> merged into a clan or tribe. Thus he saw himself all the
> time as a member of a community, but he saw no struggle
> between his own interests and those of his community, for
> his community to him was an extension of his family. He
> might have seen a conflict between himself and another
> individual member of the same community, but with the
> community itself, he saw no struggle. . . . He is not a
> member of a 'commune', some artificial unit of human
> being; he is a member of a genuine community or a
> brotherhood.[9]
>
> In our traditional African society we were individuals
> within the community. We took care of the community,
> and the community took care of us. We neither needed
> nor wished to exploit fellow men.[10]

But while these leaders see virtue in a fuzzy definition of the limits of responsibility between the individual and society, as being conducive to the establishment of socialism and therefore 'rapid economic development,' on the contrary the lack of 'structural differentiation' has been pointed out by the proponents of structural-functionalism, as being one of the prime indicators of 'underdevelopment'. What seems clear, however, is that the attempt to differentiate African socialism from its more general variety has to be seen as another indicator of the search for original concepts and the general distrust towards theories which do not take into account the different socio-economic conditions in Africa. Foreign solutions cannot be adopted and imposed over African reality.[11]

More fundamentally, however, by attempting to paint an idyllic traditional African society to the extent that it meant common ownership of the means of production (i.e. land)[12] and the existence of an organic relationship between the individual and the community, the advocates of African socialism were implying a classless society. In short, it was a justificatory theory for the uniqueness of African socialism. One of the hallmarks of the classical varieties of socialism centres around the recognition of classes in a socialist society rooted in the relations of production. Little wonder then that the search for African socialism has meant the rejection by most of its advocates of classical Marxism. The following examples from the literature of African socialism typify the pristine representation of traditional African society on classes:

> The sharp class divisions that once existed in Europe have no place in African socialism and no parallel in African society. No class problem arose in the traditional African society and *none exists today among Africans*. The class problem in Africa, therefore, is largely one of prevent-ion . . .[13]

> It is evident that African socialism can no longer be that of Marx and Engels, which was designed in the nineteenth century according to European scientific methods and realities. Now, it must take into consideration African realities. This is particularly necessary because Marx and

Engels were not anticolonial. Engels defended classical
slavery and Marx supported British colonization of
India . . .[14]

. . . our Negro-African society is a classless society, which
is not the same as saying that it has no hierarchy or division of labour.[15]

And finally,

> African socialism, on the other hand, did not have the
> 'benefit' of the Agrarian Revolution or the Industrial
> Revolution. It did not start from the existence of conflic-
> ting 'classes' in society. Indeed, I doubt if the equivalent
> for the word 'class' exists in any indigenous African lan-
> guage;* for language describes the ideas of those who
> speak it, and the idea of 'class' or 'caste' was non-existent
> in African society.[16]

Indeed, even the 'Marxist' Sekou Toure could not resist the
temptation. Thus in assessing the notion of a classless society, he
concludes:

> To introduce the notion of 'class struggle' is completely to
> misread the African situation. There can be no ground for
> class struggle in a society that is not divided into antagon-
> istic classes. When can there be talk of class antagonism?
> When one social class imposes on others a relationship of
> oppression and exploitation. And it is able to do so when
> it holds exploitation and oppression media: capital and
> privately owned production media . . . Let us ask this
> question: have we such conditions in the Republic of
> Guinea, a country where all major sectors of the nation's

---

* It must be pointed out that the fact that there is no word for 'class'
in any indigenous African language does not necessarily preclude the
existence of classes. Surely, it is highly unlikely that there is a word for
'cancer' in traditional indigenous languages but that does not mean that
there were no people suffering from cancer.

> economic life are under direct control by the state, a country where land property is abolished, a country where farmers and wage-earners work out the laws and have extensive powers of management?[17]

Notwithstanding the welter of interpretations, there emerge two discernible poles. At one pole are those political leaders[18] like Nkrumah and Sekou Toure, who argue that there is only one socialism – scientific socialism[19] – while at the other extreme are those political leaders who, in wanting to assert the independence of 'socialism' in Africa, find solace in the doctrine of 'African socialism'. The late Tom Mboya and the Kenya government represent this latter category. Thus in restating the independence of African socialism the Kenyan government's white paper on African socialism states:

> In the phrase 'African socialism,' the word 'African' is not introduced to describe a continent to which foreign ideology is to be transplanted. It is meant to convey the African roots of a system that is itself African in characteristics. African socialism is a term describing an African political and economic system that is positively African, not being imported from any country or being a blueprint of any foreign ideology, but capable of incorporating useful and compatible techniques from whatever source.[20]

Among the adherents of African socialism there are some basic commonly shared notions. But by far the most important and consistent commonly shared notion is that which deals with property (mainly in the form of land) and classes which we have already discussed.

If we consider the fact that the nineteenth-century pioneers of socialism were labelled Utopian by Marx and Engels, primarily as a result of their failure to appreciate the fact that human social development proceeded through certain stages, and because their model socialist societies did not take cognizance of the reality of class struggles,[21] African socialism too is Utopian in 'its refusal to come to grips with the class relations in which Africans are enmeshed and in its romanticised ignorance of the stages of African historical development.'[22]

To be sure, to identify areas of consensus in the conceptualization of African socialism (e.g., on class and the common ownership of land) by its proponents, is not to deny the existence of a plurality in the meaning of the term itself. Quite the contrary. We find also a considerable degree of ambiguity in the meaning of the term 'socialism', not unlike that which exists among both the adherents and opponents of the classical varieties of socialism discussed earlier. Again let us take a look at a few representative examples of the definition of 'socialism' in Africa:

> We stand for a middle course (between communism and capitalism), for a democratic socialism, which goes so far as to integrate spiritual values, a socialism which ties in with the old ethical current of the French socialists . . .[23]

> When I talk of African socialism I refer to those proved codes of conduct in the African societies which have, over the ages, conferred dignity on our people and afforded them security regardless of their station in life. I refer to universal charity which characterized our societies and I refer to the African's thought processes and cosmological ideas which regard man, not as a social means, but as an end and entity in the society.[24]

And finally,

> 'Ujamaa' then or 'familyhood' describes our socialism. It is opposed to capitalism, which seeks to build a happy society on the basis of the exploitation of man by man; and is equally opposed to doctrinaire socialism which seeks to build its happy society on a philosophy of inevitable conflict between man and man.[25]

In the light of the above discussion we can reasonably conclude that the advocates of African socialism have failed to contribute any more than the earlier attempts towards providing greater clarity and precision of meaning to the term 'socialism'. This should not be surprising, for most of these adherents, as we shall see later, not only use the rhetoric of socialism as a guide to their actual policies or objectives, but as an ideological plank among other devices for their monopoly of political power. In short, there is an apparent absence of congruence between the officially proclaimed 'ideology' and actual practice; and it is difficult to see how such an eclectic approach can yield a credible systematic and coherent body of theory to guide action. Theory, we maintain, is inextricably interwoven with practice. Besides, even those very few countries who are consciously attempting to initiate a transition to socialism (e.g. Tanzania) find themselves confronted with the fact that Marxist economic theory, as it has developed so far, does not deal adequately or satisfactorily with the problems of developing the productive forces of such economies during the transition period.[26] To be more precise, we may say that 'socialist economic theory does not deal adequately with the problems of designing an economic strategy for transforming underdeveloped economies.'[27] In this sense, then, the degree of variation in the meaning of the term is to a large extent perhaps a reflection of the unsatisfactory state of Marxist economic theory and the lack of a satisfactory strategy for transforming such economies.

What clearly emerges from our discussion is the palpable fact that 'African socialism,' in contrast to most other movements of socialism, has not been the product of a single thinker. The history of socialist thought is marked by fairly clear relationships between individual thinkers and the ideological movements to which they gave birth. African socialism differs in that no single leader has been distinctively and uniquely associated with the ideology. Rather the ideology of African socialism has been the product of diverse leaders operating within a variety of exigencies in their own countries, which helps partly to account for the lack of development of a unified theory.[28]

Let us now take a closer look at what we have referred to above as the absence of congruence between officially proclaimed ideology and actual practice. There is a considerable body of evidence (especially in the growing literature on the political economy of contemporary Africa) that most of the economies in Africa are neo-colonial* in character and dependencies of international capi-

---

* We, like Colin Leys, have no need to depart from the definition of neo-colonialism offered by Kwame Nkrumah which essentially is: the survival of the colonial system in spite of the formal recognition of

talism. One of the characteristic manifestations of underdevelopment, writes Clive Thomas, is 'the present nature of the structural dependence of the small underdeveloped economies on international capitalism.'[29] He defined structural dependence as 'the extent to which the economic structure of these economies depends on foreign trade, payments, capital, technology, and decision-making to generate domestic economic processes.'[30] We have, on our part, no intention to deviate from this definition. Although we will not explore in detail the economic aspects of dependence and underdevelopment, what interests us is the fact that most of the 'self-styled' socialist states of Africa have economic structures no different from those which have clearly opted for a non-socialist economic system; this in spite of the loud criticism levied against the material and moral excesses of capitalism which depend upon the 'exploitation of man by man'. Indeed, capitalist forms of production and organization have grown in scope and significance within these countries partly, of course, in response to the growth of international capitalism. Commenting on this existential duality, Jitendra Mohan writes: '. . . the actual economic and social policies followed by many African 'socialist' leaders differ but slightly from the policies followed by those who do not feel themselves in need of the socialist label.'[31] Thus the Kenyan government white paper on African socialism and its application to planning states in no unclear terms that, '. . . unlike many countries that have eliminated many successful economic mechanics on narrow ideological grounds, Kenya is free to pick and choose those methods that have been proven in practice and are adaptable to Kenya conditions regardless of the ideologies that others may attach to it.'[32]

But beneath the seemingly conflicting dichotomy between theory and practice lurks a basic congruence.[33] It is the existence of a congruence between the political ideologies of the 'socialist'

political independence in emerging countries which become victims of an indirect and subtle form of domination by political, economic, social, military or technical means. Cited in Colin Leys, *Underdevelopment in Kenya: The Political Economy of Neo-Colonialism* (London: Heinemann, 1975). p. 26.

leaders (which in practice are non-socialist) and their political economies (again non-socialist in practice), authenticated by the stamp of colonialism and patented by neo-colonialism. The emergence of such a situation was not unexpected given the uncritical decision of these post-independence 'socialist' leaders to maintain exploitative relations and a stratification system that they dominated. Equally significant is the fact that they are unable or rather unwilling to 'change existing relations of production and to redistribute available resources in a radically egalitarian direction.'[34] In short, they have maintained an essentially non-socialist socio-economic system reminiscent of the pre-independence era.

But our agreement with Ake stops here. For to go on from here as Ake has done, to argue that the differences that do exist between 'progressive' socialist leaders such as Julius Nyerere and Sekou Toure, and 'conservative' non-socialist leaders such as Senghor, Mobutu, Houphuet-Boigny and Kenyatta, are more 'apparent than real' poses real problems. For if it is true that the differences are not real then we can safely conclude that there are no 'progressive' leaders or countries in the world. Ake states that:

> Because in all African countries, the leaders have held tenaciously to power, change of government is brought about only by force . . . the political systems of Africa have become uniformly monolithic . . . power has become centralized, and opposition to those in power is illegitimate . . . all African countries are now de facto one party systems in which the masses have been effectively depoliticized, in the sense that their political participation has been reduced to choices which are totally inconsequential.[35]

Yet leaders such as the late Mao Tse-tung and Fidel Castro, (widely acclaimed as progressive and socialist in commitment, in the sense that they have consciously struggled to end, *inter alia*, the exploitation of man by man) have ruled and are ruling countries which fit his description almost perfectly. Let us go on. As a further proof, Ake continued his indictment of these two camps by saying that the states they rule are all undemocratic because:

> top party positions are not effectively elective, they are
> rather 'effectively co-optive' and only 'formally elective';
> . . . party elections are not free in the sense that any party
> member cannot offer himself as a candidate for office and
> in the sense that members of the party are not free to
> choose between the candidates who offer themselves for
> elective office.[36]

Again we may ask whether this is not largely true of China or Cuba
or for that matter any other socialist country? But in anticipation
of possible criticisms of his position, since he had earlier maintained that the objective forces in Africa are essentially identical
and hence it will be difficult to 'explain why some countries will
prefer the appearance of a particular ideological complexion,
while others prefer another . . . [Ake argues that] if the thoughts
we have and the images we seek to project are merely epi-
phenomenal, African leaders should seek to project the same
image.'[37] The answer to this paradox, he continues, is that far from
contradicting the thesis (on congruency) the difference in question
corroborates it. It corrobates it in the sense that the difference is
not due to caprice or choice; it is determined by objective
conditions. The difference reflects social forces that are for the
moment more potent in the African countries that we call 'progressive'. Every prognostication indicates that these social forces
are likely to become stronger in the 'reactionary' countries so that
the difference in ideological posture will be obliterated.[38]

Now, if these social forces are correctly identified as (i) desperate poverty and (ii) the consciounesss of the burden of poverty and
the injustice of economic inequality, it begs the question: is the
desperate poverty in Tanzania any more serious than that in Niger,
Chad etc.? Or is the consciousness of the burden of poverty and
the injustice of economic inequality of the masses more in
Tanzania than in these countries or even in Nigeria? The answer,
of course, is 'No'. For one thing the UN study lists Tanzania and
these countries as the 25 poorest countries in the world. No, the
reasons for the ideological identity of these leaders must be found
somewhere else. But before we identify the source, it should be
clear that we believe there are essential differences between such
progressive leaders as Nyerere and the 'conservative,' 'reactionary' leaders such as Senghor, Mobutu, Kenyatta and

Houphouet-Boigny.* In this regard, we are in agreement with Giovanni Arrighi and John Saul's evaluation of Tanzania:

> Tanzania is, perhaps, the country in contemporary Africa where socialist aspirations figure most prominently and interestingly in the development equation, and most powerfully affect the kind of policies which are being pursued.[39]

That we have devoted so much space to 'congruency' can be easily justified when seen in the context of its centrality to the thesis of this study. The presumed identity of these leaders is false in the sense that the perceived congruence between their political ideologies and political economies is more apparent than real. It is so to the extent that, in theory at least, these leaders have openly professed to be 'socialists' while in practice they have been anything but 'socialists'. The reason for this divergence, we argue, is largely a result of the absence of the appropriate ideological framework with which to determine and then guide the actual programmes of action. In other words, they lack an appropriate theoretical (ideological) framework consistent with the task of transformation in the 'unscientific gropings' for a development strategy. In the absence of the appropriate framework, the development strategy adopted has been very much, *inter alia*, a derivative of the import-substitution industrialization strategy reminiscent of the Economic Commission for Latin America. Concedes Thomas, 'Although the situation cannot be attributed simply to the absence of adequate socialist theory, the absence has not helped the struggle for socialism within these countries. Indeed, from the point of view of practical politics, neo-classical economic theories and policies have managed to maintain a nearly impregnable predominance in these countries.'[40]

Indeed, the same conclusion was reached by Fitch and

---

* This is especially true when judged against the criteria (based on key socialist principles) of the common ownership and control of the means of production, equality and democratic participation. In these, there is strong evidence to show that both Kenya and Senegal, for example, have demonstrated far less resolve *vis-à-vis* Tanzania (to put it mildly) to achieve these objectives.

Oppenheimer in their searching analysis of Ghana's 1966 military *coup d'état*:

> Pre-1961, Ghana had been guided by a development strategy formulated by W. Arthur Lewis. This strategy which emphasized total dependence on foreign capital to industrialize the country, brought nearly complete disaster . . . If all of Ghana's post-independence history was an experiment in socialism (they continue) and if that experiment failed, then it can be argued that socialism is really unworkable in Africa . . . We will try to show the failure of the socialist experiment in Ghana did not lie in the peculiarity of African circumstances, and still less in the psychology of a single man. It failed because the attempt to break with Ghana's colonial past was not made soon enough, and because when it was made it was not complete enough.[41]

At this point it is essential that we clear up what might appear as a problem in our thesis. We had suggested earlier that there is a sufficient body of evidence in the literature to show that the characteristic features of dependence and underdevelopment in the developing states of Africa and beyond are largely a direct consequence of the neo-classical capitalist economies of these countries. In other words, neo-colonialism breeds dependence relations and underdevelopment. If it is our basic position that the absence of congruence between ideological framework and practice consistent with the actual programmes of action is responsible for the failure of these countries to affect fundamental changes, then the problem should not arise where there is congruence between a non-socialist theory and a non-socialist development strategy. But it is more than this. We have seen that the neo-colonial capitalist economic system breeds dependence relations. And since most if not all of these countries see the most pressing economic task as that of breaking loose from the dependence cord, then it is illogical, indeed irrational, at least in theory, to continue to adopt a strategy of economic development that reinforces that condition. We on our part accept the proposition that only a socialist economic approach can achieve this desired objective. Thus the seeming problem with our thesis evaporates. We would submit that in the absence of a systematic and coherent theory of socialism guiding the actual programmes of action, there can be no fundamental transformation in these countries towards a transition to socialism. Clearly, there is incongruence where we have a socialist ideology with capitalist strategy of development in practice.

Returning to the question of real differences we may now ask: How different is Tanzania from the others? Our position is that Nyerere, and therefore Tanzania,* has evolved a clearer conceptualization of socialism than any other African leader during the period under study. He has demonstrated a conscious determination and commitment to transform Tanzania on the basis of his formulations of socialism. Thus the crucial theoretical differences lie in the fact that whereas Julius Nyerere's erstwhile 'socialist' counterparts (e.g. Senghor, Kenyatta, the late Tom Mboya) have been merely satisfied with the 'banal' and 'idyllic' conceptualizations of African socialism, even in the face of glaring internal contradictions, Nyrere has actually 'advanced from the ideal to the real'[42] and in his conceptualization of Ujamaa moved to a more rigorous theoretical understanding of socialism.[43] From 'socialism' being just an 'attitude of mind'[44] in pre-Arusha Tanzania, Ujamaa evolved in post-Arusha to a 'way of life,'[45] partly reflecting his growing convictions and partly as a response to national, African and international developments.

To be sure, the differences are evident not only in the theoretical formulations but also in the actual development strategy. Thus on the economic front, while Nyerere's other erstwhile counterparts of African socialism see a permanent coexistence between the private capitalist sector and a fledgling 'public' sector – euphemistically dubbed the 'mixed economy' – Nyerere sees it as a temporary stage to be phased out in the future. Hence the conscious de-emphasis on both private or foreign capital in post-Arusha Tanzania consistent with the spirit of Arusha as elaborated upon by the policy on self-reliance. For it was clearly

* It is crucial, in the context of Tanzania and for our purposes, to understand the basic fact that the evolving ideology of socialism revolves around President Julius Nyerere himself. In short, socialism as an evolving ideology in Tanzania is synonymous with Nyerere.

understood that the continued reliance on private capital meant the perpetuation of foreign control of the economy, since there was hardly any idigenous capital to speak of. Hence the key notion of self-reliance.[46]

One of the key policy statements of the Arusha Declaration was the theme of self-reliance. The document's emphasis on self-reliance and the insufficiency and shortcomings of external 'aid' was partly a constructive response to the unreliability of external sources of aid, as vividly demonstrated by the unexpected withdrawal of aid by both Britain and West Germany in the mid-1960s. These two incidents perhaps more than anything else exposed the vulnerability of a policy that indiscriminately encouraged the continued reliance on external aid for economic development. The emphatic orientation toward self-reliance in the Declaration was therefore a negation of the pervasive belief that aid was essential for development. Self-reliance had to be seen and appreciateed as a crucial adjunct to the process of building a socialist society in Tanzania within the context of the Arusha Declaration. It meant that since Tanzanian society was too poor to provide the government with the much needed capital base, the people of Tanzania had to be self-reliant in their struggle against the unholy trinity – poverty, ignorance and disease. Rather than rely on money as the indicator of advancement, the Declaration argued that Tanzanians needed to reorient themselves to depend on the resources already at their command. Land and labour, not money, were Tanzania's assets, and these were bound to be the cornerstone upon which the country's socialist development would be based.[47] In short the call, if it meant anything at all, was aimed at the mobilization of the people's forces for carrying out the much needed social transformations, as well as the increases in production, vital for a socialist reconstruction.[48]

Although self-reliance implies the ability to improvise out of one's own resources, it remains essentially a collective concept. Therefore, the application of self-reliance to a lower level – that of the family or the individual – must be viewed as counter-productive, although in practice it is possible that it may still occur.[49] The dangers in individualizing self-reliance are fairly obvious, for very often the failure to 'respond with programmes of social justice in capitalist countries, for example, has been attributed to, or cited as evidence for a traditional and enduring commitment on the part of its citizenry to individual self-reliance or "rugged individualism".'[50]

By way of summation, we would point out that we certainly do not deny, by our recognition of the differences between Nyerere and his erstwhile counterparts, the inadequacies in his 'theory' of socialism *qua* theory. We shall not strain ourselves in the manner of Walter Rodney to prove the identity of Ujamaa ('African socialism') as scientific socialism.[51] In discussing the theoretical inadequacies we shall begin our analysis by first focusing on Nyerere's approach to the question of social classes in Tanzania.

'Social Class' in Tanzania

So far we have been discusssing 'African socialism' and the problems of 'class' analysis in Africa in general. We shall now briefly examine the problem in the context of Tanzania. Like many other 'socialist' leaders in Africa, desiring to assert the independence of 'African socialism', Nyerere has denied the existence of classes ('incipient,' 'transitory,' or 'concrete') in Tanzania.[52] Nyerere denied the existence of 'class' in his pre-Arusha formulations of 'socialism'.[53] The justification for this position does not lie in any rigorous theoretical analysis of the productive forces as they exist, but on the pristine characteristic features of traditional African society they themselves have thrown up.

While we concede that the concept of social classes[54] is not the most definitive in Marx's writings, especially when seen in relation to the more systematic and rigorous treatment that he gave to other concepts,[55] in the final analysis the basic social classes of society are not a task for empirical observation but one for theoretical investigation of the mode of production. The concept of class appears as a result of analysis of the productive forces and the relations of production in the process of social production. Hence a class is defined primarily by 'the relations or modes of relations conditioning the possibilities of interaction among men given a determinate mode of production.'[56]

Clearly then, the starting point of class analysis should be the analysis of the productive process in which we can distinguish:[57]

26

1 The level of development of productive forces, taken not only as a level of technological information but also as a function of the application of technology to the productive process and the development of social and entrepreneurial division labour.
2 The levels of the relations of production.
3 A differentiation following the analysis within the social structure, the basic class of society, the intermediate classes, those in the process of formation, decline, the various sectors of class interrelating within a mode of production or a social structure.

Seen in this context, the inadequacies of the attempts by Nkrumah and others to define or rather analyze classes in Africa becomes clearer.[58] Their attempts clearly lack the rigour that is the essence of any class analysis or of any scientific classification system for that mattter. Perhaps one is unduly harsh here, given the 'fluidity' of class formations in Tanzania and elsewhere in the continent. We suggest that the 'incipient' and 'embryonic' character of social classes in Africa raises special problems in studying them and more needs to be done in this area. Perhaps we can only talk about the development of classes in tendential terms and shall therefore be well advised not to encourage the dogmatic use of the concept of classes given these obvious limitations.[59] We do not have, in Tanzania or elsewhere in black Africa, the classical types of class divisions into bourgeoisie and proletariat with the 'middle class' on the indeterminate fringes, as was the case in Europe. They have had different socio-economic formations.

It is indeed significant that even the relatively more rigorous attempt by Shivji to analyze 'social classes' in Tanzania is still marked by distinctive fuzziness. His analysis is littered with phrases and sentences such as: '. . . the broad divisions [of classes] are extremely vague and rough';[60] a class classification chart, we are told, is 'admittedly a very rough indication of differentiation among the petty-bourgeoisie . . . [and] a more precise one would have to be supported by quantitative data';[61] 'It is significant for our purposes, various overlappings between the different categories notwithstanding . . .'[62] Indeed, it took seven years (from 1961 to 1967) to 'create the bureaucratic bourgeoisie,' only to be told a few pages later that the 'bureaucratic bourgeoisie' is not yet a 'fully-fledged class'.[63] This is followed a few lines later by the statement that the 'bureaucratic bourgeoisie is very much in the process of formation. . . .'[64] And so it goes on!

Clearly, the qualifications and contradictions cited above indicate the slippery path one must necessarily encounter in a class analysis of Tanzania and perhaps elsewhere in the continent. We can, however, draw solace from Shivji's modesty: 'An attempt at a class analysis of Tanzania society runs into the inevitable complexities introduced by a racially structured social organization inherited from colonial times.'[65] It further underscores Dos Santos' conclusions on the problem:

> A special problem may arise in transitory classes, or those which do succeed in crystallizing as classes, since their conditions of existence in society are in constant transformation towards new forms of relations. By definition the consciousness of these cannot crystallize into a solid set of interests and they are subject to the constant pressure of the interests of other classes. This does not deprive the class of its specific character as transitional, but makes analysis of its class consciousness and psychology very complex.[66]

The point we want to emphasize here (the scope of this study prohibits any lengthy discussion on classes), is that until there is a more rigorous theoretical analysis of 'social classes' in Tanzania, the use of the various categories of class must be viewed as tendential.

Notwithstanding the limitations of what is available on class analysis in Tanzania, we have benefited from Shivji's relatively more rigorous analysis. Aspects of his broad categories (e.g., the 'commercial bourgeoisie' (Asian), the 'bureaucratic bourgeoisie' (the ruling sector* of the African 'petty-bourgeoisie'), peasants and workers, etc.) are useful abstractions for our purposes and we

---

* Modified to read the 'Managerial Sector'. We would also like to emphasize, though, that for our purposes we are satisfied to simply use broad categories which have aspects of 'class' in them in our analysis. This is partly to avoid unnecessary confusion and partly a recognition of the inherent problems posed by the embryonic nature of 'social classes' in formation in Tanzania.

shall apply them where necessary.* Other 'social classes' include the relatively small proletariat stratum and the peasant stratum. There is continued social differentiation in some parts of Tanzania such as exists, for example, between the 'kulaks' and poor peasants; we shall return to this later. But as an important point of distinction we suggest, at least for analytical purposes, another stratum of the petty-bourgeoisie: the 'political leadership stratum'.[67] Our distinction, it is important to note, is ideological. Specifically, the significance of this stratum must be seen in the context of our proposition that the 'struggle' between the 'bureaucratic bourgeoisie' (whose base is the small but qualitati ely important sector – the civil service) and the 'political leadership' stratum (whose base is primarily the Party) is increasingly becoming the dominant internal contradiction with wide implications for the continued progress towards the transition to socialism in Tanzania.[68] In this context, it is very significant that by far the most sustained opposition to President Nyerere's proposed cut in salaries of the top civil servants, party leaders etc., in the mid-1960s, in fact, came from the 'bureaucratic bourgeoisie' stratum of the civil service and parastatals who saw in the President's moves a real threat to their interests and privileged positions.

Although we recognize that the quintessence of the 'bureaucratic bourgeoisie' as managers of the state apparatus and economy lies in their functional specificity as well as their know-how (technical, managerial, etc.), the location of their base in the civil service concretizes their existence. Equally important, too, is the fact that most of the Regional and District directors, including the managers and directors of the numerous parastatals, have come through the ranks of the civil service. It is significant that the government of Tanzania has not instituted any radical structural changes in the country's civil service. The basic features of the colonial civil service are very much intact in spite of its politicization and the decentralization measures of 1972.[69] More importantly, it has maintained its independent role. Indeed, we are witnessing throughout most of Africa the emergence of very

---

* We would emphasize that we do not necessarily agree with the categories of Shivji either in content or with the boundaries.

powerful bureaucracies perhaps unprecedented in her history. The civil service or bureaucracy in Tanzania is no exception. Viewed in this perspective, we submit that the 'struggle' between the 'political leadership' stratum and the 'bureaucratic bourgeoisie' stratum comes into clearer relief. An equally important point is that recruitment to the civil service in the colonial era was not limited to a particular 'class'. Its labour force was essentially a 'mosaic,' albeit some social 'groups' or 'classes' were more dominant. It must be noted, however, that over and above these essential features of the civil service, is the link between the 'bureaucratic bourgeoisie' and international capitalism, accentuated and accelerated by the dominant economic role of the state apparatus.

The 'struggle' between the two strata has, of course, been exacerbated by the 'bureaucratic bourgeoisie's' link with international capitalism.[70] We recall that such a link helps to breed in part dependence relations. One consequence is that the 'bureaucratic bourgeoisie' takes on a more pragmatic ideology (non-socialist), which is more compatible with its non-colonial status, as the 'bureaucratic bourgeoisie' becomes increasingly unreceptive to the more idealistic socialist ideological demands of the 'political leadership' stratum. The 'struggle' is on, with both strata seeking to win the continued support and allegiance not only of its base, but also eventual control of the peasants and workers, and ultimately control of political power. It is important to note that in addition to the 'bureaucratic bourgeoisie's' link with international capitalism, there is yet another external link resulting from the cold war. Both strata are linked into this international struggle but at opposing ends. The 'political leadership' stratum leans towards the socialists while the 'bureaucratic bourgeoisie' stratum leans toward the capitalists. The second link plays the role of a reinforcer. A schematic representaton is presented opposite (Diagram 1).

Explanatory Note
The 'petty–bourgeoisie' is divided into two broad categories – the 'political leadership' stratum (the ruling sector of the 'petty-bourgeoisie') and the 'bureaucratic bourgeoisie'. The 'bureaucratic bourgeoisie' become, among other things, the managers of the economy as the state begins to play a dominant economic role in

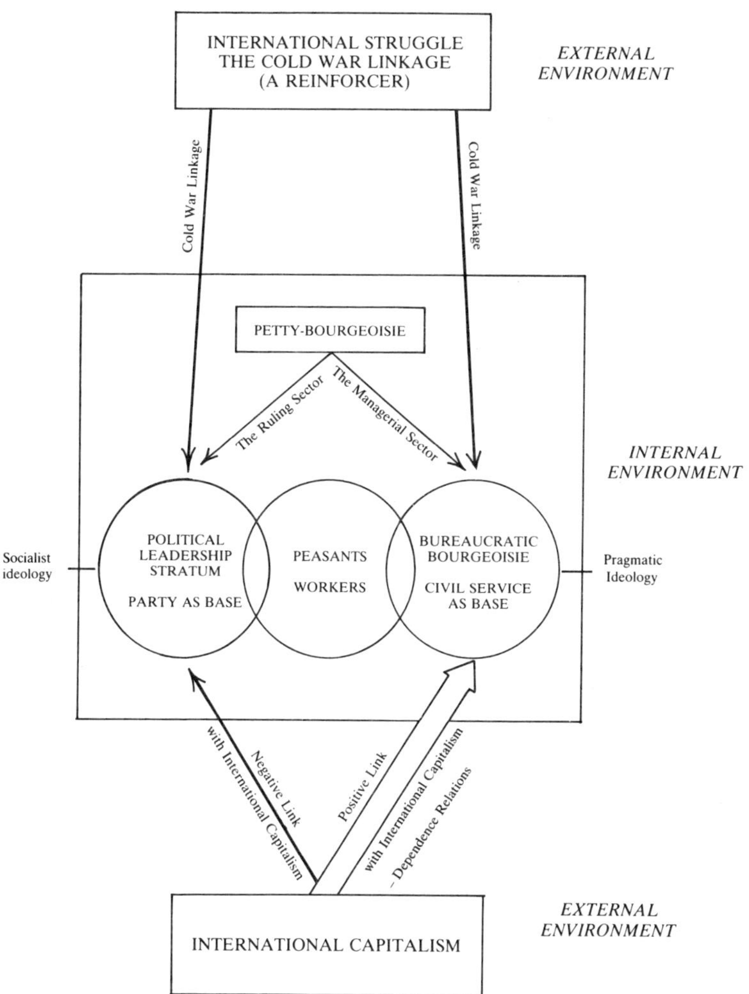

Diagram 1: *Diagram showing the nature of linkages between the political leadership and bureaucratic bourgeoisie strata and international capitalism and the 'Cold War' in Tanzania*

post-Arusha Tanzania. These two strata have bases both in the Party (for the 'political leadership' stratum) and in the civil service (for the 'bureaucratic bourgeoisie'), respectively. Both strata need the support, allegiance and the eventual control of the peasants and workers. The ultimate aim is, of course, the control of political power. However, the Party and the 'political leadership' in Tanzania happen to have a greater degree of support and allegiance of the peasant masses and the workers *vis-à-vis* the civil service and the 'bureaucratic bourgeoisie'.

The External Linkages
The 'bureaucratic bourgeoisie', through foreign partnerships, foreign consultants and managers and technical assistance, become increasingly linked, wittingly or unwittingly, with international capitalism (see later discussion on the role of the NDC in Tanzania). The greater the degree of linkage with international capitalism the more pragmatic (ideologically) they become. Besides, there is a second external linkage arising from the 'international struggle' which results from the 'cold war'. This second link reinforces the 'bureaucratic bourgeoisie' in a positive way as the 'bureaucratic bourgeoisie' tend to lean towards its ideologically more compatible capitalist camp in the 'struggle', while they become more unreceptive to the idealistic socialist ideological demands of the 'political leadership' stratum. This latter stratum, committed to a fundamental transformation of society towards 'socialism', has as its only positive external linkage that arising from the international 'struggle'. They lean more towards the socialist camp of the 'struggle'. They have a negative linkage with international capitalism in the sense that they reject any economic relationships with international capitalism that would foster dependence. Paradoxically, the act of rejection tends to radicalize the 'political leadership' who are then poised to counter the machinations of international capitalism.

The significance of the internal 'struggle' in Tanzania (and therefore the need to emphasize it), can perhaps be best understood in terms of China's Cultural Revolution. The Cultural Revolution was largely a struggle to maintain the supremacy of the Communist Party, under the leadership of Mao Tse-tung, over and above the bureaucracy of the state apparatus and the party under the leadership of the 'renegade capitalist leader' Liu Shao-Ch'i and later Teng.[71] Politics must take command! Thus the struggle between the two strata in Tanzania exhibits the nuances of a 'political leadership' wanting to maintain the supremacy of the party over the bureaucracy.[72] To the extent that previous analysis of 'social classes' and the 'political struggle' in Tanzania emphasized the external linkages over and above this aspect of the internal contradictions and hence struggle, it may well lose sight of the totality of the 'struggle' as it paints only a partial picture, and hence a partial solution to a more complex set of relations. This by no means denies the importance of the link between the 'bureaucratic bourgeoisie' and international capitalism. Far from it. It is simply a question of emphasis – but a rather important emphasis all the same.

In conclusion, then, we have argued the case for our basic thesis:

1   That the absence of an appropriate theoretical (ideological) framework consistent with the actual programmes of action, *inter alia*, is largely responsible for the failure to transform fundamentally most of the developing states in Africa along desired goals. In the absence of a congruence between political ideologies and political economies, it is virtually impossible to transform fundamentally these societies towards 'socialism'.

2   We have tried to show that there are essential differences between Julius Nyerere and his erstwhile 'socialist' counterparts in the rest of black Africa, in the realms of theory and practice. Nyerere, more than any of the others, has demonstrated a clearer understanding of the term 'socialism' as well as a conscious determination to ensure that the programmes of action are based on his formulations of 'socialism'. To this extent he has been more successful. While we concede the gains made under the leadership of President Julius Nyerere towards a transition to socialism, we equally recognize the potency of the internal contradictions – especially those posed between the 'bureaucratic bourgeoisie' and the 'political leadership' stratum – in arresting the speed of the transition, with the ever-looming possibility of a reversal of the process. With this foundation, we can now examine some key policy areas and programmes to test the validity of our propositions.

Chapter 2 Socialism and Self-Reliance in Tanzania:

A Theoretical Overview

1. Paul Sweezy, *Socialism* (New York: McGraw-Hill Book Company, 1949), p. 91.
2. This view is symptomatic of the self-styled 'African socialists' in contemporary Africa.
3. Julius K. Nyerere, *Ujamaa: Essays on Socialism* (Dar es Salaam: Government Printer, 1962), p. 10.
4. It must be noted, however, that there is the rather idyllic claim by most of the advocates of 'African socialism' that socialism has deep roots in traditional African society.
5. W.H. Friedland and Carl G. Rosberg, 'Introduction: The Anatomy of African Socialism,' in *African Socialism*, ed. by Friedland and Rosberg (Stanford: Stanford University Press, 1964), p. 1.
6. J. Mohan, 'Varieties of African Socialism', in *The Socialist Register*, ed. by Ralph Miliband and J. Saville (New York: The Merlin Press, 1966), p. 221.
7. Kwame Nkrumah, 'Why I founded *The Spark*,' *The Spark*, No. 100 (November 1964), p. 1.
8. Mohan, 'Varieties of African Socialism', in *The Socialist Register*, ed. by Miliband and Saville, p. 221.
9. Julius K. Nyerere, cited in *Africa Report*, 8 (5) May 1963, p. 20.
10. Julius Nyerere, *Freedom and Unity* (Nairobi: Oxford University Press, 1966), p. 166.
11. A. Zolberg, 'The Dakar Colloquium' in *African Socialism*, ed. by Friedland and Rosberg, p. 119.
12. On the common ownership of land, Nyerere put it aptly when he said: 'And in rejecting the capitalist attitude of mind which colonialism brought into Africa, we must reject also the capitalist methods which go with it. One of these is the individual ownership of land. To us in Africa, land was always recognized as belonging to the community. Each individual within our society had a right to the use of land, because otherwise he could not earn his living, and one cannot have the right to life without also having the right to some means of maintaining life. But the African's right to land was simply the right to use it, he had no other right to it, nor did it occur to him to try and claim one.' Nyerere, *Freedom and Unity*, p. 166.
13. Republic of Kenya, *African Socialism and its Application to Planning in Kenya*, 1965, p. 12. Emphasis mine.
14. Zolberg, 'The Dakar Colloquium' in *African Socialism* ed. by Friedland and Rosberg, p. 119.
15. Leopold Senghor, 'African-Style Socialism' in *African Socialism*, ed. by W. Friedland and Carl Rosberg (Stanford: Stanford University Press, 1964), Appendix VI, p. 264.

16. Nyerere, *Ujamaa: Essays on Socialism*, p. 11.

17. Sekou Toure, *Guinea Revolution and Social Progress* (Cairo: S.O.P. Press, 1963), pp. 182–3.

18. It is significant that almost always the 'theoretical' formulations of socialism in Africa (or any other ideology, for that matter), revolve around the national political leaders.

19. Disgusted and impatient with the various assortments of 'African socialism' in Africa (for example, 'Arab socialism,' 'Algerian socialism,' 'pragmatic socialism,' 'Senegalese socialism,' to name only a few), Sekou Toure in his despair comments: 'There is much talk of 'African socialism', and this seems to infer that there also exist a Chinese socialism, an American socialism . . . Why would people, tomorrow, not speak of the Nigerian or Togolese path of African socialism, or of Senegalese chemistry or Moroccan mathematics . . . Engaging in 'socialism for the sake of socialism' is trying to mow with the sickle's handle.' Sekou Toure, *Guinea Revolution and Social Progress*, p. 362.

20. Republic of Kenya, *African Socialism and Its Application to Planning in Kenya*, 1965, p. 2.

21. See F. Engels, 'Socialism, Utopian and Scientific' in *Marx and Engels, Selected Works*, Vol. 2 (Moscow: Foreign Languages Publishing House, 1962).

22. Walter Rodney, 'Tanzanian Ujamaa and Scientific Socialism,' *African Review*, Vol. 1, No. 4 (April, 1972), p. 63.

23. Leopold Senghor, *On African Socialism* (New York: American Society of African Culture, 1964), p. 46.

24. Tom Mboya, 'African Socialism' in *African Socialism*, ed. by W. Friedland and Carl Rosberg (Stanford: Stanford University Press, 1964), Appendix IV, p. 25.

25. Nyerere, *Freedom and Unity*, p. 170.

26. Commenting on the same fact, Clive Thomas argues that despite its general preoccupation with capitalism – and by extension with imperialism and neo-colonialism – socialist economic theory has turned its attention to the study of the economics of the transition period, the focus has been on the Soviet Union and Eastern Europe. But none of these countries, he continues, was underdeveloped in the sense in which we speak of underdevelopment today, and their transition did not occur during the neo-colonial phase, in the more or less total absence of an indigenous industrial and technological capacity. See Clive Y. Thomas, *Dependence and Transformation: The Economics of the Transition to Socialism* (New York: Monthly Review Press, 1974), p. 35.

27. *Ibid.*, p. 34.

28. Friedland and Rosberg, 'Introduction: The Anatomy of African Socialism' in *African Socialism*, p. 1.

29. Thomas, *Dependence and Transformation*, p. 31.

30. *Ibid.*

31. Mohan, 'Varieties of African Socialism' in *The Socialist Register*,

ed. by Miliband and Saville, p. 31.

32. Republic of Kenya, *African Socialism and Its Application to Planning in Kenya*, 1965, p. 8. Indeed, Colin Leys's searching inquiry into the economic structure of post-independence Kenya confirms this pragmatic approach to economic development and reveals more than ever before the increasing dependence of its economy on international capitalism and hence the 'development of underdevelopment.'

33. We have benefited greatly from Ake's article on the 'Congruence of Political Economies and Ideologies in Africa' in *The Political Economy of Contemporary Africa*, ed. by Peter Gutkind and I. Wallerstein (Beverly Hills: Sage Publications, 1976).

34. *Ibid.*, pp. 205–206.

35. *Ibid.*, p. 207.

36. Ake, 'Congruence of Political Economies and Ideologies in Africa' in *The Political Economy of Contemporary Africa*, ed. by Gutkind and Wallerstein, p. 207.

37. *Ibid.*, p. 209.

38. *Ibid.*

39. Giovanni Arrighi and John Saul, 'Socialism and Economic Development in Tropical Africa' in *Socialism in Tanzania Vol. 1*, ed. by Lionel Cliffe and John Saul (Nairobi: East African Publishing House, 1972), p. 3.

40. Thomas, *Dependence and Transformation*, p. 39.

41. Bob Fitch and Mary Oppenheimer, eds., *Ghana: End of an Illusion* (New York: Monthly Review Press, 1966) pp. 82 and 84.

42. Rodney, 'Tanzanian Ujamaa and Scientific Socialism,' p. 62.

43. To be sure, this development has not been easy. It has been marked by an ongoing struggle based on actual study of the interplay between theory and practice, particularly in the context of Tanzania. Even after the Arusha Declaration in 1967, Nyerere is known to have raised doubts in his own mind about socialism. 'It is not easy to say what socialism in our conditions means. I have frequently thought and written about this. Up to this moment, I am still not sure that we have exactly understood what is meant by socialism and the building of socialism in African conditions . . .' Interview granted by Nyerere to A. Prija, correspondent of the Belgrade newspaper *Politika* and published July 18, 1968. Cited in 'Evolution of Socialist Thought in African Countries' by Ivan Ivekovic, *Socialist Thought and Practice*, Vol. XVII, No. 1 (January, 1977), p. 92.

44. 'Socialism – like democracy – is an attitude of mind. In a socialist society it is the socialist attitude of mind, and not the rigid adherence to a standard political pattern, which is needed to ensure that people care for each other's welfare.' Nyerere, *Ujamaa: Essays on Socialism*, p. 1.

45 'Socialism is a way of life, and a socialist society cannot simply come into existence. A socialist society can only be built by those

who believe in, and who themselves practise, the principles of socialism. A committed member of TANU will be a socialist, and his fellow socialists – that is, his fellow believers in this political and economic system – are all those in Africa or elsewhere in the world who fight for the rights of peasants and workers.' *Ibid.*, p. 17.

46. The part foreign capital plays in ensuring the continuation of economic underdevelopment has been demonstrated by Colin Leys in Kenya (in his work, *Underdevelopment in Kenya*) and attested to by others in Senegal, Ivory Coast, *et al.*

47. See Nyerere, *Ujamaa: Essays on Socialism*, pp. 17–22.

48. The mobilization aspect of self-reliance was also emphasized by the Central Committee of the Korean Workers' Party in their policy formulations on self-reliance: 'The construction of an independent economy under the banner of self-reliance has been put forward as a particularly important and urgent question in our country . . . Under the banner of self-reliance our people have mobilized to the maximum all their forces and all national resources while making rational use of aid from fraternal countries.' *Self-Reliance and Independent National Economic Construction* (Peking: Foreign Languages Press, 1963), pp. 13–14.

49. There is an interesting parallel during the Cultural Revolution in China when the 'high degree of economic independence enjoyed by rural households over wide areas of China in the early 1960's is attributed to the pernicious influence of Liu Shao-Ch'i and his followers . . .' Audrey Donnithorne, 'China's Cellular Economy: Some Economic Trends since the Cultural Revolution,' *China Quarterly*, No. 52 (October-December, 1972), 607.

50. H. S. Tishler, *Self-Reliance and Social Security* (New York: Kennikat Press, 1971), p. 3.

51. See Walter Rodney's attempted proof in his article, 'Tanzanian Ujamaa and Scientific Socialism.'

52. It has been suggested that the assertion that there are no classes in Africa is often used to justify capitalist investment in the continent as well as a justification for one-party systems, and has come under criticism in recent times from progressive African thinkers. See Kwame Nkrumah, *Class Struggles in Africa* (London: Panaf Publication, 1970).

53. In fairness to Nyerere it must be pointed out that he conceded later (post-Arusha) to the existence of the elements of 'social class' in Tanzania: 'Tanzania,' he writes, 'is a nation of peasants and workers, but it is not yet a socialist society. It still contains elements of feudalism and capitalism – with their temptations. These feudalistic and capitalistic features of our society could spread and entrench themselves.' Nyerere, *Ujamaa: Essays on Socialism*, p. 11.

54. By 'social classes' we, like Dos Santos, mean 'the basic groupings of individuals in a society, opposed to one another by virtue of the role they play in the production process, from the point of

view of the relations they establish among themselves in the organization of labour and in respect of property.' T. Dos Santos, 'The Concept of Social Classes', *Science and Society*, Vol. 34, No. 2 (1972), p. 188.

55. This, it has been argued by some Marxists, was due to the fact that Marx just began the discussion of classes in Volume III of *Capital* before the manuscript breaks off. He thus had this much to say on classes: 'The owners merely of labour power, owners of capital and land owners, whose respective sources of income are wages, profit and ground-rent, in other words wage labourers, capitalists and landowners, constitute the three big classes of modern society based upon the capitalist mode of production.' See Karl Marx, *Capital* (Moscow: Foreign Languages Press, 1972), Vol. 3, pp. 863–4.

56. Dos Santos, 'The Concept of Social Classes,' p. 181.

57. *Ibid.*, p. 191.

58. Kwame Nkrumah's attempt to analyze social classes in Africa suffers from a lack of analytical rigour. See Nkrumah, *Class Struggles in Africa*.

59. In a similar vein, Shivji warns: 'In my opinion, it is a mistaken over-emphasis (especially on the part of those who come with fixed ideas about classes and appear to see classes everywhere so long as they can count a handful of farmers owning two land-rovers or a tractor) to focus attention on rural stratification out of all proportion to its role in the context of the Tanzania economy as a whole.' See I.G. Shivji, *The Silent Class Struggle* (Dar es Salaam: Tanzania Publishing House, 1973), p. 1.

60. Issa G. Shivji, *Class Struggles in Tanzania,* (Dar es Salaam: Tanzania Publishing House, 1975), p. 40.

61. *Ibid.*, p. 87.

62. *Ibid.*

63. *Ibid.*, p. 94.

64. *Ibid.*, p. 96.

65. *Ibid.*, p. 40.

66. Dos Santos, 'The Concept of Social Classes,' p. 185.

67. Under this stratum we will include: political heads of government ministries and departments – Central, Regional, District and Local – and the top leadership of the Party.

68. In the absence of any reliable social background data on the political leadership and bureaucratic bourgeoisie strata, it has been difficult to identify, for now at least, the origins of both strata. But even if this were possible, the credibility of social background data in social science analysis has come under increasing 'dissensus' in recent years. However, it remains true that the political leadership stratum continues to draw very strong support from the peasantry, as shown by the presidential election statistics in post-Arusha Tanzania – although this factor alone is not sufficient to locate the origin of this stratum in the peasantry. At

best, we can only infer. For a detailed analysis of elections in post-Arusha Tanzania, see the comprehensive study by the Election Study committee of the University of Dar es Salaam published in *Socialism and Participation: Tanzania's 1970 National Elections* (Dar es Salaam: Tanzania Publishing House, 1974).

69. Several studies on the effectiveness of the decentralization measures of 1972 have revealed that basically the bureaucracy remains as '. . . an elite, ensconced in a state bureaucracy trying with varying degrees of detachment to convince the masses to change their ways . . . The major decentralization measures implemented during 1972 and 1973 have been government's response to the set of problems which this bureaucratic method has engendered.' See J.R. Finucane, *Rural Development and Bureaucracy in Tanzania: The Case of Mwanza Region* (Uppsala: The Scandinavian Institute of African Studies, 1974), p. 10.

    Perhaps it will pay us to heed what Max Weber clearly recognized as a shortcoming: that the early socialists' emphasis on ownership patterns had minimal effect upon the bureaucratic mode of operation and had no effect at all upon the continued presence of bureaucratic features. The competition of the market, he writes, has been replaced by the scholastic hierarchy of an emoloyee society. Such an analysis recognizes that both systems are highly centralized. Weber writes: 'The bureaucratic structure is only the counter-image of partriarchalism transposed into rationality.' Max Weber, 'The Sociology of Charismatic Authority,' from *Max Weber: Essays in Sociology* ed. by Gerth and Mills (New York: Oxford University Press, 1958), p. 245.

70. 'The "bureaucratic bourgeoisie" is not an independent class because so long as the economy remains structurally linked with the capitalist world and within the world capitalist system, the "bureaucratic bourgeoisie" is a dependent bourgeoisie – dependent on the international bourgeoisie.' See I. Shivji, *Class Struggles in Tanzania*, p. 85.

71. Summing up the effects of the Cultural Revolution on the bureaucracy, Audrey Donnithorn writes: 'Since the Cultural Revolution there has been a diminution in the role, attenuated ever since 1957, of the Central ministries. This has been accompanied by a decrease in the number of ministries through amalgamations and also by a reduction in the size of their staff. No official list has been issued but it appears that some two-thirds of the pre-Cultural Revolution ministries, commissions and other offices under the state council have lost their separate identity . . .' See Audrey Donnithorne, 'China's Cellular Economy: Some Economic Trends since the Cultural Revolution,' p. 605.

    Similarly, Tang Tsou comments: 'The foregoing analysis of the Cultural Revolution shows that it has not only destroyed the Party organization and badly disrupted the government bureaucracy, but has also inflicted serious damage on the relationship of authority

which had been established in Communist China.' See Tang Tsou, 'The Cultural Revolution and the Chinese Political System,' *China Quarterly*, No. 38 (April–June, 1969), p. 91.
72. It must be noted that the bureaucracy of party in Tanzania is much weaker than its counterpart in the state apparatus.

Chapter 3

On Implementing Socialism and Self-Reliance: The Role of Education and Political Socialization

. . . those who, in learning to read and write,
come to a new awareness of self-hood and
begin to look critically at the social situation in
which they find themselves, often take the
initiative in acting to transform the society that
has denied them this opportunity of participation. Education is once again a subversive
force.

Paulo Freire

We are making great efforts to promote a new
attitude in our schools. Everything possible
must be done to replace the discredited values
of competitive individualism by the cooperative
socialist ideal . . .

Minister of Education, Tanzania

We established in our previous discussion that the problem of
Tanzania is not one of goal. The goal is 'socialism'. The problem
therefore is that of formulating the appropriate strategy to institutionalize socialism in Tanzania. Admittedly, such a strategy will
evolve partly from practice and in part from theory. In this chapter
we will therefore examine and evaluate the contribution of the
educational strategy (especially as a medium of political socializ-

ation*) towards the socialist goals and objectives of Tanzania. Are the educational policies and programmes in fact consistent with the ideological requirements of socialism? In other words, is there a congruence between the theory and practice of education in the context of the socialist goals and objectives of Tanzania?

Though the Arusha Declaration did not initially address itself specifically to the issue of education *per se*, the policy statement on 'Education for Self-Reliance' issued shortly thereafter (in March 1967) came to grips with the problem of education. It is probably the most salient document in Tanzania with reference to the problem of how the education system can best be mobilized towards the socialist goals and objectives of the country. In March 1967 Prime Minister Kawawa declared: 'the educational system in the country must be appropriate to the future of the country, and not to its [colonial] past . . . The university must produce people with socialist ideas who are also experts at different jobs.'[1] And speaking of the 'colonial past,' a useful place to begin our analysis of the educational system in Tanzania must be with the colonial educational system.

The Colonial Educational system

Briefly, the colonial system of education which Tanzania inherited at the time of independence was largely based on the traditional British pattern of education, modified to suit the needs of the colonial administration, which in this case meant the supply of a small 'elite' group of urban non-manual workers. It was designed to reach only a very small percentage of the population and those that 'benefited' from it were largely from the urban areas, as the jobs for which the educated were being trained were predominantly urban. It encouraged white-collar mentality and a contempt for manual labour. The elitist design of the system was assured of in the very nature of the selection process, the content of the

---

* We will only be looking at political socialization tangentially as it relates to the role of education.

education (which was highly academically oriented), and the privileged existence of students. The differential rewards from education led people to view it not as a means of developing the society as a whole, but primarily as a means of personal advancement, and separation from the greater reality of the society. In other words, it emphasized the individualistic values of a capitalist society – the individual gaining wealth and power in competition with others. This should not be surprising since by and large 'every prescription represents the imposition of one man's choice upon another, transforming the consciousness of the man prescribed to into one that conforms with the prescriber's consciousness.'[2] A more devastating aspect of the colonial educational system lies in the cultural invasion. It begins with the comparatively few African children who had the 'benefit' of this type of formal education. They were taught alien traditions and attitudes to life. The history, traditions and customs of their own people were thus ignored and ridiculed. Again, this is as it should be, 'for cultural invasion to succeed, it is essential that those invaded become convinced of their intrinsic inferiority. Since everything has its opposite, if those who are invaded consider themselves inferior, they must necessarily recognize the superiority of the invaders. The values of the latter thereby become the pattern for the former. The invasion is accentuated and those invaded are alienated from the spirit of their own culture and from themselves, the more the latter want to be like the invaders: to walk like them, dress like them, talk like them.'[3]

That the Tanzanian political leadership painfully recognized the awesome inadequacies of the colonial educational system bequeathed to them, when viewed from the wider perspectives outlined in the policy statement on education, can be seen from Nyerere's own evaluation. We shall quote him at length given the significance attached to the role of education in the task of social transformation:

> The education provided by the colonial government . . . was not designed to prepare young people for the service of their own country; instead, it was motivated by a desire to inculcate the values of the colonial society and to train individuals for the service of the colonial state . . . The educational system introduced into Tanzania by the coloni-

alists was modelled on the British system, but with even heavier emphasis on subservient attitudes and on white-collar skills. Inevitably, too, it was based on the assumptions of a colonialist and capitalist society. It emphasized and encouraged the individualistic instincts of mankind, instead of his cooperative instincts . . . This meant that colonial education induced attitudes of human inequality . . . colonial education in this country was therefore not transmitting the values and knowledge of Tanzanian society from one generation to the next; it was a deliberate attempt to change those values and to replace traditional knowledge by the knowledge from a different society . . .

The independent state of Tanzania in fact inherited a system of education which was in many respects both inadequate and inappropriate for the new state . . . So little education had been provided that in December, 1961, we had too few people with the necessary educational qualifications even to man the administration of Government as it was then, much less undertake the big economic and social development work which was essential. Neither was the school population in 1961 large enough to allow for any expectation that this situation would be speedily corrected. On top of that, education was based upon race, whereas the whole moral case of the independence movement had been based upon a rejection of racial distinctions.[4]

Clearly then, there is no gainsaying the fact that the cultural deprivation which the colonial situation engendered in the colonized people inevitably left behind a social psychology, conscious or otherwise, of social and cultural subordination, submission and imitation. Indeed the social psychology of submission, in no small measure, constitutes an important obstacle in the way of mobilizing a formerly colonized people for development. Therefore any strategy of meaningful social, political and economic development, more so if socialism is the professed goal, cannot but take into account this important factor. Viewed against this background, the education policy of post-independence Tanzania comes into clear relief. For the policy is based on the assumption that undesirable social attitudes are a consequence of particular characteristics of Western schooling and that more appropriate dispositions can be achieved by means of the re-structuring of school experience.

The importance of education as a medium for restructuring experience has been recognized by scholars and educationists alike. Thus Prewitt writes: 'A society seeking to bring about substantial changes in political values will find the educational system among the most effective instruments for implementing new ways of experiencing and interpreting political life.'[5] In short, education functions as an instrument of political socialization if by political socialization we mean 'the processes through which a citizen acquires his own view of the political world.'[6] And the recognition by both scholars and policy-makers alike of the critical attitudinal component of the development process in the developing countries in general has meant a preoccupation with the educational systems of these countries. Tanzania in this regard is no exception.

There appear to be two broadly opposing lines of thought on the social effects of schooling (i.e. formal schooling). One view contends that as schools are part of an elaborate economic and social context, they cannot have an independent effect upon the attitudes and values of their students. The other expresses the opposing view that schooling can be used to initiate comprehensive socialization. It is clear that the former, if seen in isolation, is the view of the Tanzanian leadership. But we would argue that a juxtaposition of the two views is not necessary, for those who hold the latter view do not claim an independent role for schools. They see them as one of the more important channels for inducing changes in the attitudes of the citizenry. The two views are therefore not mutually exclusive. Besides, whether there is an agreement amongst educators, social scientists, policy-makers, *et al* on the role of schools as instruments for inducing future political behaviour in the citizenry, it is certain that all countries (both new and old) and educational institutions have had recourse to programmes of civic training in their schools. Indeed, several important cross-national studies have shown that education induces an 'attitudinal syndrome characterized as modernity'.[7] This principle thus lends support to Tanzania's assumption that schools are important in the formation of social values.

Significantly, however, notwithstanding the early recognition of the gross inadequacies of the inherited colonial educational system, the changes that were instituted during the early post-independence period (i.e. pre-Arusha) were basically organizational. The changes did not fundamentally alter the educational orientation of the citizenry. As a result there are at least two clearly discernible periods in educational development in post-independence Tanzania. The first period covers the early post-independence, pre-Arusha period (1961–66); the second period is from 1967 onwards, beginning with the Arusha Declaration. These coincide broadly with the two distinctive phases of ideological evolution in Tanzania.

The Early Post-Independence Period

Essentially, the changes that were instituted during this period were threefold. We recall that colonial educational policy was based, among other things, on a differential selection process which favoured the children of European settlers and Asians over and above the African children. The best facilities were dispensed in that descending order. For example, before independence, in 1961, the annual expenditure per pupil was shs.3,320 and pupil:teacher ratio was 16 for the first category. The corresponding figures for the second and third categories were shs.460 and 19; and shs.200 and 54 respectively.[8] What clearly emerges from the above data is that education under colonial policy was 'generously given to the children of European settlers, more carefully dispensed among Asian children and very parsimoniously rationed among the children of the African soil . . .'[9] And to the extent that the educational system greatly favoured first, the children of European settlers, and second, the Asian children, all at the expense of the African children, colonial education policy carried with it the seeds of possible racial antagonisms.

One of the obvious consequences of this hierarchical pattern of education was the considerable restriction, especially amongst Africans, in the growth of the petty-bourgeoisie stratum. Thus, one of the first acts of the government in the wake of independence was the abolition of all racial distinctions within the

Table 1 *Population:-Educational Characteristics in 1961 by Type of Educational System*

Population	Africans	Asians	Europeans	Total
Pupils:	9,281,000	117,200	22,700	9,420,900
Standards I-IV	512,291	27,288	2,557	542,136
Standards V-VIII	450,644	11,844	1,347	463,834
Forms I-VI	6,031	5,401	387	11,819
Technical and Vocational Training	1,386	525	54	1,965
Teacher Training	1,698	50	–	1,748
Teachers	9,521	971	156	10,643
with university degree	191	399	59	649
completed secondary school	1,107	470	96	1,673
not completed secondary school	8,223	102	1	8,326
Total Expenditure	£4,950,388	£632,200*	£424,965*	£6,007,553
Pupil:Teacher Ratio	54	22	16	51
Expenditure per pupil	£10	£23	£166	£11

* Excluding contributions by voluntary agencies, which were relatively small.
Source: Department of Education, *Annual Report 1961*, Statistical Abstract.

educational system, not only in order to promote racial equality but also to end presumably the restrictive chains on the growth of the petty-bourgeoisie stratum. In its place, a national integrated system of education was established under the auspices of the Ministry of Education for overall co-ordination. Also introduced was a unified teaching service as part of the measures to rationalize the administration of education.

Secondly, there was a greater infusion of nationalistic ideas in the school curriculum to reflect better the cultural and socio-economic realities of the Tanzanian society. Kiswahili was to be emphasized as a medium of instruction in schools. On the whole, however, during this early phase of post-independence Tanzania, the content of what was being taught in schools throughout the country did not change much.

Thirdly, the shortage of schools was dealt with by a big expansion of educational facilities, especially at the secondary and post-secondary school levels, including the establishment of a university at Dar es Salaam. This included the building of numerous new primary and secondary schools and teacher training colleges. There were, for example, only 41 public and private secondary shcools with a total enrolment of 12,000 and a teaching staff of about 760 at independence. By 1971, there were 114 public and private secondary schools and a total enrolment of 43,352 (over three times that at independence), with a teaching force of 2,111. At the primary school level, there were 490,000 primary school children in 1961. By 1967 this figure had jumped to 852,000, about twice that of 1961, as the graphs in Figures 1, 2 and 3 show.[10]

The rapid expansion of the school system reflects in part the tremendous popular demand for education, as it continued to be considered a sure means for upward mobility – a stepping stone for higher income and a comfortable life-style. There was essentially no difference between what the citizenry expected of education in the colonial and early post-independence Tanzania, given the fact that the reforms introduced at the time were largely structural and organizational in nature and had therefore very little impact on either the existing social structure or the value orientations of those within the educational system. Mbilinyi has shown, in her studies on various aspects of the educational system in Tanzania, that there are signs that parental expectations of financial and status returns from education have a significant influence upon

48

Figure 1 *Enrolment in Public Secondary Schools: 1961–1973*

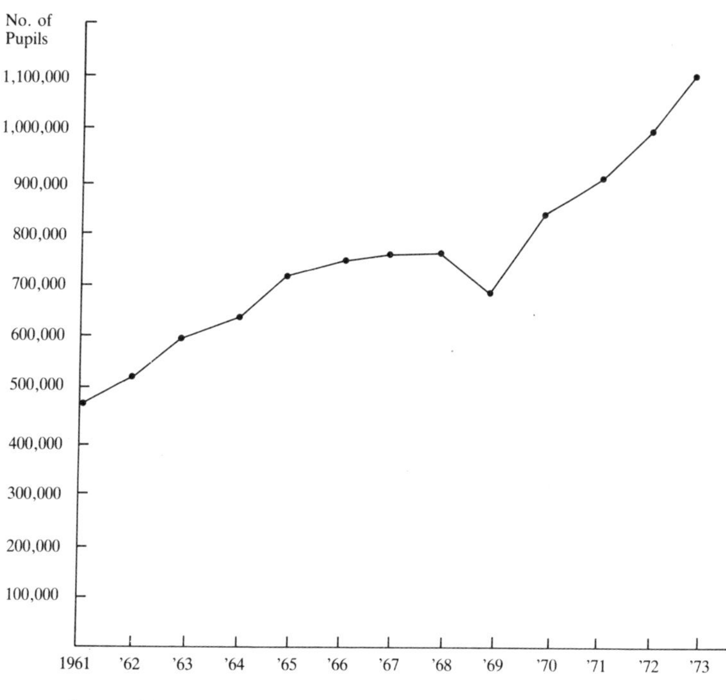

Source: *Ministry of National Education, Directorate of Planning
and Development*

student outlook. Given the structural relationship between formal
education and occupational opportunity structures, access to
formal education provides a direct measure of access to occupations, in particular to formal wage employment. Indeed, Nyerere
drew attention to the power of societal expectation in Tanzania,
where occupations were still defined largely according to education with income increasing geometrically with the level attained.

> . . . he [the student] will often find that his parents and rela-
> tions support his own conception of his difference and
> regard it as wrong that he should live and work as the
> ordinary person he really is. For the truth is that many of
> the people in Tanzania have come to regard education as

Figure 2 *Enrolment in Public Secondary Schools 1961–1974*

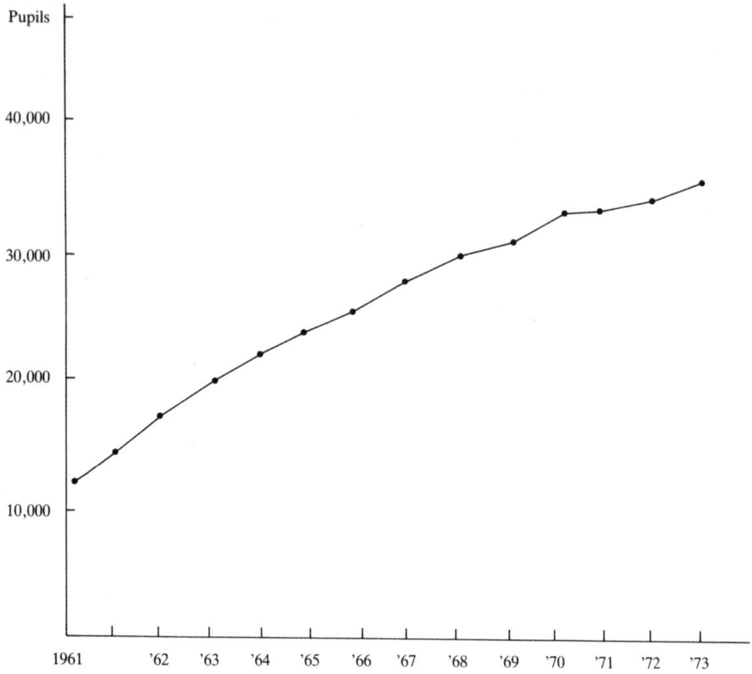

Source: *Ministry of National Education, Directorate of Planning and Development*

> meaning that a man is too precious for the rough and hard life which the masses of our people still live.[11]

Nyerere's observation was confirmed by Van de Laar's study of the structural relationship between formal education and occupational opportunity structures. He concluded that 'it is the general opinion of parents, teachers and pupils that those who are not selected for secondary school have failed. For their children the most important ambition of parents seems to be that at last one or two of their sons will acquire a salaried post . . .'[12] To this end, the plea of the university students who demonstrated against the requirement of national service in 1966 was their need to gain what they saw as their just reward for years of schooling, in order perhaps to pay back the investment of their parents in them. In

50

Figure 3 *Enrolment in Public and Private Secondary Schools: 1965–1973*

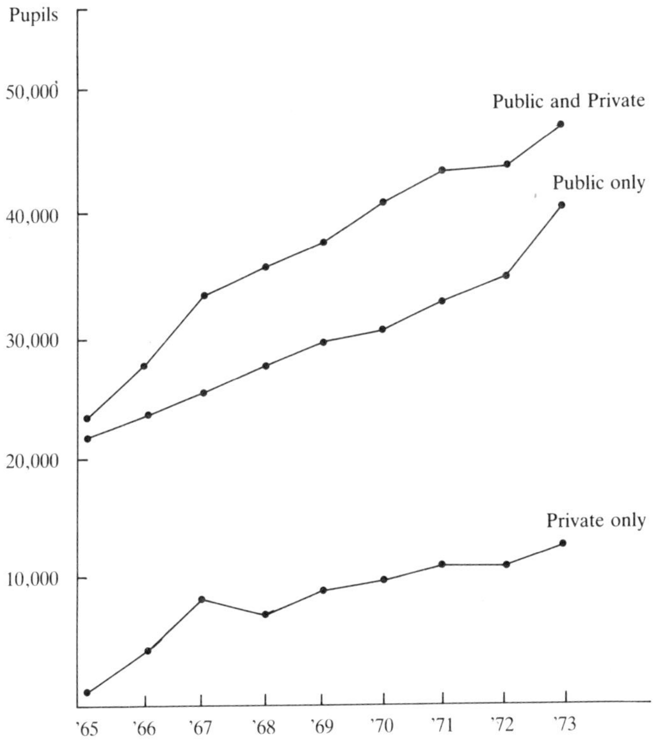

Source: *Ministry of National Education, Directorate of Planning and Development*

fact, Mbilinyi goes further to show 'how an investment philosophy still guides parental decisions on the allocations of scarce school fees between boys and girls.'[13]

The rapid expansion of the educational system reflected the manpower supply problem, as more qualified personnel were required to fill up the vacant and new posts created in state apparatus. Both the expanding bureaucracy and replacement of colonial personnel by locals (localizaton) all entailed increased output from the education system. And consonant with the lop-sided pattern of economic development, high-level manpower almost invariably meant white-collar and administrative personnel.[14] Commenting on the emphasis put on the supply of middle and high-level manpower requirements in Tanzania's educational policy, Walter Rodney writes:

> The emphasis on middle and high level manpower requirements in Tanzania's educational policy was an extension of the missionary atmosphere which produced white collar workers in the colonial pariod. The schools of independent Tanzania, in spite of reforms, continued to alienate their products from the type of labouring activity in which the overwhelming majority of the people engaged – namely, agricultural and other forms of manual work. The higher levels were providing a locally trained bureaucracy, who would strengthen the existing petty-bourgeois social formation, appropriating to itself a great part of the fruits of the nation's labour, and conducting a holding operation for international capitalism. Meanwhile, even the primary school pupils were becoming misfits in their own agricultural environment after a few years of education had set their sights on petty-bourgeois privileges.[15]

Table 2 *Demand and Supply of High-Level Manpower in Tanzania 1964/65 to 1968/69*

Job	Demand	Supply	Shortage
Category			
A	2,905	1,962	943
B	6,555	5,401	1,154
C	17,262	541	16,721

Source: Manpower Planning Unit.

Note: High-level manpower in Tanzania is defined as comprising those jobs which require a completed secondary school education.

For Category A jobs, a university degree is required.

Category B jobs require four years of secondary school, plus one to three years of further training.

Category C jobs require four years of secondary school as a minimum.

The pervasive white-collar mentality in the educational policy of Tanzania meant a relative de-emphasis on technical education. It is not surprising that the expansion of technical education lagged behind in the early post-independence period, as shown in Table 1. Both government and educationalists agreed that plans to develop Tanzania's supply of manpower should be the prime consideration in the development of education. Whatever may be said of the importance of cultural and social aspects of education, remarks one spokesman from the Ministry of Education in February 1966, it would hardly perform its functions if it did not serve economic development efforts to the fullest possible extent.[16] In short, education was committed to serving the purposes of economic development which was essentially neo-colonial in type.

It is clear that there were no essential differences in the value expectations of pupils, teachers, parents and educationalists as regards the benefits of education even during this period. Education both in the colonial and early post-independence period was viewed not as a means of developing the society as a whole, but primarily as a means of personal advancement, and separation from the greater reality of the society.* The reforms which were initiated in the wake of independence were not based on any new ideological re-orientation in spite of the pronouncements of Ujamaa (African socialism) during this period. To this extent, the publication of Ujamaa in 1962 had little or no impact at all on the general population and the 'socialist' sentiments expressed therein were no more than platitudes, for such changes that there were took place within the same inherited capitalist milieu, and for this reason 'the revamped educational system failed to serve the best interests of the workers and peasants of Tanzania.'[17] Neither within nor without the educational system did the end of colonial rule induce ideological re-orientation. It did not deviate from the capitalist-oriented policies of the colonial period and in most crucial respects the 'fundamental structure of the colonial school system was designed to further the capitalist way of life.'[18]

---

* Conversations this author had with both students and some faculty members at the University of Dar es Salaam, as well as some high school students, tended to confirm this aspect of the Tanzanian educational system – although the views expressed may be of little significance if seen in the context of a rigorous study.

We have seen that the organizational and structural reforms introduced in the early post-independence period did not yield any fundamental changes in the basic educational system, especially in the value expectations and judgements of its broad citizenry. However, several familiar problems arose as a result of these limited reforms, especially in regard to the rapid quantitative expansion of the school system. The problems are familiar in that the tremendous expansion in educational investment is one of the characteristic features of virtually all the development programmes of the newly independent African countries. At the same time, however, since the early 1960s there has been undisputable evidence from Kenya, Ghana, Nigeria, the Cameroons, Sierra Leone etc., that the adjustment to the dramatic rise in the number of people with educational qualifications has not been as smooth as had perhaps been hoped. Thus, for example, the structural change that the rapid expansion of the educational system has imposed on African wage labour markets has coincided with the emergence of serious problems of 'urban utilization'. The 'school leaver problem' refers to the fact that there are growing numbers of educated people in the urban areas who are not being utilized at all; or are being utilized less productively than used to be the case with people at their educational level. In short, the social returns to increases in the level of education of the urban population are on the decline.

In Tanzania also, some of these familiar weaknesses of the post-independence educational policies experienced by other African countries began to appear in 1966. Having provided a substantial increase in the number of primary school places, the Tanzanian Government soon found that it could offer neither a comparable number of secondary places nor paid employment that could satisfy the expectations that had been fuelled by the educational processes. It became apparent that the inherited capitalist economic system would not be able to generate enough jobs to absorb all of the increases in the numbers of people leaving primary school. Thus the country faced the so-called 'problem of primary school leavers,' as well as the more localized problem of about 400 students from the university and other institutions of higher learning demonstrating against a proposed enlistment in the National Service programme. Commenting on these two educational crises in 1966, Walter Rodney writes:

These two experiences not only revealed weaknesses in the schools but they also helped to expose the sterility of neo-colonialism from a Tanzanian viewpoint. Taken at its best, the nationalist bourgeoisie honestly aimed to educate the maximum number of people and give them jobs in the modern sector. They had assumed the mantle of the colonial state and were prepared to carry out tasks which capitalism in the colonial era had failed to fulfil. But they were to find that capitalism in the post-colonial era was equally barren. The capitalist ethic was proving incompatible with the ideal of service to the community, while international capitalism was not permitting the Tanzanian economy to expand fast enough to meet the aspirations of those who completed their education at the primary school level . . .

These two educational crises demonstrated, at least in part, that there was apparently little in the educational system which helped in creating a realistic appraisal of what the Tanzanian realities were at the time. It showed that the instrumental use of schools for socialization was limited both by their existing institutional properties and by the nature of the societal expectations which apply to them. This was affirmed by the study of Prewitt and others into school experiences and political socialization among Tanzanian school students when they wrote, 'Our findings do indeed offer some empirical support for President Nyerere's (1967) recent declaration that the source of the social dispositions of Tanzania's students is to be found in the character of their schools.'[20] Indeed, the events of 1966 did suggest, in the President's words, 'that a more thorough examination of the education we are providing must be made. It is now clearly time for us to think seriously about this question: "What is the educational system in Tanzania intended to do – what is its purpose?"' Having decided that, we have to look at the relevance of the existing structure and content of Tanzanian education for the task it had to do. In addition to the painful experiences of the educational crisis there were also economic and foreign policy problems. Both the amount of foreign investment (which was very much welcomed at this period) and loans, for example, had fallen well below expectations, coupled with the sudden withdrawal of economic aid by both Britain and West Germany.

Table 3 *Educational Output and Job Openings 1964 and 1970*

	1964	1970
University Output (East Africa and Overseas)	421	679
Form II Output	761	1,389
Entered University	506	758
Entered Labour Force	255	631
Form IV Output	3,630	6,713
Entered Form V	780	1,584
Entered Labour Force	2,950	5,129
Standard VII Output	9,121	65,624
Entered Secondary School	4,196	7,372
Entered Labour Force	4,925	58,252
Total Entered Labour Force	18,466	64,691
Primary Leavers Entered Labour Force	15,046	58,252
Post-Primary Leavers Entered Labour Force	3,426	6,439
Increase in Non-Agricultural Employment	12,856	13,229
Allowance for Turnover 10%	1,285	1,320
Allowance for Turnover 12%	11,542	1,587
Total Job Openings	15,683	16,136

Sources: *Annual Manpower Report to the President 1970*, pp. 50–63.
Employment and Earnings, 1964, 1970.

   The consequence of all this was the proclamation of the Arusha Declaration in February 1967, which set out major changes in the economic and political policies of the government with a clear commitment to building a socialist Tanzania. To be sure, the Arusha Declaration has become generally acclaimed as an important landmark in the politics of Tanzania. It formed a watershed between a Tanzania groping and unsure of the type of society it wanted and that with a confident new-found goal – socialism. However, the major policy statement 'Education for Self-Reliance' was to be issued later in March 1967. As a counterpart of the Arusha Declaration, the policy paper on education had the theme of countering the assumptions that education automatically makes one human being better than another, and that manual labour is demeaning for the learned. The role of education as a tool to equip youth for rural living received renewed attention, when the authorities were faced with the clear recognition that the creation of wage-earning jobs was doomed to lag far behind the increases in the number of people entering the labour market for a long time to come. The policy pointed out that the education to be promoted in Tanzania must encourage the growth of socialist values. It demanded a 'revolution' in attitudes and values from the inherited colonial and 'conservative' traditional norms. For Tanzania, the important task was how to modify the terms of school-inspired elitism in line with the objective of creating socialist-self-reliant citizens. And 'Education for Self-Reliance' clearly identified the pivotal agency for the re-socialization of its citizenry as the educational system.

Education has long been recognized as an instrument of socialization – used to facilitate integration of the younger generation into the logic of the present system and bring about conformity to it. To this extent every learning process carries with it the ideological values of the ruling class of the given historical time. Hence, in this sense, all educational institutions including universities are ideological institutions whether the ideology is bourgeois, as in Britain, or socialist, as in China. More concretely, Marx summed up the position of education thus: 'Education is determined by the social conditions under which you educate, by the intervention, direct or indirect, of society by means of schools, etc. Communists have not invented the intervention of society in education; they do but seek to rescue education from the influence of the ruling class.'[22] Indeed, education has been accepted as the process of transmitting accumulated knowledge and experience to the younger generation so as to ensure the survival of the society's structures (we might add, no matter how oppressive these may be). Viewed in this context, the political content passed on 'is a reflection of an actual society, serves to justify that society: its economic structures, its societal customs, its ethical and artistic concepts, in short the culture of the society.'[23]

Furthermore, education ensures the reproduction of the productive forces, i.e., it enables the transmission and expansion of scientific knowledge and technical skills from generation to generation. It is an essential tool, or rather, indispensable for the production of social wealth insofar as these skills and knowledge are necesssary for the production of this wealth, and hence it contributes to the size of the social surplus. And in a related sense, education contributes to the maintenance of the existing relations of production by its role in the realm of consciousness.

Now, if education is to become an effective agent of socialization, it must go beyond the realm of formal education to include, *inter alia*, the informal aspects of education especially in a society such as Tanzania where one of the consequences of the colonial education policy was the mass illiteracy of the colonized. Broadly conceived, socialization encompasses all social learning both formal and informal, at every stage of the life cycle of human development,[24] for social values are formed not only 'by the school but by family, school, and society – by the total environment in which a child develops.'[25] If the school is only one of several formal agencies of socialization, then any strategy that emphasizes school alone impairs the success of effective socialization in Tanzania.

Notwithstanding this obvious factor, the educational reforms of the early independence period were largely limited to the field of formal education with the result that the bulk of the illiterate adult population was left untouched.[26] This suggests that such a policy assumes, implicitly at best, that the adult population is already imbued with the new socialist culture to be inculcated. But this cannot be true for we know too well that socialism is not established in any society just by simple pronouncements or fiat. In this respect, the question of who should be socialized first – the child or the adult – becomes a crucial one, as we shall see later.

Post-Arusha Educational System 1967–72: Education for Self-Reliance

Let us now consider the objectives of the major policy document on education – 'Education for Self-Reliance'. This was Tanzania's response to the important task of how to modify the school-inspired elitism of the colonial and early post-independence educational system, in line with the objective of creating socialist, self-reliant citizens. Nyerere writes:

. . . there are four basic elements in the present system which prevent, or at least discourage, the integration of the pupils into the society they will enter, and which do encourage attitudes of inequality, intellectual arrogance and intense individualism among the young people who go through our schools . . . The most central thing about the education we are at present providing is that it is basically an elitist education designed to meet the interests and needs of a very small proportion of those who enter the school system. Although, only about 13% of our primary school children will get a place in a secondary school, the basis of our primary school education is the preparation of pupils for secondary school. Thus 87% of the children who finished primary school last year – and a similar proportion of those who will finish this year – do so with a sense of failure, of a legitimate aspiration having been denied them. Indeed we all speak in these terms, by referring to them as those who failed to enter secondary schools, instead of simply as those who have finished their primary education. On the other hand, the other 13% have a feeling of having deserved a prize – and the prize they and their parents now expect is high wages, comfortable employment in towns, and personal status in the society. The same process operates again in the next highest level, when entrance to university is the question at issue. In other words, the education now provided is designed for the few who are intellectually stronger than their fellows; it induces among those who succeed a feeling of superiority, and leaves the majority of the others hankering after something they will never obtain. It induces a feeling of inferiority among the majority, and can thus not produce either the egalitarian society we should build, nor the attitudes of mind which are conducive to an egalitarian society. On the contrary, it induces the growth of a class structure in our country.[27]

Against this rather incisive and comprehensive assessment of the existing state of the educational system of Tanzania in 1967, the President went on to suggest changes that must not only be quantitative but must also have a strong qualitative dimension.

Education must 'prepare young people for the work they will be called upon to do in the society which exists in Tanzania – a rural society where improvement will depend largely upon the efforts of the people in agriculture and in village development. It must produce good farmers and education must inculcate a sense of commitment to the total community, and help the pupils to accept the values appropriate to our kind of future not those appropriate to our colonial past.'[28] In more concrete terms the President suggested diverse policies such as:

1 raising the age of entry from 5 years to 7 or 8 years so that primary school leavers would be old enough to productively enter into farming on completing their education;
2 integrating schools and farms in such a way that children can learn modern practices and become aware of the fact that their living standards and those of the nation as a whole depend upon agriculture, since 'Tanzania will continue to have a predominantly rural economy for a long time to come';[29]
3 restructuring the school calendar so that students can help their fellow villagers at times of peak labour demand;
4 lessening the reliance on formal examinations as a means of evaluating student performance;
5 generally restructuring the curriculum, giving emphasis to subjects more directly relevant to problems of rural development.[30]

The essential thrust is on functional education, for schools must become self-reliant communities engaging in agricultural and other practical activities. The all-pervasive attitudes of competition and individualism must give way to attitudes of co-operation and service to the community with the socialist objectives of Tanzania. 'Instead of primary school activities being geared to the competitive examination which will select the few who go on to secondary school, they must be a preparation for the life which the majority of the children will lead.'[31]

It has been pointed out by some that the changes that flowed from the policy document on education represented a reintroduction of a feature of colonial education which the people and the nationalist party had totally opposed.[32] It is true the colonial legislative council proceedings for the year 1928 clearly stated that:

'. . . in any vision of future development, agriculture must occupy the foremost place . . . Everything, therefore, points to agriculture as the basis of our educational system in the elementary stages.'[33] And the 1953 primary school syllabus is even more specific in the importance attached to agriculture and 'community service' in schools.

> In the teaching and education in school it would be wrong
> to consider the pupils and their individual progress alone,
> we must consider also their responsibility in the community
> and the environment, so that their lessons may lead them
> to actions which will benefit their country . . . it is obligat-
> ory that every primary school should have a sufficient
> farm. . . . The purpose of this farm is educational,
> that is to show the practice of good farming and to
> accustom them to follow these practices.[34]

And finally two years later, the new syllabus for middle schools reiterated similar sentiments:

> The middle school course is designed to be complete in
> itself so that those who pass through it, whether they
> proceed further or not, will have received an education
> which will assist them to follow in a more intelligent and
> capable manner whatever pursuits they take up and,
> generally, to play a more useful part in the development of
> the locality to which they belong.[35]

But it would be most misleading to equate the changes in the educational system in post-Arusha Tanzania with those expressed in these colonial legislative council proceedings of 1928, or even with the comments on the primary and middle school syllabus of 1953 and 1955 respectively. For one thing, agriculture was the lowest form of labour activity with regard to prestige, in the view of the dominant colonial culture. More importantly, as Rodney himself pointed out, under colonialism, genuine scientific, technical and agricultural education to promote the comple-mentary development of industry and agriculture was ruled out. Besides, the introduction of farming and other manual work was meant only for the African schools. The children of the 'metropolitan bourgeoisie' and the Asian 'commercial bourgeoisie' were spared these 'ignoble' and demeaning demands on their superior intellect. In short, the colonial policy, in spite of the sentiments expressed above, was based on the assumption that manual tasks in society are reserved for the Africans and thus it served to perpetuate the colonial class structure in which the Africans were at the bottom rung of the ladder. It helped to maintain the exploitative relations of production and helped to reinforce the 'inferior mentality' of the Africans which the colonizers meticulously sought to establish and sustain.

The fundamental objective which emanates from 'Education for Self-Reliance' is a determination to strive for a social order based not on inequality, exploitation etc., but on '. . . equality and respect for human dignity; sharing of resources which are produced by our efforts; work by everyone and exploitation by none. . . Hence the education system needs to be transformed so that it serves to foster the social goals of living together and working together, for the common good.'[36] In this regard, the policy pronouncements of the colonial educationists bear no real resemblance to those changes introduced in post-Arusha Tanzania, for the latter were designed to complement the other comprehensive changes introduced in the other sectors of society (e.g., in the economic field) in order to fundamentally transform Tanzania towards its goal of socialism. Surely, if schools function, as we have argued, to reproduce the skills and consciousness necessary to maintain a given way of life, we would be right to expect schools in a society where the capitalist way of life is dominant – both in terms of their internal relations and their links with society as a whole – to reflect this reality and vice versa.

Other changes intended to implement 'Education for Self-Reliance' included a further re-evaluation of the curricular aspects of school experience, aimed at eliminating the colonial character of Tanzanian education. These include the more intensive use of Kiswahili, the achievement of virtual self-sufficiency in pre-university teachers, the removal of foreign references from school names, the localization of the syllabus content at all levels and the introduction of political education, paramilitary drills and defence training. The changes amounted (it was thought so at least) to a major nationalization of education in Tanzania, in the sense of removing the most viable legacies of inherited colonial practice with the hope, of course, that these changes would lead to a corresponding nationalizaton in the frame of reference of students.

As expected, the job of implementing thee changes was placed squarely with the teachers, in recognition of the crucial role teachers play in any education process.

> It is teachers more than any other single group of people who determine the attitudes of society, and who shape the ideas and aspirations of the nation. This is power in its reality. . .[37]

Indeed, the importance of teachers in the implementation process is underscored by the evidence gleaned from several studies which show that, 'teachers [in Tanzania] enjoy the trust of over 3 in 4 Tanzanian secondary pupils; in the primary schools the figure reaches 86 per cent . . . That 35 per cent of the primary and 56 per cent of the secondary school pupils in the sample mentioned teachers as having taught them the most about being good citizens – percentages that place teachers at the head of the list containing parents, TANU leaders, clergymen and a residual category of other agents.'[38]

Problems in Implementing 'Education for Self-Reliance'

It has been argued by some observers of the Tanzanian educational scene that despite 'all the organizational changes and reorientation of curriculum in the wake of "Education for Self-Reliance", in practice education in Tanzania is still elitist and bourgeois in its philosophy.'[39] Indeed, seven years after 'Education for Self-Reliance' President Nyerere declared in May 1974:

> . . . I am becoming increasingly convinced that we in Tanzania either have not yet found the right educational policy or have not yet succeeded in implementing it . . . or some combinaton of these two alternatives.[40]

Putting it even more bluntly, Foster writes:

> It is unlikely that his [Nyerere's] attempts to harness the schools to a major programme of 'egalitarian socialization' will change the largely instrumental view of education held by most of the population.[41]

Admittedly, there is a considerable body of empirical evidence to substantiate the largely 'instrumental view of education' held by students from primary school to university level. In an opinion survey on the attitude of pupils, teachers, parents, politicians and educational administrators about 'Education for Self-Reliance' in 1971, Lema concluded:

> Still in the minds of most teachers, pupils, and parents, education is interpreted simply as an academic book learning. The importance of practical education in skills such as handicrafts, and of social education in human relations, patterns of behaviour, and other attitudes of life is ignored. Success in academic education has been accepted and is projected as the highest goal a young person should strive for . . . It is no wonder then that almost everyone has come to regard academic studies as the most valuable prize in life – worth almost any sacrifice – while manual work is despised as an activity fit only for the illiterate and the 'school failures'.[42]

It cannot be denied that as long as these kinds of attitudes continue to be accepted in the community at large, especially by parents and teachers, pupils will find it difficult to interpret the value of education in a different perspective as called for in 'Education for Self-Reliance'. Indeed, the influx of children to towns from rural areas in search of the better paying white-collar jobs, for example, bears witness to this prevailing conceptualization of education.* It is little wonder then that the parents with this wrong valuation of education have been reported to be rather unhappy with the so-called self-reliant activities at school. They have been critical of

---

* See Tables 4 and 5 for patterns of migration.

the policy, and believe that the cause of their children's weakness in academic education is due to excessive work on the school *shamba* (farm) or on self-reliant projects.

> Our children don't study how to read and write nowadays. They only go to work on school farm. The farming business has become more important than writing and reading. After seven years of primary sschool, children can't even write their names.[43]

It is most significant and revealing (from evidence provided in the research findings) that the old attitudes, which venerate academic education as a symbol of wealth and status, are still held by a large number of school teachers and parents. This certainly underscores the question we posed earlier as to who should be socialized first – the child or the adult. The empirical evidence gleaned from surveys on the attitudinal component of education, leads us to speculate that no substantial political, cultural or ideological transformation of the children is feasible through the school system, as long as the adults themselves remain unsocialized and untransformed. The task of transformation and socialization is not an easy one since there is the cardinal need to make the new socialist values, attitudes and norms not only comprehensible and acceptable but internalized as well.[44] The appropriate strategy to adopt becomes even more crucial. For it is an understatement to say that Tanzania (like many of the developing states of Africa) has socialization problems quite different from those encountered by the well-established developed states of the world. In the latter, values, mores and socio-political practices are, by and large, no longer in dispute by the majority or the majority of the citizenry are imbued with the same values.

> In established developed countries formal and informal agents of socialization do reinforce the established and accepted pre-dispositions, thus inculcating the future generation with political information, values and socio-cultural practices. It should be noted here that the adults in established states do not need to be transformed – they are the very embodiment of that particular culture. Furthermore unlike young nations all agents – formal as

Table 4 *Male Migrants: Education by Time of Arrival in Town 1970 (Percentages)*

	No Education	Some Education	Standards 1–4	Standards 5–8	Forms 1–6	University
Before Independence	33	67	29	28	9	1
After Independence	14	86	21	44	20	2

Source: Adapted from R.H. Sabot, 'Education, Income Distribution, and Rates of Urban Migration in Tanzania,' *Economic Research Bureau Paper 72.6*, University of Dar es Salaam, 1972.

Table 5 *Male Migrants: Rates of Urban Migration by Age and Education (Percentages)*

Age	No Education	Some Education	Standards 1–4	Standards 5–8	Forms 1–6	University
14–19	0.15	1.62	.60	2.65	5.0	3.33
25–34	0.28	1.88	.81	3.45	11.11	22.22
35–44	0.47	2.00	1.00	3.61	11.81	20.00
45–59	0.46	2.62	1.63	4.69	15.00	50.00
60 and Over	0.55	4.00	2.09	12.10	30.00	–

Source: *Ibid.*, p. 9.

well as informal ones – reinforce the same cherished values, cultural traits, beliefs and norms. As total integration in any one state can hardly be achieved, it is true that they do have a segment of diverse if not antagonistic population. However, the segment may be small in size or disorganized or dispersed or it may be weak and so by use of either the carrot (e.g. by giving more schools for the disadvantaged, school welfare etc.) or by the use of the big stick (e.g. prisons, detentions and shooting by police) the establishment does contain that segment and are able to disarm any elements of potential instability.[45]

In Tanzania two socialization strategies have beeen employed in the attempt to ensure the comprehension, acceptance and internalization of the new political values, attitudes and norms enshrined both in the Arusha Declaration and subsequent major policy documents including 'Education for Self-Reliance'.

1 Through voluntary 'Ujamaaization' – which will be taken up in the next chapter. Suffice to say here that it means essentially the encouragement of peasants, especially in those less developed areas at the beginning, to start commercial Ujamaa villages where they would live and work together and share the proceeds of their communal co-operative efforts.

2 Socialization through the formal education system. But we have already shown that both teachers and adults (in large numbers) remain apathetic towards the ideals expressed in 'Education for Self-Reliance'. They still maintain the old attitudes which venerate academic education as a symbol of wealth and status. Since adults (including the teachers) in Tanzania have not yet been changd in sufficient numbers, it could be argued that the other channels of socialization – the family, the peer group, the factory, the civil service etc. – are incapable of imparting the new ideals of Ujamaa. Ujamaaization requires a radical transformation of old values and attitudes. Old attitudes die hard (so the popular saying goes), and to bring about socio-cultural transformation requires an alteration in adult attitudes. Recognizing the inadequacies of the formal school system in the task of re-socialization, a major

drive towards adult education was embarked upon following the President's speech on adult education on New Year's Eve 1969.*

Aims and Objectives of Adult Education in Tanzania

With the Arusha Declaration and the attendant change in emphasis, adult education increasingly gained more attention. Earlier attempts in the realm of adult education had lacked a coherent ideology that would define the direction and the degree of change, and provide the required motivation for the nation to move in that direction. The absence of an appropriate ideological framework had led to the absence of a national adult education development front. There is no denying the fact that the role of adult education in effecting development, particularly in the rural areas, can best be appreciated in a situation where there is a clear national policy. That policy should state in clear terms what strategies will be employed in mobilizing the necessary human and other resources, and should take into account the need to motivate and activate the rural population whose participation in every programme at all the stages of its development is essential. The Arusha Declaration gave it the much needed ideological content and clarity. Broadly speaking, therefore, the objectives contained in the subsequent documents** and summarized by the President himself were:

* It must be pointed out that the Arusha Declaration itself had two major implications for adult education: 1) being a socialist policy it theoretically provided for equal educational opportunity to all citizens, young and old, and 2) the policy of Self-Reliance and Rural Development required full participation by all the citizens – irrespective of age and sex. Thus eradication of illiteracy among adults came to be regarded as a political imperative.
** These include:
1 The second 5-Year Plan (1969–74);
2 The President's Adult Education Year Speech in 1969;
3 The 15th and 16th TANU Biennial Conference Resolutions (1971 and 1973, respectively); and
4 The Prime Minister's Directive on Workers Education in 1973.

1   To learn how to improve our lives.
2   To make everyone understand our national policy of socialism and Self-Reliance.

Following the President's speech the Ministry of National Education put out the following elaborations on its operating goals:

1   To mobilize the rural and urban masses and arouse them to consciousness of Ujamaa socialism.
2   To give knowledge and skills that will improve the productivity of the people and help raise their standards of living.
3   To eradicate illiteracy.
4   To provide follow-up education to primary and secondary school leavers and to adults with a view to settling them in Ujamaa villages and rural areas.
5   To provide leadership training in various aspects of rural life.[46]

What clearly emerges from these aims and objectives is the fact that the political leadership in Tanzania has recognized fully that adult education is essential in promoting a well-integrated kind of development as required by the new national goals and objectives. It is the kind of development that means participation by people in the major decisions which affect their lives. It means liberation from colonial or neo-colonial ways of thinking. A significant role was played by the media (especially radio and to a lesser extent print).[47] Thus in 1971 the Institute of Adult Education, University of Dar es Salaam, experimented with radio-study-group campaigns in a major attempt to reach people who had been outside the formal educational system – the rural population. The message for Tanzania was clear in the Arusha Declaration: the key to development, it said, is the improvement of agriculture, which implies the development of better agriculturalists.

The importance attached to adult education by the leadership is further borne out by later directives on adult education, which called upon the government, the party and parastatal offices throughout the country to draw up and conduct education and training programmes for their workers of all levels of education, in order to improve their productive and intellectual capacities. Indeed, Tanzania is often singled out among many developing countries as a country having a well-formulated adult education policy, a declared commitment to it, and well-designed implementation machinery. 'As has often been stated, a great asset for the educational planner in Tanzania is its well defined and consistent taxonomy of goals and objectives.'[48] Similarly, the international symposium on adult education for development held in Dar es Salaam in 1974 noted that for many adult educationalists in the world, Tanzania not only exhibits a clear national policy regarding adult education but also demonstrates a unique approach to the subject. Furthermore, it stated, in terms of financing, 'In Tanzania, adult education is allocated more than 10% of Ministry of National Education budget, in addition considerable financial support is given to many other organizations involved in adult education noting that the eradication of illiteracy is regarded as a social duty and the target date for the complete victory over illiteracy is 1975.'[49]

However, in his study to find out the extent to which adult education policy in Tanzania was actually being translated into action at the district level, Mlekwa concluded: 'that while Tanzania has boldly declared her stand *vis-à-vis* adult education and has gone even to the extent of declaring deadlines for accomplishing certain programmes such as eradication of illiteracy by 1975, there still are a number of problems to solve in order to achieve complete victory.'[50] Such problems include absenteeism by those enrolled for classes, as well as the diversity of meanings which the different categories of people seem to attach to the whole question of adult education.

Before concluding our discussion on the role of schools in the implementation of socialism in Tanzania, we would like to emphasize the place of teachers in the scheme of things. We have shown that there is a considerable body of empirical evidence revealed by Lema, Mbilinyi, etc., that the schoolteachers themselves still hold attitudes of worshipping education as a 'symbol of wealth and status'. We have also shown that teachers in a number of schools in Tanzania are highly esteemed, well remunerated and quite non-socialist in orientation. Above all they have had a bad effect on the majority of the student body, who have also continued to view education as a symbol of wealth and status.[51] We have also shown that self-reliance projects are held in contempt by staff and, consequently, by the students. If the cornerstone for the implementation of Ujamaa are teachers (as rightly emphasized by the country's leadership), then these shortcomings seriously undermine the successful implementation of education for self-reliance. Even more crucial for the successful implementation of education for self-reliance is the significant role played by the expatriate staff who originate from the capitalist world in the educational system at both the secondary and university level.[52] This is not to deny the fact that a number of expatriate staff indeed view socialism favourably but there is no gainsaying the fact that

> The vast majority consider themselves either 'apolitical' or are explicitly and consciously hostile to socialist ideas . . . Even more crucial and pernicious, however, is the implicit and sometimes explicit organization of curricula and courses around textbooks and concepts which carry an anti-socialist bias. Indeed most of the teaching and reference material, especially that used in the social sciences, originates from the United Kingdom and the U.S.A. and, therefore soaking with the official and widely shared anti-socialist and anti-communist orthodoxy.[53]

This is equally true in the fields of research and publishing. Many major research projects on various aspects of Tanzanian politics were carried out by expatriates during the period of study. It must however be pointed out that a lot more has been done since then to rectify the situation. The establishment of the Tanzanian Publishing House, for example, has meant the publication of volumes that would not have had the chance to see the light of day, as well as the publication of much more relevant textbooks for primary and secondary schools in particular. Equally, a growing proportion of the research done on Tanzania is now undertaken by Tanzanians themselves within the country. The efforts so far are far from being self-reliant in both areas. The important thing is that a qualitative start in the right direction has been made.

Not the least contradictory in terms of self-reliance, is the fact that even at the strategic Kivukoni College – the ideological Institute for Tanzania – where socialist cadres are to be trained in large numbers (for there cannot be socialism without socialists), there were a significant number of expatriate staff in its formative years, as well as during the period of our study. At the February 1967 National Conference called to discuss the Arusha Declaration, loud criticisms were voiced against Kivukoni's continued dependence upon expatriate staff. 'It is certainly not an ideal situation to have an expatriate teaching about the removal of existing privileged position. When the teacher's voice is alien, it is difficult to be really convincing when explaining the meaning of self-reliance as having confidence in the people to develop their own resources in their own interests.'[54] Similarly, commenting on the unsuitability of expatriate teachers as agents of programmed political education, Muhll writes:

> . . . It is at least unlikely that an African pupil will fully identify with a teacher of a different race or cultural background; and to that extent the legitimacy of the expatriate teacher as an exponent of any doctrine is seriously impaired. Moreover, an expatriate teacher is unlikely to discuss civic issues as candidly and as fully as he would in his own country. The Peace Corps, for example, has unequivocally admonished its members not to teach or engage in politics; and while individual members may vary in their definitions of 'politics' or their disposition to obey the injunction the rationale for the rule is clear.[55]

But perhaps even more crucial for our purposes is the relationship between the students who graduate from the secondary schools, the universities and other higher institutions of learning. The relationship is crucial to the extent that the vast majority of the middle- and higher-level positions of the country's civil service are staffed by these graduates (see Tables 6, 7 and 8), who are now called upon to take key policy decisions both in the economy and elsewhere in the state apparatus. (Of course, they become teachers too.) For it is obviously incorrect to think of 'big decisions' as springing full-blown from the politicians. With some exceptions, it would be rare for politicians, faced with the choice of a well-articulated plan backed by the full weight of 'technical' opinion or their own vague preferences, to choose the latter.[56] And of course, 'one of the myths that must be exorcised from the outset is that haloing the figure of the "non-political" civil servant giving "purely technical advice"'.[57]

If as we have shown, the vast majority of students are largely

Table 6 *High- and Middle-Level Employment 1968–9*

	Citizens*	Non-Citizens	Total	Vacancies
I. University level				
Science/Maths-based	446	1,491	1,937	326
Arts-based	966	1,177	2,143	285
Total[a]	1,403	2,673	4,076	613
II. Sub-professional	8,797	2,146	10,943	668
III. Secondary School requirements[b]				
Skilled office	18,074	2,256	20,330	2,415
Skilled manual	7,412	1,341	8,753	192
Total	25,486	3,597	29,083	2,607

[a] Totals are as given in the source.

[b] Many of these posts were, however, filled by individuals without a secondary school certificate. The terminology used in the report is that these are jobs 'requiring a secondary school education for adequate performance of the full array of tasks involved.'

Source: Tanzania, *Tanzania Second Five Year Plan, 1969–74*, Vol. IV, Tables 4, 5, 6.

Table 7 *African Higher Incomes 1964 and 1970*

	1964	1970
Exceeding shs.100 per month		
A. Enterprise sector	2,246	6,707
B. Public sector	–	4,890
Total	2,246	11,597
Between Shs.500 and 999 per month		
A. Enterprise sector	7,269	11,148
B. Public sector	–	14,762
Total	7,269	25,910

Source: Tanzania, *Survey of Employment and Earnings, Tanzania, 1970* (Dar es Salaam: 1972).

imbued with elitist mentality, being 'technocratic and bureaucratic' in outlook – much more interested in their own eventual perquisites and economic well-being (though the avenues for conspicuous consumption, for example, have now been severely restricted), than in the imperatives of Tanzanian socialism – then we can reasonably conclude that they would favour the continued maintenance of their privileged positions, political, economic and otherwise, in the vital decisions they are called upon to make.* To this extent they will be more disposed to the non-socialists/pragmatists of the bureaucratic bourgeoisie stratum, since there is a congruency of interests, and hence exacerbate the struggle between the political leadership and the bureaucratic bourgeoisie strata in their swollen numbers. The more their numbers, the

---

* It is illuminating and fitting that one of the placards held up during the student demonstrations at the University College, Dar es Salaam, in 1966 read: 'Colonialism was Better.' Indeed, the conversations this author had with several undergraduate and graduate students, as well as some faculty members at the University of Dar es Salaam, confirm the view that there is a great degree of cynicism and lip-service about Ujamaa at the Hill.

Table 8 *Localization of the Senior- and Middle-Grade Civil Service as at December 31 1971: Citizenship of Officers*

	1962	1963	1964	1965	1966	1967	1968	1969	1970	1971
Tanzanian Citizens	1,821	2,469	3,083	3,951	4,364	4,937	6,208	6,379	8,042	9,708
Non-Citizens	2,902	2,580	2,306	2,011	1,710	1,817	1,619	1,410	1,377	1,015
Total Officers	4,723	5,049	5,389	5,962	6,074	6,754	7,827	7,789	9,419	10,723
Localization*	38.5	48.9	57.2	66.3	71.8	73.1	79.3	81.9	85.6	90.5

* These percentages refer only to officers actually holding posts in civil service. If the vacant posts to be filled by overseas recruitment are included in the exercise, the percentage of localized posts would be much lower.

Source: Central Establishment Division, President's Office.

greater and more intense the struggle and the stronger their link with international capitalism.

The above discussion suggests that the successful implementation of 'Education for Self-Reliance' depends to a considerable degree on the successful reorientation of the adults (including teachers) in Tanzania. On a more general level, graduates from the higher institutions of learning, in the higher echelons of the bureaucracy, perhaps pose even a more formidable problem, given the crucial economic role they play in the state apparatus. However, notwithstanding these problem areas, it appears that the educational policies and programmes in post-Arusha Tanzania tend to be more consistent with the evolving socialist theoretical framework. The problems encountered in its implementation are, of course, not entirely unexpected. But more importantly, some noticeable attempts are being made by the political leadership to re-examine, adapt and change any of the programmes that have been found to be unsuitable in the light of practical experiences while still remaining under the ambit of socialist objectives. Indeed, even Lema's critical study of the attitudes of teachers in Tanzania concedes that the majority of teachers, pupils and parents who were interviewed, expressed some satisfaction in what has been achieved since 1967. Many expressed the feeling that education was now for the first time developing in the 'right direction' for Tanzanian society. 'There is no question at all that in the organization of study programmes and in the general administration, most schools are more than ever before in line with the concept of "Education for Self-Reliance"'[58] The rather contemptuous attitude towards manual work as being below the dignity of a person undertaking academic studies may still not have disappeared completely, but it is dying out gradually. For after all, rarely if ever have a people's traditional values been successfully changed in a generation. To that extent, Tanzania is unique among its erstwhile 'socialist' counterparts in the rest of Africa – not to mention the avowed capitalists. It is not only confronting the fact that the inherited educational system reflects considerations having little or nothing to do with the intended objectives of creating socialist citizens; it is also committed to bringing about much needed fundamental transformations in the system.

We began our discussion by noting the critical attitudinal component of the development process in the developing nations

76

of Africa and the strategic role of education in this process. We also noted that in Tanzania the educational role goes beyond just mere formal education. It includes education efforts designed to mobilize not only students and workers, but also peasants, into socialist, self-reliant, democratic economic units. These must take into account the situation in the villages in the countryside, and it is to this we now turn.

Chapter 3 On Implementing Socialism and Self-Reliance: The Role of Education and Political Socialization

1. Cited in Goran Hyden, *Political Development in Rural Tanzania* (Nairobi: East African Publishing House, 1969), p. 46.
2. Paulo Freire, *The Pedagogy of the Oppressed* (New York: Herder, 1970), p. 31.
3. *Ibid.*, p. 151.
4. Julius K. Nyerere, *Ujamaa: Essays on Socialism* (Dar es Salaam: Oxford University Press, 1968), pp. 46–48.
5. Kenneth Prewitt, ed. *Education and Political Values: An East African Case Study* (Nairobi: East African Publishing House, 1971), Introduction.
6. Dawson and Prewitt, eds., *Political Socialization* (Boston: Little, Brown and Company, 1969), p. 6.
7. See for example, J. Kahl, *A Study of Values in Brazil and Mexico* (Austin: University of Texas Press, 1968); and A. Inkeles, 'Participant Citizenship in Six Developing Nations,' *American Political Science Review* (January, 1970).
8. A. Van de Laar, 'Towards Manpower Development Strategy in Tanzania' in *Socialism in Tanzania* edited by Cliffe and Saul (Nairobi: East African Publishing House, 1972), p. 226. See also Table 1 for the educational characteristics of 1961.
9. Walter Rodney, 'Education and Tanzanian Socialism' in *Tanzania: Revolution by Education* edited by Idrian N. Resnick (Dar es Salaam: Longmans of Tanzania, 1968), p. 71.
10. *The Economic Survey 1971–72* (Government Printer, Dar es Salaam, 1972), p. 131.
11. Nyerere, *Ujamaa: Essays on Socialism*, p. 56.
12. Van de Laar, 'Education and Educational Planning in Tanzania,' Economic Research Bureau No. 67.2, University College, Dar es Salaam (1967), p. 167.

13. M. Mbilinyi, 'Education of Girls in Tanzania.' (Dar es Salaam: Institute of Education, 1969).

14. Thus in 1962, out of a total of 4,723 senior and middle grade civil servants 38.5 per cent were Tanzanians. In 1971, the total had gone up to 10,723 out of which local personnel constituted 90.5 per cent. See *The Economic Survey 1971–1972*, p. 133. However, we are aware of the fact that the attainment of 'flag independence' which was accompanied in some cases by a sizeable exodus of foreign and technical personnel, necessitated the rapid training of local personnel to fill the created gaps.

15. Rodney, 'Education and Tanzanian Socialism' in *Tanzania: Revolution by Education* ed. by Resnick, p. 75.

16. A. C. Mwingira, *Education Policy and Development Policy in Tanzania* (Dar es Salaam: Institute of Education, February 1966), mimeo.

17. Rodney, 'Education and Tanzanian Socialism' in *Tanzania: Revolution by Education* ed. by Resnick, p. 74.

18. J. P. Breeden, 'The Struggle for Socialist Education in Tanzania' in *Papers in Education and Development*, Department of Education, University of Dar es Salaam, 1975.

19. Rodney, 'Education and Tanzanian Socialism' in *Tanzania: Revolution by Education* ed. by Resnick, p. 76. Table 3 gives us an idea of the magnitude of the problem of finding jobs for the primary school leavers in particular.

20. K. Prewitt, G. von der Muhll, D. Court, 'School Experiences and Political Socialization: A Study of Tanzanian Secondary School Students', *Comparative Political Studies*, Vol. 3, No. 2 (July, 1970), pp. 203–222.

21. Nyerere, 'Education for Self-Reliance' in *Ujamaa: Essays on Socialism*, p. 49.

22. Quoted by Grant Kamenju, 'In Defence of a Socialist Concept of Universities' in *Socialism in Tanzania*, ed. by Cliffe and Saul, Vol. 2. *Policies* (Nairobi: East African Publishing House, 1972), p. 286.

23. Samora Machel, 'Educate Man to Win the War, Create a New Society and Develop the Country' in *Mozambique: Sowing the Seeds of Revolution*, ed. by John Saul (Toronto: Toronto University Press, 1974), p. 38.

It must, however, be pointed out that this rather narrow view of the role of educaton must not blind us to the fact that in a broader context education as a tool for independent reflection (expressed in such popular phrases as 'education for the sake of education,' 'knowledge for the sake of knowledge' etc.) has been an essential part of the philosophy of education in the West.

24. F. I. Greenstein, 'Political socialization' in *International Encyclopaedia of the Social Sciences* Vol. 14, p. 551.
25. Nyerere, 'Education for Self-Reliance' in *Ujamaa: Essays on Socialism*, p. 74.
26. The 1967 census showed that 26 per cent of the work force were of lower primary school education, 4 per cent of the entire force had one year of secondary education and above. By 1971 about 51.9 per cent were not having formal education at all. Only 45.6 per cent could enter Standard 1; 2.64 per cent in Form 1; 0.2 per cent in Form 5 and only 0.3 per cent were able to enter university. Furthermore, although there has been a 5 per cent decrease in illiteracy within a decade, there were about 4 million illiterates out of a total population of 14 million in 1970. Thus while the illiteracy rate was decreasing, the absolute numbers were increasing during the period of our study. See The Economic Affairs and Development Plan, Ministry of Manpower Planning Division, *Annual Manpower Report to the President, 1971*, (Dar es Salaam).
27. Nyerere, 'Education for Self-Reliance' in *Ujamaa: Essays on Socialism*, pp. 54–55.
28. *Ibid.*, p. 52.
29. *Ibid.*, p. 51.
30. *Ibid.*, p. 52.
31. *Ibid.*, p. 61.
32. Rodney, 'Education and Tanzanian Socialism' in *Tanzania: Revolution by Education* ed. by Resnick, p. 77. Philip Forster also alluded to the similarity when he said, 'efforts to make the schools productive agencies and centres for agricultural education merely reflect the pattern of far earlier efforts and proposals and are unlikely to be viable.' See Philip Forster, 'Education for Self-Reliance: A Critical Evaluation' in *Education in Africa: Research and Action* edited by R. Jolly, (Nairobi: East African Publishing House, 1969), p. 81.
33. J. Cameron and W. A. Dodd, *Society, Schools and Progress in Tanzania* (Oxford: Pergamon Press, 1970), p. 69.
34. *Ibid.*, p. 109.
35. No information – see p.96 of text.
36. Nyerere, 'Education for Self-Reliance' in *Ujamaa: Essays on Socialism*, p. 52.
37. Julius Nyerere, quoted in George von der Muhll, 'Education, Citizenship and Social Revolution in Tanzania' in *Education and Political Values: An East African Case Study*, ed. by Kenneth Prewitt (Nairobi: East African Publishing House, 1971), p. 23.

38. See D. Koff and G. von der Muhll, 'Political Socialization in Kenya and Tanzania: A Comparative Analysis,' *Journal of Modern African Studies*, Vol. 5, No. 1 (1967), pp. 22–27.
39. By way of elaboration, Ndonde further contends that the elitist education of the educators, their job training and their bourgeois notions about their role of developing the 'traditional' peasant, the inherent contempt and mistrust for the same peasants as well as the low cultural level of the peasants themselves due to many years of underdevelopment, put the educators and the rest of Tanzanians *vis-à-vis* the peasants in a situation analogous to that of an exploiter and exploited, oppressor and oppressed. Given such social relations, he argues that it is difficult for educators to use educational methods which will arouse the people's awareness and enable them to unleash their potential creativeness which is a prerequisite for self-reliant development. Emile C. Ndonde, 'Educational Methods for Self-Reliant Development,' *Maji Maji*, No. 25 (January, 1976), p. 22. See also K. F. Hirji, 'School Education and Underdevelopment in Tanzania,' *Maji Maji*, No. 12 (September, 1972).
40. Cited in 'Education for Liberation' in *Documents on Adult Education* No. 1, Institute of Adult Education, Dar es Salaam, 1974.
41. Forster, 'Education for Self-Reliance: A Critical Evaluation' in *Education in Africa: Research and Action* ed. by Jolly, p. 81.
42. A. A. Lema, 'Education for Self-Reliance: A brief Survey of Self-Reliant Activities in some Tanzanian Schools and Colleges,' Institute of Education, University of Dar es Salaam, (1972), p. 27.
43. This was a parent's answer to one of the survey questions in Lema's study. To some extent some of the negative attitudes of pupils towards self-reliant activities at school is attributable to talk of motivation as well as the failure on the part of teachers to consult with or explain to the pupils the entire planning of the projects in the true spirit of 'Education for Self-Reliance.' For instance, in early 1971, the pupils in one of the schools had harvested several sackfuls of maize from the school *shamba*. Later on they learned that they could not get lunch because the school was short of maize flour; they became puzzled and very angry. They were puzzled as to why the maize they had harvested only a few months before had not been used for their lunch. Apparently all the maize had been sold without the knowledge of the pupils. Lema, 'Education for Self-Reliance: A brief Survey. . . ,' pp. 33 and 35.
44. Speaking about comprehensiveness, Lema argued, on the basis of the empirical evidence from his study, that many of the negative

attitudes revealed during the interviews are caused by misconceptions about the true meaning of 'Education for Self-Reliance'. Some teachers, for instance, did not fully understand the implications of the new policy, nor were they sure how to interpret its significance to their pupils.

45. F. I. Greenstein, 'Political Socialization' in *International Encyclopaedia of the Social Sciences*, Vol. 14, p. 551.

46. See *SASA* No. 2, Institute of Adult Education, University of Dar es Salaam (November, 1971).

47. The need to use radio became evident when it was discovered that the evening-class activities of university adult education programmes were in fact aiding the process of increasing social stratification by offering courses of an academic nature to those who were already comparatively well educated.

48. O. Osterling, 'The Literacy Campaign in Tanzania: A Short Introduction,' *The Directorate of Adult Education*, Ministry of National Education, Dar es Salaam (1972), p. 11.

49. *Ibid.*, p. 9.

50. V. M. Mlekwa, 'The Policy and Practice of Adult Education in Tanzania Since the Adult Education Year 1970: A district case study,' (M.A. thesis, University of Dar es Salaam, 1975).

51. Indeed, Lema found out in his study that it was not uncommon in his village today for the elders to voluntarily give up the seats they might be sitting on at a meeting to young men who are home on vacation from secondary or university studies and happen to attend the meetings. The highly educated are seen as clean, sophisticated and enjoy an enviable reputation in the community, even if they do very little for the society itself. The educated men may be arrogant, lazy and unconforming to the ways of the society but in the village they will still be 'admitted for inexplicable reasons'. Lema, 'Education for Self-Reliance: A brief Survey . . . ,' p. 27.

52. In 1965, there were for example 82 established posts for education officers in the Secondary School Division of the Ministry of Education. Only 17 of these were held by Tanzanians, with 41 non-citizens being employed and a further 24 posts being vacant. Similarly, there were 451 secondary school teachers who were grade 2 officers, only 41 of these were citizens. See C. Pratt, *The Critical Phase in Tanzania 1945–1968* (Cambridge: Cambridge University Press, 1976), p. 131.

53. G. Kamenju, 'In Defence of a Socialist Concept of Universities' in *Socialism in Tanzania* edited by Saul and Cliffe Vol. 2 (Nairobi: East African Publishing House, 1972), p. 286.

54. Belle Haris, 'An Ideological Institute for Tanzania' in *Tanzania: Revolution by Education*, ed. by Resnick, p. 159. All this may be reminiscent of nationalist politics carried out in the wake of independence in most of Black Africa (some of the educational reforms in Tanzania have been undertaken in countries ideologically as diverse as Nigeria and Ghana etc.) Similarly, some of the concerns expressed about expatriate staff from capitalist countries have also been voiced by officials even in those countries, e.g., Nigeria, that have opted for some form of capitalism. The indigenization policy in Nigeria, for example, is a classic case in point. To this extent it could be argued that the reforms in Tanzania's educational system may simply be a reflection of an ongoing nationalism not unlike what is taking place in the rest of Africa. While we agree that it is virtually impossible to divest completely the element of nationalism in the educational reforms of post-Arusha Tanzania, we would point out that there is a significant difference between the reforms in Tanzania and countries such as Senegal, Ivory Coast, Kenya etc., at least in one major respect. That is, the reforms and the concerns expressed in Tanzania have tended to reflect a commitment on the part of the political leadership to work towards the realization of congruency between ideology and practice.
55. Von der Muhll, 'Education, Citizenship and Social Revolution in Tanzania' in *Education and Political Values*, ed. by Prewitt, pp. 42–3.
56. John Saul, 'High-Level Manpower for Socialism' in *Socialism in Tanzania*, ed. by Saul and Cliffe, Vol. 2 *Policies* (Nairobi: East African Publishing House, 1972), p. 277.
57. *Ibid*.
58. Lema, 'Education for Self-Reliance: A brief Survey . . . ,' p. 51. Similar trends were established by David Court in his 1975 survey of schools in the Coast Region, Tanga Region, Kilimanjaro, when compared to his earlier 1966 survey. See some of the results of the survey in the Appendices. David Court, 'School Experiences and the Making of Citizens: A Study of Tanzanian Secondary School Students,' (Ph.D. dissertation, Standfort University, 1975), pp. 199–210.

Chapter 4

On Socialism in Rural Tanzania: The Policy and Implementation of Ujamaa Vijijini

For while other people can aim at reaching the
moon, and while in future we might aim at
reaching the moon, our present plans must be
directed at reaching the villages . . .

Julius K. Nyerere

In this chapter we shall argue that the political leadership in
post-Arusha Tanzania had recognized the need to develop the
Ujamaa Village programme in order to create the basis for future
economic and social transformation consistent with the goals of
socialism. We shall attempt to show that the slow pace in the
implementation of rural socialism in this period was partly due to
the fact that the bureaucracy, in its role as implementors of
Ujamaa Vijijini, was more interested in Ujamaa villages (which
they saw as mere settlement schemes) than in Ujamaa Vijijini *per
se*.

We have already noted that the education system in Tanzania
was designed to mobilize not only students and workers but also
peasants into socialist, self-reliant and democratic economic units.
The proposition that socialist transformation can be achieved by
means of peasant mobilization in traditional structures is not new
in socialist theory. The Narodiniks held the view that the Russian
village commune could become the basis for a socialist society and

that the major political effort ought to be concentrated on the peasantry.* Replying to the Narodiniks, Marx and Engels wrote in the preface to the Russian edition of *The Communist Manifesto* of January 21, 1882 that:

> The question is now whether the Russian village commune – a form of primitive collective communal property which has indeed already been to a large extent destroyed – can pass immediately into the highest communist form of landed property or whether, on the contrary, it must go through from the beginning the same process of disintegration as that which has determined the historical development of the west. The only answer to this question today is as follows: if the Russian revolution becomes the signal for the workers' revolution in the West, so that the one supplements the other, then the present form of land ownership in Russia may be the starting point of an historical development.[1]

What interests us in these views is the fact that they left open the possibility that a predominantly peasant country can make substantial advances towards socialism without going through capitalism – a view that later gained wide recognition and indeed acceptance especially under the ideological tutelage of the late Mao Tse-tung. And as if to salvage Marx and Engels and, consequently, Marxism from their implied rejection of the Narodiniks' view in the above dialogue, Hobsbawn points out that Marx 'increasingly stressed the viability of the primitive commune . . . and even . . . its capacity to develop into a higher form of economy without prior destruction.'[2] In fact, continues

---

* For our purposes we shall refer to the peasantry in the manner of Redfield, as consisting of small agricultural producers who, with the help of simple equipment and the labour of their families, produce mainly for their own consumption and for the fulfilment of obligations to the holders of political and economic power. Such a definition implies a specific relation to land, and the peasant family farm and the peasant village community as the basic units of social interaction. See R. Redfield, *Peasant Society and Culture* (Chicago: University of Chicago Press, 1956), p. 23 and 25.

84

Hobsbawn, Marx 'had always admitted the positive social values embodied, in however backward a form, in the primitive community.'[3] Certainly, Hobsbawn declares, Marxism does not consider the commune a 'worthless' institution.

The pertinence of these views to the African and, in particular, the Tanzanian situation lies in the fact that there is a growing recognition on the part of many of the national leaders in Africa that the mobilization of the peasantry is fundamental for any meaningful social advance in Africa. But, although the strategies for implementation may differ, there is the widely shared recognition too that the village structures must be taken into account in the process of mobilization in the rural sector. In Tanzania the importance attached to the rural peasantry in the task of socialist transformation becomes evident in the President's policy document titled 'Socialism and Rural Development' of September 1967, which followed the publication of the Arusha Declaration earlier that year:

> For the foreseeable future the vast majority of our people
> will continue to spend their lives in the rural areas and
> continue to work on the land. The land is the only basis
> for Tanzania's development; we have no other. Therefore,
> if our rural life is not based on the principles of socialism
> our country will not be socialist, regardless of how we
> organise our industrial sector, and regardless of our
> commercial and political arrangements. Tanzanian
> socialism must be firmly based on the land and its workers.
> This means that we have to build up the countryside in
> such a way that our people have a better standard of
> living, while living together in terms of equality and
> fraternity. It also means that, in the course of time, the
> advantages of town life in the way of services and personal
> pleasures and opportunities must become available to
> those who work in the rural sector as much as those in
> urban areas.[4]

In short, the battle for socialism in Tanzania would be lost or won in the countryside. This is not to deny the fact that rural development must be situated within its wider economic and socio-political environment and also related to overall development strategies, especially if the move towards a programme of integrated rural development, which leads in the direction of the kind of socialist society Tanzania is attempting to establish, is to be taken seriously. Thus, for example, the international market-place and Tanzania's dependence on it, the presence or absence of an effective industrial strategy, the urban-rural relationships, the character of national class formations, etc., can all have an impact upon the continued ability to mobilize genuine enthusiasm in the peasantry for local development efforts. Notwithstanding these relationships, however, it is fair to say that the rural policy process as contained in the policy document 'Socialism and Rural Development', has its own dynamic as well. We shall therefore in this chapter focus more concretely on the specific policies towards the formation of Ujamaa villages – the institution designed to effect rural socialist transformation – in the countryside within the context of the existing agricultural systems of Tanzania. In effect, this means an examination, first, of earlier efforts at conventional agricultural development schemes or programmes within an essentially capitalist rural economic structure in such areas as settlement, cooperatives and extension and other related activities; and secondly, of the post-Arusha attempts by the political leadership of Tanzania to 'evade the logic of capitalist development' by challenging the spontaneous emergence of rural capitalism, and postulating development upon the construction of a collective mode of production in line with the imperatives of Tanzania's socialist objectives.

> But the basic difference between Tanzania's rural life now
> and in the past stems from the widespread introduction of
> cash crop farming. Over large areas of the country
> peasants spend at least part of their time – and sometimes
> the larger part of it – on the cultivation of crops for sale –
> crops like cotton, coffee, sisal, pyrethrum, and so on. But
> in the process the old traditions of living together, working
> together, and sharing the proceeds, have often been
> abandoned. Farmers tend to work as individuals, in
> competition and not in cooperation with their neighbours.
> And in many places our most intelligent and hard-working
> peasants have invested their money . . . in clearing more
> land, extending their acreage, using better tools, and so

on, until they have quite important farms of 10, 20 or even more acres. To do this, they have employed other people to work for them . . . The result has been an increase in production for the nation as a whole . . . and still further increase in the wealth of the man who owned, managed and initiated the larger farm . . . But the moment such a man extends his farm to a point where it is necessary for him to employ labourers in order to plant or harvest the full acreage, then the traditional system of Ujamaa has been killed . . . And the result is that the spirit of equality between all people working on the farm has gone – for the employed are the servants of the man who employs them. Thus we have the beginnings of a class system in the rural areas . . . If this kind of capitalist development takes place widely over the country, we may get a good statistical increase in the national wealth of Tanzania, but the masses of the people will not necessarily be better off. On the contrary, as land becomes more scarce we shall find ourselves with a farmers' class and a labourers' class, with the latter being unable either to work for themselves or to receive a full return for the contribution they are making to the total output. They will become a rural proletariat depending on the decisions of other men for their existence, and subject in consequence to all the subservience, social and economic inequality, and insecurity, which such a position involves.[5]

Early Post-Independence Attempts at Rural Development

We shall examine the earlier versions (i.e. colonial and early post-independence period) of agricultural development schemes in rural Tanzania. In essence, Tanzania's post-Arusha rural development strategy of co-operative farming has evolved from two earlier approaches or phases: the 'improvement approach' of colonial days and the 'transformation approach' initiated by the Government in the early post-independence period, all in an attempt to increase rural agricultural production and consequently to increase foreign exchange earnings.

The Improvement Approach

Cognizant of the fact that the various colonial methods (involving different types of co-operatives) used as instruments for controlling both production and the peasants were more or less inadequate for increasing agricultural productivity, the government of Tanzania decided to make changes in its agricultural policy based on the report of the World Bank Mission which had advised on the economic development of Tanganyika in 1960.[6] The World Bank report identified two approaches to agricultural development: the 'improvement' approach and the 'transformation' approach. In the period between gaining independence in 1961 and the beginning of the Ujamaa Village programme in 1967, the government of Tanzania adopted a two-pronged strategy to agricultural development in Tanzania's First Five Year Plan (1964–69) involving the use of both the 'improvement' and 'transformation' approaches. In essence both approaches were inherited from the colonial government and, hence, their origins and essence can be found basically in colonial prescriptions. Thus Ellman writes: 'prior to independence the chief method used by the colonial government to improve the standard of farming in Tanganyika was the provision of agricultural extension officers to advise individual farmers on their own farms. This method has been called the "improvement approach"'.[7]

The objective of this approach, as the term itself denotes, is to achieve a 'progressive improvement in present methods of crop and animal husbandry by working on the peasant farmer on both psychological and technical plans, to induce an increase in his productivity without any radical changes in traditional and social and legal systems.'[8] To this extent, it is no more than a continuation of the traditional policy pursued by colonial governments in an effort to foster 'development' in rural areas of the colonies. It meant the maximization of the exploitation of the peasant without, however, creating any imbalance that could cause local resentment.

The approach focused on 'progressive farmers'. The main weight of government effort to generate rural development under the improvement approach was directed at encouraging the responses of individual producers by a variety of incentives in order to achieve overall targets in the development of various cash crops on an extensive scale. It thus sought to exercise controls in a very indirect manner – statutory measures, marketing arrangements, training and demonstration centres, the use of extension and community development personnel, etc. In general, the results of this approach in Tanzania for the early post-independence period were dismal failures as testified to by the various area studies. In assessing the effect of the improvement approach on Sukumaland, Hulls concluded '. . . the failure to communicate modern agricultural technology to the vast majority of the farmers of Sukumaland appears to have been almost total.'[9] But the failure of the improvement approach cannot be attributed to the problem of communication alone or even to the resistance to new farming techniques on the part of peasant farmers. Its failure ultimately lies in the faulty premise on which the approach was based: that an agricultural system based on small-scale individual peasant holdings should provide the base for long-term economic and social development[10] without changes in the existing, essentially capitalist, relations of production in the countryside. We would contend that in order to build socialism in a predominantly agricultural society such as Tanzania, it is imperative, indeed a prerequisite, to initiate programmes that will necessarily change the existing relations of production in the rural sector.

The Transformation Approach

Having recognized the fact that an agricultural system premised on small-scale individual peasant holdings could not provide the necessary conditions for the long-term economic and social development of the country in general, and the countryside in particular, the government then decided to broaden its developmental strategy to include the alternative approach recommended by the World Bank Report of 1960 – the 'transformation' approach. This was viewed as the appropriate medium through which the government could overcome the economic disadvantage inherent in small-scale agriculture. It therefore emphasized resettlement schemes with the capital intensive techniques then deemed essential to large-scale agricultural production. It aimed at concentrating resources in a few select areas (which happened to be the more fertile parts of the country) where conditions could be created for the peasants to produce certain crops intensively. Its basic rationale was that it is difficult for peasants just emerging from colonialism to adopt modern techniques of agriculture since they are limited, on the one hand, by their lack of technology, and on the other, by the traditional socio-economic environment which militates against individuals trying new ideas and practices. The answer then would be in separating – both physically and socially – select peasants who would subsequently be provided with the requisite technology and under close supervision. Furthermore, it was hoped that by grouping together the farmers and bringing them in close contact with their extension advisers, farmer education would increase in efficiency. There was the added benefit of enjoying greater social services such as schools, dispensaries and water supplies made possible by a government now in a better position to provide these amenities to farmers not in scattered homesteads but living in 'gathered' villages. It is true, writes Rene Dumont, 'that the scattered population characteristic of the Tanzania countryside is an obstacle to the spread of technical progress, to the commercialization of crop production and to easy access to schools, dispensaries, mosques and churches. The creation of villages throughout Tanzania would also bring down the cost of community services . . .'[11] Although this aspect was perhaps not discernible at the time of the First Five Year Plan, it later gave the needed impetus to the government's policy of creating co-operative farming villages in which the members worked together on the basis of human equality as the essential step towards a socialist society for Tanzania.[12] In 1963 an Act was passed in Parliament establishing a Rural Settlement Commission as the policy-making body for the transformation approach to agriculture.

With the establishment of the Rural Settlement Commission, plans were drawn up to start 74 village settlement schemes in the First Five Year Plan period. In addition, four pilot projects were started in 1963, three more in 1964 and two in 1965, and assistance was given to a number of other settlement schemes. By the end of 1965, there were a total of 23 settlement schemes with some 15,000 acres of crops and about 3,400 households,[13] with an estimated cost to the government of some 3 million shillings for basic infrastructure facilities. In terms of co-operative existence – one of the essential elements of the programme – although the degree of co-operation to be practised between farmers was not clearly defined in the government's directives, in general, and on the great majority of these schemes, farmers had individual plots on which varying degrees of co-operation was practised between neighbours. On one scheme in Upper Ktete, 'the major cash crops (wheat, cattle) were grown on a communal basis, as dictated by technical efficiency considerations, although each family had in addition a three-acre homestead plot for its private use.'[14]

But barely two years after the start of the programme, it had to be abandoned as it became obvious that those schemes already launched were showing anything but success. The dismal failure of the scheme should not be surprising, when one considers the objective and the method of implementation. In the first place, there was very little dependence on the farmers' initiatives or for that matter self-reliance, as all the major decisions were taken by the government. Little attempt was made to explain to the farmers what the government's intentions were, or to involve the farmers in the planning and establishment of their schemes, in spite of the fact that the programme was conceived as one of the means of mobilizing the otherwise 'conservative' peasantry in the overall task of rural transformation towards socialism. Surely if, as the President has often pointed out, the people of Tanzania have long been an oppressed people (to the extent that they did not participate in the decisions that affected their lives), then the oppressed must be allowed to participate in the revolutionary process in the countryside, with an increasingly critical awareness of their role as subjects of the transformation. As Paulo Freire aptly remarked, 'If true commitment to the people, involving the transformation of the reality by which they are oppressd, requires a theory of transforming action, this theory cannot fail to assign the people a fundamental role in the transformation process. The leaders cannot treat the oppressed as mere activities to be denied the opportunity of reflection and allowed merely the illusion of acting, whereas in fact they would continue to be manipulated – and in this case by the presumed foes of manipulation.'[15]

Little wonder then that 'few of the farmers genuinely identified themselves with the schemes, considering themselves rather as temporary and underpaid employees on government estates, whose aim was to do the least possible work and to exploit the

Settlement Agency for what they could get out of it.'[16] But it has been suggested that even if the farmers had been ready to regard the farms as their own and to put all their efforts into them, it would have been very unlikely for them to succeed, particularly as a result of poor planning – physical and economic. One scheme, for example, was established in a flood plain which had to be abandoned after the first year. Similarly, in almost all cases mechanization was introduced automatically without due regard to whether it was economically justifiable or technically feasible and, above all, in the best interest of the overall objectives. Besides, as a rule the unique feature of the settlement schemes was their basic orientation toward cash-crop production and, consequently, the nature and location of the settlement schemes were determined by what cash crops they were expected to produce. But as it turned out this emphasis on production backfired partly because the government tended to oversponsor them initially, and in part due to the fact that the settlements were overcapitalized and the excessive protection of the villagers led to lethargy and failure to provide returns. Like its predecessor, the settlement programme had to be abandoned just after two years since it was obvious that the schemes already launched were showing anything but success.

In his diagnosis of the failure of the settlement schemes, the Second Vice-President, Mr. Kawawa, said: 'In the first place they have been heavily over-capitalized and the need to repay this great debt will be a life time burden on the settler-farmer and will swallow up his crop proceeds . . . Moreover the settler-farmers . . . in general show far less enthusiasm, and are less hardworking, than 'settlers' in spontaneous and unassisted schemes. They are also full of complaints and expect government to give them everything.'[17] Thus the one major attempt to bypass the dependence on farmers' responses in order to achieve overall production targets in agriculture turned out to be a somewhat disastrous village settlement programmme. Most of the settlement shemes, write Lewin and Cunningham, 'have proven economic and social failures, if not disasters.'[18]

The attempt by the government to concentrate its efforts on 'programme farmers', as evident in its settlement policies and practices, produced a 'yeoman' type of progressive farmer in the countryside. The kind of development that was taking place was creating individual peasant producers who were 'gradually adoping the incentives and the ethics of the capitalist system.'[19] Various researchers in Tanzania (e.g., Van Velsen, Feldman, Awiti, Raikes etc.) have documented the growth of non-socialist economic and political tendencies in the rural settlements of Tanzania. Specifically, Raikes, Feldman and Awiti have shown through their respective studies, the manner in which mechanized production of given crops in certain areas of Tanzania has spread and led to a capitalist mode of production largely 'uninhibited by any pre-existing property relationships, if not by other social ties.'[20] Clearly then, the mere offering of technical improvements (in this case through mechanization and the provision of extension facilities) within existing production relations seldom has sufficient effect on total production* since, as we have seen, the mechanisms through which the government sought to promote such improvements were themselves a product of capitalist production. It is significant that neo-classical economics clearly marked agriculture as playing a secondary role to industrialization in development. As a rule, therefore, agriculture's role in the development of the economy was to provide foreign exchange, through the production of primary goods for export, and labour for the 'developing' industrial sector. To this extent, the efforts of the Tanzanian government were simply a reflection of the neo-classic development strategy prescriptions of economists like Arthur Lewis.[21] The emphasis of the government remained on production of primary commodities (cash crops, to be more specific) for export so as to increase foreign exchange earnings, rather than laying the foundations of a nationally integrated economy through comprehensive planning and mass mobilizaton. But, as Clive Thomas suggests, the reason for this trend 'is simply a failure to accept that whatever may be the need for foreign exhange, and whatever are the short run pressures on employment and income, primary export production in this historical era does not contain enough dynamic demand potential to transform agriculture.'[22] In addition, the government's failure to view agricultural development as part of a wider economic and socio-political environment and as related to overall development strategies (and hence the failure of these earlier

---

* Despite the investment put in the agricultural sector at the time of these schemes, output continued to be less than expected.

schemes), was largely due to the absence of a basic conceptual foundation on which to premise the various schemes. This should not be surprising because, as pointed out earlier, even though 'Ujamaa: The Basis of African Socialism' had been published in 1962, socialism in this document and therefore in Tanzania remained simply 'an attitude of mind' not a 'way of life'. Surely, it is difficult under such circumstances for the appropriate agricultural policy to emerge to guide actual programmes of action. Echoing the need for a basic conceptual foundation on which to premise rural development programmes, President Nyerere remarked (while commenting on the failure of the settlement schemes) that, 'when we tried to promote rural development in the past, we sometimes spent huge sums of money on establishing a resettlement. . . All too often, therefore, we persuaded people to go to new settlements by promising them that they could grow rich there, or that the Government would give them services and equipment which they could not hope to receive either in the towns or in their traditional farming places. In very few cases was any ideology involved.'[23] Thus the failure of the first experiments in settlement schemes was explained by the President also in terms of the lack of ideological consciousness on the part of the leadership and rural population alike in Tanzania. To this extent it underscores the claim by Potter, for example, that 'ideology is important in rural development . . . because the social force needed to overcome social resistance and to mobilize a conservative peasantry to participate in development programmes can apparently come in no other way.'[24]

Before we end our discussion on the earlier settlements, it must be pointed out that a few of the voluntary and co-operative schemes which had existed were showing greater prospects of survival and development. These promising ones did not escape the weary eyes of the government and in fact later won the favour of government after the fiasco of the settlement schemes and became the basis for the formulation of the Ujamaa Village policy.*

* The most successful of the 'voluntary and cooperative' schemes were in the south. The Litowa settlement in Ruvuma region, started in 1960, was one of these. In fact, President Nyerere specifically stated in the policy paper 'Socialism and Rural Development' that the

Ujamaa Villages

The Arusha Declaration of February 1967 was in recognition of the essential role of an appropriate ideology in the strategic move to establish the relevant institutional arrangements for promoting rural development in Tanzania. The Ujamaa Village policy was initiated partly as a response to the growth of 'kulak' or 'progressive farmers' whose wealth was growing significantly through the use of hired labour on privately farmed plots. The greater wealth meant inequality and the hired labour meant at least the beginning of exploitation. Indeed, the importance of emergent large-scale kulak farmers as a potential obstacle to the realization of government policy of rural socialist transformation finds its clearest expression in the following statement by President Nyerere:

> The present trend is away from the extended family production and social unit towards the development of class system in the rural areas. It is this kind of development which would be inconsistent with the growth of a socialist Tanzania in which all citizens would be assured of human dignity and equality and in which all were able to have a decent and constantly improving life for themselves and their children.[25]

Since the overwhelming majority (about 90 per cent) of Tanzania's population lives in the rural areas, success in achieving the country's goal of socialism and self-reliance will clearly be determined by the extent to which the peasants understand, accept and formulate the policy's implications. It ultimately meant the creation of the necessary institutions at the local level. In this regard, the philosophy and direction of rural socialism in Tanzania, clearly summarized in the President's policy paper 'Socialism and Rural Development' issued in September 1967, was meant to initiate the desired structural changes in rural areas, to

experience of the Ruvuma schemes should be utilized in the construction of the new Ujamaa villages. He had apparently been impressed, among others, by the 'high degree of democratic control and participation' during his 1965 visit to the Litowa scheme.

begin the transition towards the goals of the Arusha Declaration. The publication of the document committed Tanzania to revolutionize its rural areas through voluntary and gradual formation of socialist Ujamaa villages. It called upon the peasants to organize themselves into viable socio-economic and political communities – the Ujamaa villages intended to transform production that is private and scattered into communal and planned production. But before we discuss the means by which the objectives of the Ujamaa policy were to be achieved as set out in 'Socialism and Rural Development,' let us outline briefly the objectives of the Ujamaa development strategy as outlined in the Second Five Year Plan (1969–74). The Plan defines Tanzania's Ujamaa policy as follows:[26]

> To create a society based on co-operation and mutual respect and responsibility in which all members have equal rights and equal opportunities, where there is no exploitation of man by man, and where all have a gradually increasing level of material welfare before any individual lives in luxury.

Within the context of rural Tanzania, the document continues, this means groups of families farming their land collectively, and collectively deciding upon the distribution of the proceeds, with the following objectives in mind:

1. Creation of self-reliant and self-determining communities following the tenets of the Arusha Declaration.
2. Avoidance of exploitation and excessive differentiation in wealth, income and power.
3. Raising the status of agriculture and reduction of the gulf between urban and rural life.
4. Economies of scale in purchasing, marketing, provision of services (schools, hospitals etc.) and some field operations requiring mechanization (including intermediate forms of technology).
5. Facilitating national planning both as to formulation of overall goals and decentralized implementation.
6. Better utilization of rural labour to raise productivity potentially obtainable through groups of peasants working

together compared to equal numbers of individuals working in isolation.

7. Openness to technical innovations, through increase in scale, readier access to farmer education, and removal from conservative influence of traditional environment.

And in a move to further concretize the interpretation of the Ujamaa agricultural programme, the President explained that:

> This means that most of our farming would be done by groups of people who live as a community and work as a community. They would live together in a village; they would farm together; market together; and undertake the provision of local services and small local requirements as a community. Their community would be the traditional family group, or any other group of people living according to Ujamaa principles, large enough to take account of modern methods and the twentieth century needs of man. The land this community farmed would be called 'our land' by all the members; the crops they produced on that land would be 'our crops'; it would be 'our shop' which provided individual members with the day-to-day necessities from outside; 'our workshop' which made the bricks from which houses and other buildings were constructed, and so on.[27]

Having outlined the broad objectives of the Ujamaa strategy, let us now examine the means by which these objectives are to be achieved as set out in the policy document, 'Socialism and Rural Development'. As a first step in areas of scattered settlement, people are to be persuaded to come together to live in villages so that (according to the government) it becomes feasible for them to work together and enjoy the economic and social benefits that go with such a co-operative existence, such as schools, hospitals or dispensaries, water supply etc. The next task is to persuade not 'coerce' people to start work on a communally owned plot that will be harvested in common, with the proceeds being shared in common. It is hoped from this point on, that once sufficient 'confidence in the community farm' has been gained, all the land can be pooled that way, with the exception of individual gardens around the houses for vegetables; it will lead to a full-fledged socialist village.

In terms of the developmental process of Ujamaa villages in Tanzania, three stages become readily discernible during the period of this study (see Tables 1 and 2).

Table 1 *Stages in Development of Ujamaa Village by Region*

Region	Number of Villages			
	Stage 1	Stage 2	Stage 3	Total
Arusha	38	5	1	44
Coast	31	26	1	58
Dodoma	132	17	1	150
Iringa	349	–	1	350
Kigoma	93	15	–	108
Kilimanjaro	9	2	–	11
Lindi	162	26	–	188
Mara	226	20	4	250
Mbeya	191	–	3	194
Morogoro	21	2	1	22
Mtwara	651	21	–	672
Mwanza	38	3	–	41
Ruvuma	105	15	–	120
Shinyanga	131	1	–	132
Singida	42	15	–	57
Tabora	35	43	4	82
Tanga	113	32	1	146
West Lake	43	–	–	43
Total	2,410	243	17	2,668

Source: *Economic Survey 1970–71*

The first stage is a formative one, when villages have not yet attained social and economic viability. The main requirements at this stage are infrastructural for which funds are usually provided through, for example, the Rural Development Fund.

Table 2 *Ujamaa Village Statistics (Continued)*

Region	In December, 1971 Stages			Registered Co-operative Societies May, 1972*	
	I	II	III	Full	provisional
Arusha	47	11	1	1	–
Coast	(95)	–	(26)	28	1
Dodoma	227	17	2	15	22
Iringa	628	–	23	59	4
Kigoma	(117)	(15)	–	1	–
Kilimanjaro	11	–	–	–	–
Mara	308	54	14	22	–
Mbeya	490	3	–	6	–
Morogoro	112	–	1	1	–
Mtwara	727	21	–	–	–
Lindi	524	66	2	–	–
Mwanza	(124)	3	–	–	–
Ruvuma	(190)	(15)	–	–	–
Shinyanga	150	–	–	1	–
Singida	194	7	–	5	–
Tabora	59	2	20	12	–
Tanga	96	35	1	1	–
West Lake	26	12	8	8	–
All Regions	4,125	261	160	160	27

*The number of villages registered as Co-operative Societies has been provided by the Registrar of Co-operative Societies.

The second stage in development of an Ujamaa village is reached when the community has gained sufficient experience of living and working as a unit, has a workable constitution and has become economically viable. It is then registered as an agricultural association and is then entitled to credit from the Tanzania Rural Development Bank as well as other infrastructural investments.

And thirdly, the village becomes a full-fledged multipurpose co-operative society and has adequate security to attract commercial credit from any source including the national Bank of Commerce, Marketing Boards, etc.[28]

It is important to note that the emphasis, in the implementation of the Ujamaa policy, was in principle at least on the voluntary establishment of co-operative Ujamaa activities among the peasants, rather than of forced massive resettlement of the rural population. The choice of persuasion and voluntarism, rather than coercion, as the country's approach to socialist rural transformation is based on at least two main considerations. The first is related to the emphasis on local initiatives and self-reliance as methods of implementation of the country's Ujamaa Vijijini programme. Thus in Ujamaa Vijijini the President warns:

> It is essential to realize that within the unity of Tanzania, there is also such diversity that it would be foolish for someone in Dar es Salaam to try to draw up a blueprint for the crop production and social organization which has to be applied to every corner of our large country. Principles of action can be set out, but the application of these principles must take into account the different geographical and geological conditions in different areas, and also the local variations in the basically similar traditional structures. For example, in the Kilimanjaro Region not only is the practice of individual land-holding almost universal, but also there is no unused land on the mountain . . . Again, some parts of our country suffer from great water shortage or uncertainty . . . It would be absurd to try and settle all these questions from Dar es Salaam, particularly as such variations as those of the type of soil sometimes occur within a very small area. Local initiatives and self-reliance are essential.[29]

The emphasis therefore reflects an awareness on the part of the national political leadership that it was impossible, indeed unwise, to draw up uniform blueprints for Ujamaa villages in a country like Tanzania which has important geographical and cultural variations.

Secondly, there is the President's basic belief in the superiority of persuasion as a method of influencing behaviour. Once people know what they are doing and why they are doing it, it is argued, they will not only exert themselves to the maximum but will also see more point in development because they are carrying it out for themselves. In addition to realizing their potential creativity and energy will be channelled into development, it was hoped that leaving the initiative to manage change in the hands of the rural population would force them to rely more on themselves and their hard work instead of relying on government. We would argue that it is this aspect of the strategy (i.e. persuasion) more than any other aspect perhaps, which makes it different from the previous settlement schemes where the hand of the government was conspicuously dominant. It is more likely, should such a strategy succeed, that the rural property which will result from this type of development will not only assure equality but will also have come about as a result of the efforts of the villagers themselves, rather than the sweat and efforts of other taxpayers through subsidies.

While the policy statements on Ujamaa Vijijini were characteristically flexible enough to permit the implementation of different forms of Ujamaa villages (in recognition of the different local situations), there was no mistake about the importance attached to rapidly achieving at last some movement towards Ujamaa in all parts of the country. This was because the impetus for Ujamaa and villagization was premised on the expectation that transferring traditional peasant farmers from scattered homesteads to village communities would bring about major attitudinal changes, which would speed the 'modernization' of agricultural practices and provide dramatically increased opportunities and motivation for transferring otherwise idle labour time into productive capital assets through various kinds of self-help efforts.*

There was also no doubt about the key role party and government officials were supposed to play as the primary initiators of the

---

* The choice of the 'frontal approach' (where the whole range of governmental and political institutions is mobilized behind the principles of Ujamaa) rather than the 'selective approach' (whose effort is concentrated on limited areas which can move to complete socialist living after a short period of time), in the implementation of the Ujamaa programme, was essentially to ensure rapid achievement (and thereby avoid the development of a basically stagnant rural economy under the 'selective approach') of the movement towards Ujamaa Vijijini in accordance with the President's directives and as defined in the Plan.

implementation of the policy. Both the Second Five Year Plan and the 'Presidential Circular No. 1 of 1969' stressed that it is to the building of Ujamaa villages that government must turn its attention: 'We have to organize our government and party machinery to assist their establishment; we have to give them priority in all our credit, servicing, and extension services – at the expense of the individual producer.'[30] Furthermore, detailed instructions on the institutional organization were given, emphasizing that 'no department of the party and no ministry of government is exempt from the requirements to participate and to contribute to the success of the policy.'[31] This was followed in subsequent years by more directives and reorganizations within the individual ministries, parastatals, party organizations and in the region. However, while it is true that the President strongly emphasized in his circular that both party and government agencies must give their strongest support and encouragement to the formation and development of Ujamaa villages, he still maintained that the decision to start an Ujamaa village must come from the farmers themselves and the establishment of the village must be through the efforts of the farmers. The Plan, for example, stressed the importance to balance the need for vigorous leadership and official encouragement, against the need to avoid the dangers of bureaucratic control, coercion and overcapitalization, which would negate the very principles of self-help and co-operation which the villages are intended to embody.[32]

An Assessment of the Development of the Ujamaa Programme During the Period of Study: Progress and Problems

The speed with which Ujamaa villages were established throughout the country in response to the President's call for a rapid achievement of some movement towards Ujamaa can be surmised from the available figures. Whereas in 1967 about 50,000 peasants lived in 'pre-Ujamaa' villages, 1,250,000 in other villages and 6,500,000 in isolated tiny units, by 1973 after six years of ceaseless campaigns including sometimes the mass movement of whole regions into Ujamaa villages, the official count for Ujamaa villages stood at 5,556 across the country involving a total population of over 2 million or about 15 per cent of all Tanzania.[33] It must be noted that these figures are estimates; their accuracy cannot be verified and it is not unusual to find discrepancies about the numbers of Ujamaa villages from different government sources, as borne out by Tables 3 and 4.[34] Besides, the figures cover a broad range of extremely different situations not only in terms of the distribution between regions (see Tables 5 and 6), but also with regard to the socio-economic and social organization of the villages and with regard to the manner by which they were initiated, reflecting flexibility in the implementation of the programme. Equally important is the fact that initially, the majority of the Ujamaa villages were established in areas where there was no shortage of land to develop. This was generally in the economically less developed parts of the country where there are few permanent crops and relatively little social and economic differentiation to act as a barrier to co-operative organization.[35] Gumbel noted that in some regions the majority of the population were already enrolled in Ujamaa villages, while in others the Ujamaa villages included only a single-figure percentage of the inhabitants.[36] In a similar vein, Boesen writes: 'There were completely collectivized new settlements; settlements where the people had (been?) moved together to become more accessible to government help and services, but with hardly any communal

Table 3 *Number of Ujamaa Villages 1967–71*

Date	Number of Villages	Total Population of Villages	Total Population as percentage of mainland total
February 1967	48	5,000	0.04%
December 1968	180	58,000	0.5%
December 1969	650	300,000	2.5%
September 1970	1,200	500,000	4.2%
June 1971	2,668	840,000	6.3%

Source: *Ministry of Rural Development report: Economic Survey 1970–71.*

Table 4 *The Development of Ujamaa Villages 1968–1972*

Region	December 1968		December 1969		December 1970		December 1971		December 1972		December 1973	
	No. of villages	No. of villagers	No. of villages	No. of villagers	No. of villages	No. of villagers	No. of villages	No. of villagers	No. of villages	No. of villagers	No. of villages	No. of villagers
Arusha	a	a	20	a	25	5,200	59	14,018	92	19,818	95	20,112
Coast	a	a	46	a	56	48,300	121	93,503	185	111,636	188	115,382*
Dodoma	a	a	40	a	75	26,400	246	239,366	299	400,330	336	278,915*
Iringa	a	a	60	a	350	11,600	651	216,200	630	207,502	659	243,915*
Kigoma	a	a	14	a	34	6,700	132	27,200	129	114,391	129	114,391
Kilimanjaro	a	a	7	a	9	2,700	11	2,616	24	5,009	24	4,934
Mara	a	a	19	a	175	84,700	376	127,371	376	127,370	271†	108,068
Mbeya	a	a	22	a	91	32,900	493	64,390	713	98,571	715	103,672
Morogoro	a	a	16	a	19	6,000	113	10,513	116	23,915	118	19,732*
Lindi	a	a	412	a	750	70,673	592	263,128	626	175,082	59†	169,093
Mtwara	a	a	10	a	–	173,027	748	371,560	1,088	441,241	1,103	446,098*
Mwanza	a	a	10	a	28	4,600	127	18,841	211	32,099	284	49,846
Ruvuma	a	a	26	a	120	9,000	205	29,430	205	29,430	242	42,288
Shinyanga	a	a	6	a	98	12,600	150	12,265	123	15,292	108†	12,052*
Singida	a	a	12	a	16	6,800	201	51,230	262	59,420	263	59,420
Tabora	a	a	41	a	52	16,700	81	18,408	148	25,115	174	29,295
Tanga	a	a	37	a	37	7,700	132	35,907	245	77,858	245	77,957
West Lake	a	a	21	a	22	5,600	46	9,491	83	16,747	85	13,280
TOTAL	180	58,500	819	300,000	1,957	531,200	4,484	1,605,437	5,555	1,980,826	5,098	1,908,450

Unconfirmed figures.

* In some cases small villages had to be merged.

† Figures not recorded, the totals are based on estimates.

Source: Nyerere. J. K. *Mkatano Mkuu wa TANU, 1973: Taarifa va Rais wa Chama* (Dar es Salaam, Government Printer, 1973). p. 25.

Table 5 *Distribution of Ujamaa Villages, March 1971*

Region	No. of Ujamaa Villages	Average population per village	Approximate Population	
			Total population in Ujamaa Villages	Percentage of regional population liiving in Ujamaa Villages
Arusha	44	200	9,000	1.3
Coast	58	940	55,000	6.0
Dodoma	150	310	47,000	5.9
Iringa	350	240	84,000	10.8
Kigoma	108	300	32,000	6.3
Kilimanjaro	11	190	2,000	0.3
Lindi	188	420	79,000	18.3
Mara	250	380	95,000	15.5
Mbeya	194	260	50,000	4.6
Morogoro	22	210	5,000	0.7
Mtwara	672	420	282,000	44.1
Mwanza	41	190	8,000	0.7
Ruvuma	120	100	12,000	2.7
Shinyanga	132	100	13,000	1.3
Singida	57	230	13,000	2.7
Tabora	82	240	20,000	3.2
Tanga	146	160	23,000	2.7
West Lake	43	250	11,000	1.5
Total	2,668	315	840,000	6.3

*The figures for Dodoma exclude most of the new villages which are being established as a result of the current mass mobilization campaign (q.v.)

Source: *Economic Survey 1970–71* (Dar es Salaam: Government Printer).

production activities; old traditional villages, where some inhabitants cultivate a communal field while retaining their private farms as their main occupation; and many other types of Ujamaa villages.'[37]

Table 6 *Distribution of Ujamaa Villages in Tanzania by Regions, March 1973*

Regions	Number of Villages	Village Population	Average per Village	% of Villages to Population
Arusha	95	20,112	212	3.3
Coast	188	115,382	613	22.6
Dodoma	336	378,915	1,128	53.4
Iringa	659	243,527	370	35.4
Kigoma	129	144,391	1,119	30.4
Kilimanjaro	24	4,934	206	0.8
Lindi	589	169,093	287	40.2
Mara	271	108,068	399	19.8
Mbeya	715	103,677	145	10.7
Morogoro	118	19,732	167	2.9
Mtwara	1,103	466,098	423	75.0
Mwanza	284	49,846	176	4.7
Ruvuma	242	42,385	175	10.7
Shinyanga	108	12,052	112	1.3
Singida	263	59,420	226	12.9
Tabora	174	29,295	168	5.2
Tanga	245	77,957	318	10.1
West Lake	85	13,280	156	2.0
Totals	5,628	2,024,418	361	16.9

Source: *Economic Survey 1972–73* (Dar es Salaam: Government Printer, 1973).

In general we can identify at last three types of Ujamaa Village organization during the period of our study. First, where the Ujamaa village coincides with the natural village. Here all or an overwhelming majority of the people at a particular settlement have joined the new Ujamaa organization, The houses of all these people are close to each other so that the Ujamaa village is in actual fact a real physical entity. Also the internal dynamics of the village organization are, perhaps more than any other type, allowed full play. The dominant interactions are those within the village organization rather than those with non-Ujamaa peasants. Factors such as the relationship between the leaders and the led, between collective and individual interests, etc., become concrete issues for the development of the village organization, rather than being submerged in an effort to solve contradictions (real or imaginary) between village and non-Ujamaa peasants.

Second, where the Ujamaa Village organization constitutes roughly half the population at a natural village or locational settlement – a more or less equal balance of forces between the Ujamaa organization and the non-Ujamaa population. Sharp competition between the two groups is characteristic of this type. The internal dynamics of the Ujamaa village are more or less submerged in favour of the play of relations between the two sides.

Third, where the Ujamaa Village organization is insignificant in proportion to the total population within which it is enmeshed. Here there is no real competition to speak of; the non-Ujamaa side is overwhelming. In this sense, it is a conceptual village – not a physical entity. Here forces outside the village organization tend to play the most dominant role in determining developments in the villages.[38]

In evaluating the progress made in the development of Ujamaa villages, the speed of implementation of the programme is not a sufficient criterion on which to judge the degree of success. The Ujamaa Village programme, we would argue (but we do not deny that there may be other criteria), cannot be evaluated realistically outside the context of Tanzania's overall developmental goals of transition to a socialist, egalitarian, participatory, self-reliant society. More concretely, Ujamaa is conceived to prevent the rise of a rural 'kulak' class with a corresponding rise in landlessness and inequality. Factors such as the productive viability of the Ujamaa villages, peasant participation in decision-making, the degree of self-reliance, urban-rural differentials, increased agricultural output, etc., and above all the progress towards Ujamaa Vijijini, must all form the basis for a realistic evaluation of the programme.

Ellman suggests that the criteria on which progress towards socialism must be judged are. 'the proportion of land or other assets which are communally owned and used, the level of co-operation practised between farmers on individual holdings, the amount of hired labour which is used and how it is rewarded, the way in which the proceeds are distributed and . . . the amount of popular participation in the government of the village communities.'[39] We basically agree with the above citeria even though the dearth of reliable data on several of these factors has made it virtually impossible to reach any firm conclusions. There are, however, some recognizable trends, as can be gleaned from Table 1, on the degree of progress towards Ujamaa. All that can be said based on the available data is that many of the Ujamaa villages made very little progress towards socialism during the period of our study. Indeed, various field researchers working in different parts of the country have come to similar conclusions.[40] The reasons for this will become clear below.

This is not to deny the fact that there are very notable exceptions, especially in Tanga and Ruvuma regions, though there were no more than twenty to thirty of them across the country. In these cases, the land was owned and farmed by the village as a whole, with the exception of small privately owned homestead plots near each family's house. They are all characterized by a

> high level of ideological commitment, strong internal leadership, and closely defined norms and sanctions for maintaining unity. They have a high degree of popular participation in village government, with a Village Assembly of all the members as the final authority, and subsidiary committees for various functions such as farm management, accounting, education, health etc., on which a large population of the members, both men and women, are elected to positions of responsibility . . . The distribution of proceeds from the communal farms is in every case in proportion to work contributed. No Ujamaa villages have as yet fully adopted the Communist principle of 'to each according to his need, from each according to his ability', though a number of villages have elderly or crippled members who are given a share of the proceeds, generally equivalent to the average paid to the other members.[41]

It has been suggested by observers like Ellman that in all of these exceptional cases, the establishment of the Ujamaa village was voluntary and spontaneous. Besides, the motivation of the membership must be high, given the level of individual participation in the decision-making process.

With regard to the level of productivity in the agricultural sector,* the performance was rather sluggish despite the importance attached to rural development in the country's development strategy since 1967. Agricultural output increased by only 2.7 per cent between 1967 and 1973 (see Table 7), barely enough to keep up with population growth. Similarly, the growth in volume of the six principal unprocessed agricultural exports (coffee, cotton, sisal, cashew nuts, tea, tobacco), which together accounted for 50–60 per cent of total commodity exports between 1967 and 1972, was even slower, barely 2 per cent a year.[44]

Table 7 *Growth rates in GDP and Selected Sectors*

	1967–73	1967–70	1970–75
GDP (factor cost)	4.5	4.3	4.7
Agriculture	2.7	2.7	2.6
Manufacturing	7.6	7.8	7.4
Transport and Communications	8.8	10.8	6.8
Construction	5.5	4.1	6.7
Public Administration and Services	7.7	5.3	10.2

Source: *World Bank Reoort on Tanzania, 1977*, Table 4, p. 6.

Several reasons have been advanced to explain the weak performance of the agricultural sector. These include, among others, the meagre allocations of capital received by this sector as

* It cannot be overemphasized that agriculture dominates the Tanzanian economy, contributing 40% to GDP, 80% of exports (in terms of both processed and unprocessed agricultural products) and employing about 90% of the labour force.

shown in Table 8; lack of leadership and skill; inadequate extension services; defects in supply and marketing systems; insufficient research on appropriate technical packages, especially for food crops; weak infrastructural base; the price fluctuations of commodity prices in the international capitalist market; natural disasters such as the droughts of 1972, etc. But perhaps even more crucial is that the agricultural sector, more than any other sector, bore the brunt of the major institutional changes which characterized this period of Tanzanian development.

> While in many respects these changes, especially the 1971 decentralization of government, increased the potential for broad-based rural development, it is difficult to escape the conclusion that during the period of transition, the upheavals and uncertainties in framework, organization and management of the supporting services for agriculture and rural development took their toll in terms of foregone potential output.[43]

Table 8 *Fixed Capital Formation by Industry (per cent shares)*

	1966–69	1970–73	1966–73
Agriculture	9.6	5.8	7.1
Manufacturing and Mining	16.4	15.7	15.9
Electricity and Water Supply	6.6	8.2	7.6
Transport and Communications	35.9	46.9	43.9
All Other	31.5	23.4	26.2
Total	100.0	100.0	100.0

Source: *World Bank Report on Tanzania, 1977*, Table 9, p. 7.

That there is a strong correlation between a sluggish performance in the agricultural sector and massive institutional changes in the rural sector has been amply demonstrated in several socialist countries, especially the USSR under Stalin. However, although the scope of our study more or less prohibits a detailed examination of other factors that might be responsible for the continued poor performance in the agricultural sector of several socialist countries, we would like to mention at least some of the

Table 9 *Marketed Production of Major Food and Cash Crops (Tons)*

	*1967–68	1968–69	1963–70	1970–71	1971–71	**1972–73
Maize	104,308	127,502	54,081	186,440	42,987	106,476
Paddy (rice 60%)		46,156	45,581	93,495	68,585	73,094
Wheat	5,037	24,639	20,950	42,968	56,849	46,947
Cassava					9,156	14,265
Groundnuts					3,295	3,454
Sesame					8,170	7,336
Castor					12,934	10,243
Sunflower					6,199	9,464
Cotton Lint				76,272	65,723	76,910
Cashew Nuts					126,409	125,622
Tobacco				11,970	14,154	13,069
Pyrethrum (flowers)				2,667	4,277	4,016
Coffee				46,404	52,112	47,207
Tea (made tea)				9,182	11,613	13,363
Sisal (calendar year)				202,000	181,000	157,000

* 1967 – Arusha Declaration
** 1972 – Siasa ni KILIMO

Source: Adapted from Tanzania Government, Agriculture Ministry.

major reasons which might in fact be more decisive. Particularly relevant to our study is the continued oppositon by the peasants in those countries to collectivization, as well as the closely related problem of the lack of incentives. It is instructive that some of the socialist countries, such as Poland and Yugoslavia, have now revitalized the system of private plots in a much bigger way. The authorities in some of these countries have apparently become more sympathetic to the idea of incentives, perhaps in recognition of the continued poor performance of the agricultural sector.

In his searching assessment of the agricultural sector ten years after the Arusha Declaration, the President observed:

> Since the Arusha Declaration was passed, we have talked a very great deal about rural development and the expansion of agriculture as the basis of Tanzania's future. And we have spent large sums of money on rural development – some of it from friends abroad. Thus, for example, whereas in 1967 something like shs.45 million was spent on agricultural development, the figure has been around shs.400 million in each of the past two years! . . . However, the truth is that the agricultural results have been very disappointing . . . Looking back it is possible to see many contributory factors to this lack of sufficient agricultural growth. . . . But the real failure seems to have been a lack of political leadership and technical understanding at the village and district level. Despite the call in 'Politics is Agriculture' for all political leaders to learn the basics of good husbandry in their areas, and join with the peasants in production, we have continued to shout at the peasants, and exhort them to produce more, without doing much to help them or to work with them in a relationship of mutual respect. Many of our leaders know nothing about agriculture; what is more, they don't want to learn![44]

The problem of lack of leadership applies not only to agricultural output but also to the whole range of the rural transformation programme. As far back as 1970 the government had identified 'the chief bottleneck to the development of Ujamaa'[45] in the rural sector as the shortage of leadership and skills. The solution was seen in terms of increased education, particularly adult education, including a large element of political education relevant to Ujamaa living. Thus under TANU, a special division for Ujamaa Village development was charged with organizing seminars for party and government leaders lasting for about 2–4 weeks on the broader aspects of the ideology and organization of Ujamaa.

Although the shortage of leadership cadre must be seen in the overall development context of Tanzania, especially in this stage of transition, the problem has been made more acute in the Ujamaa programme because no particular body has been charged with the creation of Ujamaa villages.[46] This is perhaps one of the weakest links in the programme, for one would have expected that such a herculean task as the radical transformation of contemporary rural life in Tanzania into the principles of Ujamaa Vijijini would require high political organization. The creation of social and economic communities, which answer to a definite political philosophy, demands in certain contexts close supervision, organization, and general direction – as the Chinese and Russians would testify.[47] If there is one feature common to all countries that have successfully accomplished agricultural collectivization, it is their use of cadres (in a leadership role) in the task – cadres being a core of grassroots level personnel, scrupulously screened and trained to act as propagandists, agitators, organizers, and mobilizers of the peasant masses. In Tanzania, however, this idea seems to have been relegated to the bottom, if not rejected officially, as the emphasis has been on spontaneity and voluntarism.[48] The effect of all this is that generally the basic conception of the Ujamaa Villages programme becomes ambiguous when placed within a wider context. One could easily discuss the particular village in isolation and show convincingly, perhaps, that its members would develop socialist relations. Yet there cannot be 'socialism in one village'; in the final analysis, it is the social relations in the total socio-economic network in which the village is integrated that would determine what mode of production pertains in society.

Closely allied with the problem of leadership is the role of 'kulaks' in the task of rural transformation in Tanzania. As noted earlier, various researchers (e.g. Freyhold, Velzen, Mbilinyi, Senders, Hyden, Mapolu, etc.) have all reported the 'diabolical' role (understandably, of course) played by 'kulaks', including resistance to the establishment of Ujamaa villages in various parts of the country, especially in the relatively more prosperous agricultural regions of the country such as Kilimanjaro, Mwanza, Morogoro and Ismani.[49] The regional distribution of the Ujamaa villages in Table 5 demonstrates this point. For example, Mushi found that in Morogoro District 'the majority of the people live in the mountains and are relatively well-to-do farmers. They have been little interested in or perhaps indifferent to Ujamaa.'[50] Even more crucial is the fact that they have dominated leadership positions in the Village Development Committees (VDC), TANU Ten-house-cells, etc., given the dearth of leadership cadres in rural Tanzania. (See Tables 10 and 11.)

Table 10 *Official functions occupied by the richest 20% of peasant Households, Itumba (Rungwe District)*

Official Functions	Total Number Available	Occupied By The Richest 20%
Branch Chairman TANU	1	1
Secretary TANU	1	–
Chairman VDC 1967	1	1
Secretary VDC 1967	1	1
Chairman Self-Help Committee	1	1
Chairman Parents' Committee	1	1
Members VDC resident in Itumba	6	3
Recruited as wage labourers in Government services	8	5
Assessors Primary Court	3	3
Chairman TANU cell	15	9
Representative District Council	1	1
Total	39	26
%Total Functions	(100%)	(66%)

Source: Adapted from Van Velzen 1973, Table B, p. 165.

Table 11 *Peasant Participation in Local Leadership Positions and Organizations in Mwanza and Tanga*

Region	Ten-cell Leader	School Committee	Adult Education	U.W.T.	VDC	TANU Committee	Total Households
Mwanza							
Rich*	11	11	9	11	2	1	24
Middle*	6	6	5	6	–	2	25
Poor*	3	2	3	3	1	–	23
Tanga							
Rich	7	–	1	–	–	–	22
Middle	4	1	–	2	–	–	22
Poor	1	–	–	–	–	–	7

Source: Adapted from Mbilinyi 1974, Table 27, p. 32.

* The available data on the incomes of rural peasants has been, to say the least, less than satisfactory. We have therefore classified the peasant stratum into Rich (Kulak), Middle and Poor not by income but by the number of acres of land cultivated in the manner of Awiti.

Thus:

Rich Peasants	– Cultivating anywhere from between 40–350 acres and over;
Middle	– 15–39.9 acres;
Poor	– 5.9–14.9 acres.

For full details, see Appendix B

Thus Senders found in the Western Usambaras that:

> . . . in an area of marked inequality in the distribution of resources, those with a disproportionate share of resources seem to dominate the leadership positions in the Ujamaa and other local organizations. Through their corruption, they have managed to use their positions to appropriate village income or other resources for their own purposes, thereby ensuring that the financial incentives for Ujamaa work do not operate as they should. Nor in some cases is the leadership itself prepared to work in the Ujamaa shamba, the fruits of which they later control.[51]

We would caution that this may not be representative of all the Ujamaa villages during this period. Clearly then, on a local level the richest farmers have political power. This suggests (at least as implied in Table 10) that the rich peasantry share in political rule with the bureaucratic stratum. Indeed, the relationship between the urban bureaucrats and local kulaks should not be surprising in the African context. Indeed, some of the kulaks happen to be bureaucrats from Dar es Salaam and other urban centres. It is an open secret in Tanzania that bureaucrats own shambas, houses etc., in the villages and around some urban centres, in spite of the Mwongozo (TANU) Guidelines of 1971. It is a common practice in all of Africa for the urban bureaucrat to maintain his roots in his village through various means – including the building of houses. Tanzania has so far been no exception in this regard.

It is only fair to say that a more equitable distribution of income has been a major focus of development policy since the Arusha Declaration. Though we are concerned here with the urban-rural and intra-rural income differential, there is yet a third dimension of distribution – the intra-urban. All three have witnessed important policy initiatives with varying degrees of success. Although fairly reliable figures (showing a significant narrowing of the gap*) are available for the intra-urban income differentials, there are no

---

* In 'Ten Years after Arusha,' the President gave the proportions in income differentials between 1967 and 1976, after direct tax is taken into account, as 20:1 and 9:1 respectively.

116

'reliable statistics' available in the areas of urban-rural and intra-rural income differentials, as of now.[52] Nevertheless, 'it appears that since 1967 the hard working peasant (especially in areas with a good cash crop) has improved his lot faster than an equally hard working wage-earner in the towns.'[53] In this regard, even the World Bank Report grudgingly conceded that the situation between 1967 and 1973 'was a vast improvement on the previous record of sharply diverging living standards,' while at the same time maintaining that there 'was not significant change in urban-rural real income differentials between 1967 and 1973.'[54]

The full effect of the decentralization measures of 1972 has been mitigated by the continued dominant role of the bureaucracy in the decision-making process within the rural institutions of Tanzania, except in those few cases alluded to above. The Arusha Declaration states that the development of a country is brought about by the people; the Mwongozo (TANU) Guidelines of 1971 marked a firmer spelling out of the commitment to participation, egalitarianism, etc. in rural Tanzania. 'In preparing development plans, our main emphasis at all times should be the development of the people not things. If development is to benefit the people, the people must participate in considering, planning and implementing their plans.'[55] The decentralization policy was based on the assumption that measures for the mobilization of local resources for development cannot be planned realistically, except in the context of the needs, aspirations and economic condition of the people. But it became obvious quite soon that decentralization measures (which were aimed at, among other things, decentralization of responsibility and the participation of larger portions of the population in proposals and implementation), while helping to rationalize and speed up administrative action and processes in the regions and districts, do not necessarily increase popular participation of the masses in the decision-making process. Commenting on the continued dominant role of the bureaurcrats, Goran Hyden writes:

> A main reason why the socialist results of the Ujamaa
> programme so far have been meagre is that any
> revolutionary strategy is ultimately a class strategy and not
> a development strategy that can bc bolstered by, for
> example, bureaucratic control and technical assistance

inputs. For many reasons, some clearly beyond the control of a poor country like Tanzania, its socialist rural development strategy has been on the latter terms.[56]

And in a similar vein, Saul writes:

> The Ujamaa strategy was changed to conform closely with the preconceptions and interests of the bureaucratic bourgeoisie who control its implementation . . . Just as they tend to distrust the intentions and capabilities of the peasants . . . so do they distrust the major political changes which would have to occur before and during a socialist transformation. This would go further to threaten their very reason for existence.[57]

There is an inherent contradiction in interests between the peasants and bureaucrats. Ujamaa villages therefore bear some resemblance to the pre-Arusha settlement schemes in their bureaucratic monopoly of direction and decion-making.

We recognize that the government's desire to decentralize decision-making powers has to be balanced against the need for central guidance of popular support. For decentralization and institutionalization of popular participation at the District, Regional and local levels may generate centrifugal forces contrary to the leadership's desire for a unified national ideology in the transition phase. The total impact of the decentralization proposals suggests that the balance between central government guidance and local popular participation is heavily loaded in favour of guidance. We would argue that effective participation in development planning can best take place in representative institutions, especially at the local level where people can relate planning proposals by, for example, the administration to their immediate problems and experience. Moreover, the practical role of the bureaucrat at the grassroots level is difficult to differentiate from that of the government administration, insofar as each consists essentially of periodic visits by individual personnel to the Ujamaa villages to offer 'advice' in a more or less commandist fashion. This perhaps gives credence to the suggestion that the bureaucracy was more interested in Ujamaa villages (which they see as mere settlement schemes) than in Ujamaa Vijijini (and the slow pace of implementation will tend to underscore this view-point). In this crucial context the policy changes of 1974 and the more recent policy reversals of 1977 must be watched.[58] In the words of the World Bank Report of 1977, 'much will depend on whether the organization of village activity continues to be heavily governed and dominated by the Government and Party bureaucracies which spearheaded the implementation of villagization or whether the scope for peasant participation in decision-making will increase'; if 'dramatically increased opportunities and motivation for transforming otherwise idle labour time into productive capital assets' through various kinds of self-help efforts is to be achieved, the scope of peasant participation in decision-making must necessarily be increased.[59]

What must be emphasized about the Ujamaa programme (the scale of which has no parallels in the rest of Black Africa) is that, at least in the initial stages, its emphasis was not on maximization of economic growth in the rural areas. To be sure, it aimed at economic viability but this is a far cry from maximization of economic growth. Quite often the Tanzania leadership has shown itself prepared to modify policies, even at the cost of reducing its economic growth, in order to achieve long-term ideological aims.[60] In short, her production outcomes in the rural economy will in many cases rest on non-economic considerations. It is important to grasp this fundamental aspect of the developmental strategy in Tanzania, for too often it is easily ignored by scholars in their attempt to measure economic performance in Tanzania. The World Bank Report (1977) recognized this aspect when it said, 'though rural development has been at the center of the Government's development objectives since 1967, the government strategy has stressed the creation of institutions appropriate for broad-based, long-term equitable development rather than quicker income/output gains from provision of incentives and supporting infrastructure and services to progressive farmers.'[61] It nevertheless turns round to say '. . . villagization has blurred the distinction between directly productive investments and social and economic infrastructure. For example, in some drier regions the provision of rural water supplies has become a necessary concomitant for the continued viability of villages as productive units.'[62]

We conclude our discussion on rural socialism in Tanzania by restating that the emphasis on rural development stressed in both the Arusha Declaration and the policy document 'Socialism and Rural Development' is politically aimed, among other things, at the reduction of social distinctions and income differentials in a socialist economy. There is also a growing emphasis on grassroots participation by the rural peasantry (though with limited effectiveness, so far), and the quest for self-reliance does inform major village, district, etc. policies to an increasing extent. Even more crucial is the evidence of increasing political consciousness among the peasantry of the national objectives of socialism, 'especially in those areas where rural stratification is well advanced.'[63]

Above all is the realization by the leadership that the Ujamaa Village programme (and hence agriculture) must be developed to 'create the basis for future conomic and social transformation.' In short, the rural sector is seen as the best potential source of surplus for economic development. It is not argued that industrial development is unimportant, but rather that industrial and urban development cannot be carried out as desired without growth in the rural sector. Thus a holistic conception of the economy becomes a prerequisite. Up until this time economic development in Tanzania has been seen in fragmented terms so that agriculture, for instance, was presumed to be capable of development through its own dynamics – which illustrates the lack of a conceptually integrated strategy to create a nationally integrated economy, as was the case in pre-Arusha Tanzania. To the extent that the Arusha Declaration of 1967 marked a firmer and clearer commitment to socialism, it provided the required impetus for the beginnings of a conceptually integrated strategy for the creation of a nationally integrated economy.

Chapter 4 On Socialism in Rural Tanzania: The Policy and Implementation of Ujamaa Vijijini

1. Karl Marx and Friedrich Engels, *The Communist Manifesto* (Moscow: Foreign Languages Publishing House, 1969), Preface.
2. Eric J. Hobsbawn, *Precapitalist Economic Formations* (London: Lawrence, 1964), p. 50.

3.   *Ibid.*, p. 50.
4.   Julius K. Nyerere, 'Socialism and Rural Development' in *Ujamaa: Essays on Socialism* (Dar es Salaam: Oxford University Press, 1968), p. 118.
5.   *Ibid.*, pp. 112–115.
6.   See the *Report of the International Bank for Reconstruction and Development: The Economic Development of Tanganyika* (Dar es Salaam: Government Printer, 1960).
7.   A. Ellman, 'Development of Ujamaa Policy in Tanzania' in *Rural Cooperation in Tanzania* edited by Cliffe and Lawrence (Dar es Salaam: Tanzania Publishing House, 1975), p. 312.
8.   *Five Year Plan for Economic and Social Development 1964–69* (Dar es Salaam: Government Printer, 1966).
9.   R. H. Hulls, 'An Assessment of Agricultural Extension in Sukumaland in Western Tanzania,' Economic Research Bureau Paper 71.13 (University of Dar es Salaam, 1971), p. 30. Similar conclusions were reached by A. O. Ellman. See A. O. Ellman, 'The Introduction of Agricultural Innovations through Cooperative Farming: A brief Outline of Tanzania's Policies,' *East African Journal of Rural Development*, Vol. 3, No. 1 (1970), 1–15.
10. *Ibid.*
11. Rene Dumont, *Socialism and Development* (London: Andre Deutsch, 1973), p. 145.
12. Ellman, 'The Introduction of Agricultural Innovations through Cooperative Farming,' p. 2
13. Tanzania Government *Report on the Village Settlement Commission to 31st December 1965*, Dar es Salaam, Ministry of Lands, Settlement and Water Development, 1966.
14. Ellman, 'The Introduction of Agricultural Innovations through Cooperative Farming,' p.4.
15. Paulo Freire, *The Pedagogy of the Oppressed* (New York: Herder, 1970), p. 120. We are witnesses to the critical role played by peasants in the Chinese revolution and in particular in the task of socialist transformation in the countryside. For a brilliant account of the process, see William Hinton, *Fanshen* (New York: Monthly Review Press, 1966).
16. Ellman, 'The Introduction of Agricultural Innovations through Cooperative Farming' p.4.
17. R.M. Kawawa, 'New Approaches to Rural Development,' speech at a seminar on Rural Development, at the University of Dar es Salaam, 1966, and reprinted in *Mbioni*, Vol. 11, No. 11 (1966), p.7.
18. R. Lewin and G. Cunningham, 'The Prospcts for Ujamaa Villages' in *Self-Reliant Tanzania* edited by K. Svendsen (Dar es Salaam: Tanzania Publishing House, 1969), p. 274.
19. Nyerere, 'Socialism and Rural Development' in *Ujamaa: Essays on Socialism*, p. 143.
20. See for example, T. van Velsen, 'Staff, Kulaks and Peasants: A

Study of a Political Field' and 'Some Obstacles to Ujamaa: A Case Study from Rungwe' (Leiden: Afrika-Studiecentrum, 1970); R. Feldman, 'Custom and Capitalism: A Study of Land Tenure in Ismani-Tanzania,' Economic Research Bureau Paper (Dar es Salaam: University of Dar es Salaam, 1970); P. Raikes, 'Ujamaa Vijijini and Socialist Development,' Social Science Conference Paper (Dar es Salaam: University of Dar es Salaam, 1973); A. Awiti, 'Ismani and the Rise of Capitalism' in *Rural Cooperation in Tanzania* edited by Cliffe and Lawrence (Dar es Salaam: Tanzania Publishing House, 1975).

21. See W. Arthur Lewis, *The Theory of Economic Growth* (London: Allen and Unwin, 1955).

22. Clive Thomas, 'The Transition to Socialism: Issues of Economic Strategy in Tanzania-type Economies,' Economic Research Bureau Paper 72 (Dar es Salaam: University of Dar es Salaam, 1972).

23. Julius K. Nyerere, *Freedom and Development: A Selection from Writings and Speeches 1968–1973* (Dar es Salaam: Oxford University Press, 1973), p. 66.

24. D. Potter, 'Modernization Processes and Rural Development in Developing Countries: An Anthropological View' in *Rural Development in a Changing World* edited by Raanan Weitz (Cambridge: M.I.T. Press, 1971), p. 358.

25. Nyerere, 'Socialism and Rural Development' in *Ujamaa: Essays on Socialism*, p. 117.

26. Tanzania, *Second Five Year Plan for Economic and Social Development, 1st July, 1969 – 30th June, 1974*. (Dar es Salaam: Government Printer, 1969), p. 26.

27. Nyerere, 'Socialism and Rural Development' in Ujamaa: *Essays on Socialism*, pp. 124–5.

28. A. Ellman, 'Development of Ujamaa Policy in Tanzania' in *Rural Cooperation in Tanzania* edited by Cliffe and Lawrence (Dar es Salaam: Tanzania Publishing House, 1975), p. 323.

29. *Ibid.*, pp. 121–2.

30. Julius K. Nyerere, 'Presidential Circular No. 1 of 1969: The Development of Ujamaa villages' (Dar es Salaam: Government Printer, 1969), p. 3.

31. *Ibid.*

32. Tanzania: *Second Five Year Plan for Economic and Social Development, 1st July, 1969 – 30th June, 1974* (Dar es Salaam: Government Printer, 1974), p. 4.

33. M. H. Y. Kaniki, 'TANU: The Party of Independence and National Consolidation' in *Towards Ujamaa: Twenty Years of TANU Leadership*, ed. by G. Ruhumbika (Nairobi: East African Literature Bureau, 1974), p. 23. Not only has there been an increase in the number of Ujamaa villages in post-Arusha Tanzania, there has also been an increase in the size of the villages. Whereas most of the original villages had about 50

families, those found in subsequent years often contained 200 to 300 families and some, such as in the Rufiji Valley, more than 1,000. This may have been due to the activities of overzealous 'cadres' as well as a lack of understanding on their part of the policy directives (which were in themselves vague in certain respects) on Ujamaa Vijijini. See G. Huizer, 'The Ujamaa Village Programme in Tanzania: New Forms of Rural Development,' *I.S.S. Occasional Papers* (The Hague: The Netherlands, 1971), p. 20.

34. Thus Lewin and Cunningham assessed the number of real Ujamaa villages in 1968 as no more than twenty, though they included only those villages which had already reached the final objective of fully communal farming. See R. Lewin and G. Cunningham, 'The Prospects of Ujamaa Villages' in *Self-Reliant Tanzania* edited by E. Svendsen (Dar es Salaam: Tanzania Publishing House, 1969), p. 274. The *Daily News* reported in May 1972 that only 1,545,000 people in Tanzania mainland lived in Ujamaa villages out of a population of 12 million. (*Daily News*, 21 July 1972).

35. Ellman also reported that in some special cases and for security reasons people were obliged to abandon their old farms after moving to Ujamaa villages, e.g., villagers in Mtwara and Ruvuma along the Mozambique border, or in the Rufiji Valley where whole communities were moved to higher ground to escape floods. Also, in general, areas of high population density like Kilimanjaro and Mwanza regions etc., have the lowest record both in terms of number of villages and percentages of population in Ujamaa villages, as shown in Tables 5 and 6. To some extent the regional variations in the distribution of villages can be attributed to the enthusiasm of the local government and party officials.

36. P. Gumbel, 'Ujamaa: Tanzaniskt Experiment in Socialism' (Stockholm, 1973), p. 23.

37. J. Boesen, 'Tanzania: From Ujamaa to Villagization,' Institute for Development Research Papers A. 76.7, p. 3.

38. In fact, Gerrit Huizen identified 7 types of Ujamaa villages. These include: 1) villages established by regional authorities; 2) villages established voluntarily by the people; 3) traditional villages beginning co-operative activities; 4) villages which were started as settlement schemes in the early 1960's and are now being transformed into Ujamaa villages; 5) villages initiated by missions; 6) 'block farms' which will be transformed into Ujamaa villages at a later stage; 7) a few villages of young people where it is hoped that the parents will join later.

39. Ellman, 'Development of Ujamaa Policy in Tanzania' in *Rural Cooperation in Tanzania* edited by Cliffe and Lawrence, p. 328.

40. See for example: M. von Freyhold, 'Rural Development through Ujamaa Vijijini: Some Considerations based on Experiences in Tanga Pangani and Handeni Districts' (University of Dar es

Salaam, Department of Economics, 1973); A. Awiti, 'The Development of Ujamaa Villages and the Peasant Question in Iringa District: A Study Outline,' Economic Research Bureau Paper (University of Dar es Salaam, 1971); S. Sumra, 'Problems of Agricultural Production in Ujamaa Villages in Handeni District,' E.R.B. Paper (University of Dar es Salaam, 1973).

41. Ellman, 'Development of Ujamaa Policy in Tanzania' in *Rural Cooperation in Tanzania*, ed. by Cliffe and Lawrence, p. 329.

42. *World Bank Report on Tanzania*, April 1977, pp. 5 and 8.

43. *Ibid.*

44. Julius K, Nyerere, *The Arusha Declaration: Ten Years After* (Dar es Salaam: Government Printer, 1977), pp. 12–13.

45. *The Economic Survey and Annual Plan 1970–71* (Dar es Salaam: Government Printer, 1970), p. 25.

46. What comes closest to such a body, was the establishment in the Ministry of Rural Development of a Planning Research Training Unit for Ujamaa at the time of the ministerial reorganizations.

47. It has been suggested that the failure to identify a particular organ that would be charged with the implementation of the programme caused, for example, delays in the specification of task and responsibilities and, hence, in implementation. It was not until another directive in 1969 (following the President's Circular No. 1 1969) that the role of both the government and Party were made specific.

48. The 1974 policy changes on villagization, dubbed, 'Operation Planned Villages,' have in an apparent volte-face accepted the use of coercion as an essential tool in the implementation of the new policy changes – which to some extent negates the very essence of socialism as discussed above.

49. See G. Huizer, 'The Ujamaa Village Programme in Tanzania: New Forms of Rural Development,' *I.S.S. Occasional Papers* (The Hague: The Netherlands, 1971), p. 25.

50. S. S. Mushi, 'Ujamaa : Modernization by Traditionalization,' *Tamuli*, Vol. 1, No. 2 (March, 1971), p. 23.

51. John Senders, 'Some Preliminary Notes on the Political Economy of Rural Development in Tanzania, Based on a Case Study in the Western Usambaras,' Economic Research Bureau Paper (University of Dar es Salaam, 1974), p. 19.

52. *Ibid.*, p. 10.

53. *World Bank Report 1977*, p. 11.

54. *Ibid.*, p. 12.

55. See the *Mwongozo (TANU) Guidelines* (Dar es Salaam: Government Printer, 1971).

56. Goran Hyden, 'Ujamaa, Villagization and Rural Development in Tanzania,' *Odi Review*, 1 (1975), p. 70.

57. John Saul, 'African Peasants and Revolution,' *Review of African Political Economy*, No. 1 (1974), p. 61.

58. In 1974 the Government of Tanzania embarked on 'Operation

Planned Villages' partly in response to the fact that only 'a few of the rural population were leading socialist lives,' and in part as a result of the slow pace of Ujamaaization. More significantly, however, for the first time coercion was seen as essential in the implementation of this phase; the President himself argued that the move had to be compulsory because Tanzania could not sit back and watch the majority of its peoples leading a 'life of death'. Following the recommendation of the TANU National Executive it was resolved that the 'settlement of people in rural villages must henceforth be a compulsory matter.' The target date of 1976 was set as when the whole population of Tanzania was to be living in clustered villages. Everybody liked development! Beyond this the 1977 policy initiatives seem to have shelved the communal organization aspects of the original Ujamaa vision and newly settled farmers were allowed, for example, to farm on an individual basis. Indeed, the World Bank Report 1977 concludes that since 1974 'The Government has shown *increasing pragmatism in the execution of policy in the rural sector.*' (Emphasis mine.) Indeed, we too have noted the increasing pragmatism of the bureaucracy.

59. *World Bank Report on Tanzania, April 1977*, p. 38.
60. See Nyerere, 'Principles of Development,' (Dar es Salaam, 1966). In the appendix to this paper he cited ten decisions, when policy choices made by the Tanzanian Government might have involved some material sacrifice in order not to compromise objectives.
61. *World Bank Report on Tanzania, 1977*, p. 24.
62. *Ibid.*, p. 37.
63. See Peter Lawrence, 'Socialism, Self-reliance and Foreign Aid in Tanzania: Some Lessons from the Socialist Experience,' (University of Dar es Salaam, Department of Economics, 1972).

Chapter 5

The Role of the National Development Corporation in Building a Socialist and Self-Reliant Tanzania

If our nation is to develop . . . we cannot continue to have an exclusively agricultural economy.

Julius K. Nyerere

The real ideological choice is between controlling the economy through domestic private enterprise, or doing so through some state or other collective institution. But although this is an ideological choice, it is extremely doubtful whether it is a practical choice for an African nationalist . . . He will find that the real choice is between foreign private ownership on the one hand and local collective ownership on the other . . . Private investment in Africa means overwhelming foreign private investment. A capitalist economy means a foreign dominated economy. These are facts of the African situation. The only way in which national control of the economy can be achieved is through the economic institutions of socialism.

Julius K. Nyerere

We noted in the preceding discussion that too often in Tanzania (especially in pre-Arusha Tanzania) economic development was conceived in fragmented terms, largely because it lacked a strategy for the creation of a nationally integrated economy consistent with the objectives of socialism.[1] Agriculture, for example, was presumed to be capable of development through its own dynamics. While it is not possible to generate development for the entire country without a clear industrialization strategy which takes into consideration the development of agriculture, agricultural development *per se* cannot be an end in itself. Indeed, in Tanzania's specific socio-economic conditions of under-development, it has to act as an instrument for pushing ahead with industrializaton. Agriculture must be developed to create the basis for the future economic and social transformation. Observes Professor Szentes:

> No growth rate . . . in agriculture can secure independence
> of the national economy in the absence of industrialization
> . . . or attain higher productivity necessary to implement
> the socialist objectives; in other words, it is unable to
> create the economic preconditions for 'self-reliance' and of
> 'socialism.'[2]

Indeed, the Arusha Declaration recognized this and, consequently, it marked a firmer and clearer commitment to the long-term creation of a nationally integrated economy consistent with the objectives of socialism.

In this chapter we examine the role of the National Development Corporation (NDC), by far the single most important parastatal[3] agency, in the task of formulating and promoting the overall national strategy for industrial development in Tanzania. We shall argue that the lack of a national industrial strategy, as well as the absence of any clear national ideological guidelines for the implementation of programmes, indercut efforts to lay down the foundations for a nationally integrated economy. To focus on the NDC is not to deny the importance of other parastatals. The choice has been determined partly by the scope of our study plus the fact that the NDC has been the centrepiece of the industrialization process. Most of the companies nationalized at the initial stage, in the wake of the Arusha Declaration (with the exception of finance, trading and sisal concerns) were placed under the management of the NDC acting as a holding company.[4] The decentralization of the NDC did not take place until much later in the mid 1970s. At the peak of its activities it was controlling about 40 subsidiaries and 25 associate companies. These included the National Agricultural and Food Corporation (NAFCO), the Tanzania Tourist Corporation (TTC), and the Tanzania Wood Industries Corporation (TWICO).

Before attempting to discuss the role of the NDC in promoting a national strategy for industrial development, it is necessary to outline sections of the Arusha Declaration relating to the creation of a nationally integrated economy.

The Arusha Declaration and A National Industrial Strategy

It has often been pointed out by critics of Tanzania's economic structure (e.g., Shivji, Szentes) that the pre-Arusha strategy for economic development for Tanzania differed hardly at all from the development plans of most other Black African countries less committed to socialism, or indeed from those of the other self-styled African socialist countries. It was characterized by its emphasis on private investment, both local and foreign,* as the major engine of growth. It is not surprising, therefore, that in the First Five Year Plan (1964–69) private investment in Tanzania was earmarked to contribute 47 per cent of total fixed capital formation as opposed to 27 per cent in the Second Five Year Plan. As we shall see later, the NDC's primary role was seen in terms of attracting private capital rather than promoting a national strategy for industrial development or extending the control of the govern-

---

* This, of course, meant overwhelming foreign private investment as there was hardly any indigenous private capital to speak of in these countries. The major as well as most other industrial, extractive, financial and commercial enterprises in Tanzania, for example, were owned and controlled by foreign interests and a 'comprador' Asian commercial stratum. This is clearly illustrated by the quote from Nyerere at the beginning of this chapter.

ment over the economy. But it soon became obvious that the economic viability of such a development strategy, if at all possible, could only be achieved at the expense of the objective of socialist transformation. In other words, Tanzania could only move towards socialism if it altered the capitalist basis of the economy. We have already mentioned the forces behind the events that led up to the re-evaluation of the development strategy and the subsequent change in policy as spelled out in the Arusha Declaration. On the industrial front the document committed the government to exercise effective control over the principal means of production, and pursue policies which facilitate the way to collective ownership of the resources of Tanzania.[5]

The principles, enumerated in the Declaration and in subsequent policy documents, were implemented through 1967 and 1968. This involved wholesale nationalizations of the large industrial enterprises, including large-scale agricultural processing; the major step of nationalizing the commercial banking system; and the nationalization of 60 per cent of the sisal industry (which was almost wholly organized in large-scale estates by non-Africans). The government acquired complete control of the National Insurance Corporation. Under the Industrial Acquisition Act, majority ownership was acquired in seven firms, the largest industrial concerns in the country. Also nationalized were seven major milling operations, later formed into the National Milling Corporation. As a result of the implementation of the Arusha Declaration, by mid-1968 the public sector 'controlled' a sizeable majority of large-scale productive activity. Indeed, it was estimated that 'jointly, parastatals, co-operatives, Government bodies and Tanzanian small farmers accounted for perhaps three-quarters of monetary gross domestic product.'[6]

However, it is now generally agreed by even the most rabid nationalist and supporter of nationalizations that the act of nationalization itself does not necessarily bring the commanding heights of the economy under the effective control of the national government. Indeed, nationalization in most of Black Africa has come to mean no more than a symbolic act of completing the process of flag independence.[7] As has become so painfully obvious, nationalizations in most cases pose no problems (just minor irritants) for the foreign firms in Africa, because by and large they keep managerial control to get a return (hardly different from the pre-nationalization levels) on their investments. Little wonder then that in Zambia, for example, foreign firms gladly queued up to be nationalized, perhaps to the amazement of the Zambian government! The words of the *Economist* following the Zambian nationalizations clearly underscored the cosy feelings foreign firms have developed towards the once repugnant act of nationalization. It declared:

> It will be a pity if the realities of President Kaunda's move last week to nationalize Zambia's copper mines are overlooked in a useless debate on the ethics of it. It will be a tragedy if potential investors in Africa are mistakenly led to believe that there is no longer a place for them there. Although doing business in independent Africa now calls for a high degree of political acumen, the opportunities available to those who possess it are good. The risks are greater than in more settled parts of the world but so are the returns . . . The questions that anyone either possessing or contemplating a financial stake in Zambia ought now to be asking have to do with the future political and economic stability of the country, rather than with the principles of nationalization or the mechanics of compensation.[8]

It must be clear by now that natonalization *per se* does not automatically change industrial and social relations in the direction of a transition to socialism. It is a step – in certain industries a necessary step – but no more. In other words, nationalization is not socialization. And though socialization during the period of transition may mean different things to different sectors of the population (for some it may mean workers' control in the manner of Shivji and Mapolu; for others stronger government control over the nationalized industries; for others a larger say for the masses), in the Tanzanian context it was designed to foster the government's control over the economy in the interests of the country and in accordance with the socialist objectives of the government. In the short run, however, the conceptualization of take-overs by the political leadership can only be described as unclear, as we shall see later. More importantly, control over the economy is not without its problems. Attitudes towards state control are not as

130

clear cut as they were once thought to be. Many now question whether it is necessary to have greater central control of the nationalized industries, and have in fact suggested decentralization of nationalized industries. (In the context of Tanzania, the decentralization of the NDC in the mid-1970s becomes pertinent.) The call for decentralization no doubt is based on the fact (especially with political hindsight) that the concentration of economic and political power in the same hands may, in the absence of measures to avert the dangers, be a threat to the freedom and independence of the individual. His very existence becomes more and more dependent upon forces which, by their very nature, are inclined to sacrifice him for the sake of the collective good. These are issues that cannot be ignored, especially in the context of Tanzania where the development of the individual has been a central theme of the country's objectives.

As regards nationalization in Tanzania, it must be pointed out that shortcomings in implementation do not lie, in the first instance, with the machinations of the 'economic' or 'bureaucratic' bourgeoisie to sabotage the exercise (as claimed by Shivji, Hirji, Mapolu, Babu, *et al.*) as a result of their web-like links with the 'international bourgeoisie'. In addition, writes Shivji, 'state ownership allows the bureaucrats to dull the consciousness of the exploited masses of the population thereby serving very well the interests of the international bourgeoisie.'[9] We would argue that the shortcomings in the implementation of the programme lie, in the first instance, with the lack of clarity in the purpose and meaning of nationalization. While the Arusha Declaration clearly committed the government to the public ownership and control of the major means of production, the nationalizaton exercise, which was seen as an essential prerequisite in the process, is described as no more than an act of 'economic nationalism' no different from what obtains in other capitalist or socialist countries embarking on similar actions, and hence ideological. Nyerere declared on the 28 February, 1967 while opening an extension of the Tanzania Breweries plant in Dar es Salaam:

> . . . we decided to secure majority ownership in these
> industries because they are key points in our economy, and
> because we believe that they should therefore be under the
> control of Tanzania. Our purpose was thus primarily a

nationalist purpose; it was an extension of the political control which the Tanzanian people secured in 1961. Such an economic expression of nationalism is nothing new in the world; although the manner of the action may have been peculiarly Tanzanian, its motivation is common enough. Every country – whether it be capitalist, communist, socialist or fascist – wants to control its own economy. It does not necessarily exclude foreign participation in economic life, but it does insist as soon as it can that the major means of production, distribution and exchange are in the hands of its own nationals . . . This economic nationalism has nothing to do with the ideologies of socialism, capitalism, or communism.[10]

Clearly then, well before the 'bureaucratic bourgeoisie' was called upon to implement the nationalization act under the aegis of the NDC (which was described by the President himself as the major instrument for restructuring the colonial economy into a nationally integrated one), the latter was already endowed with an elastic mandate at interpreting the purpose and meaning of the nationalizations. As it turned out, the bureaucratic bourgeoisie were very much at home with the President's interpretation of nationalization as an act of economic nationalism rather than the far-reaching ideological significance of the act. A more sympathetic Packard writes: 'It is difficult to argue, therefore, that nationalization was more than the first possible step towards a socialist public sector.'[11] What may have been a tactical political ploy on the part of the President designed to placate the fears of a jittery private sector, turns out to be a negation of the very efforts of the political leadership at socialist development on the industrial front.

The de-emphasis of the ideological component of nationalization gave further incentive to the bureaucratic bourgeoisie who were already unsympathetic to the ideological demands of the Arusha Declaration. Thus, the economic performance of the NDC, in the absence of any counter ideological constraints or clear socialist guidelines for industrial strategy,[12] hardly reflected the broad socialist objectives of the Arusha Declaration during the period of our study. Surely the act of nationalization must ultimately address itself to the essential question of how to build a socialist and self-reliant economic system, which is based on comprehensive central planning that encourages and allows local participation, and attempts at the same time to relate and rationalize the different sectors and aspects of the economy by integrating them, so that they support and depend on each other.

It cannot be overemphasized that it is not enough to take over foreign-owned institutions. It is imperative that, in order that the act of taking over may meaningfully contribute to the effort of developing productive forces, there be a conscious attempt at creating an independent local economic base that replaces the foreign economic base in the supplying and distribution of basic economic needs. Proper capital allocation therefore becomes very crucial and all along a clear socialist line becomes the means test of what is or is not proper capital allocation. Against the above background, we are now in a better position to examine the role of the NDC in building a socialist and self-reliant Tanzania.

The NDC and Socialist Industrial Development: The Historical Setting

Briefly, the NDC was established by an Act of Parliament in January 1965 following the dissolution of the two public corporations which had hitherto existed as separate bodies. The NDC thus preceded both the Arusha Declaration and the attendant nationalizations of 1967 through 1968. While it is not essential for our purposes to go into the details of the Act, it must be noted that the enabling Act of Parliament specifically stated an operational requirement that is of interest to us:

> In carrying out its business the corporation shall have
> regard to the economic and commercial merits of any
> undertaking it promotes, finances, develops, manages or
> assists and the economic position and potentialities of
> Tanganyika as a whole and shall use the best endeavours
> to ensure that its business as a whole is carried out at a net
> profit taking one year with another.[13]

This specification is instructive and interesting in the sense that it is rather silent on the social. welfare components of Ujamaa. The corporation was essentially a business and commercial venture whose overall activities were to be determined primarily by the profit motive. That this was the case in 1965 is not startling as Tanzania was operating essentially a 'neo-colonial capitalist economy' at the time, plus the fact that the conceptualization of Ujamaa during this period did not in any fundamental way challenge the profit motive as the main determinant of economic policy in the parastatals. Its significance lies in the fact that even after the Arusha Declaration in which the NDC was ascribed the enviable role of the 'major instrument of socialist development' it was still expected to 'operate on a commmercial basis' including, of course, the maximization of profit.

The issue of profitability versus social welfare, as objectives (compatible or incompatible) of a socialist economic policy, has engaged the attention of scholars and fierce academic battles have been fought. Sometimes the issue has been agonized over.[14] However, the debate to our mind is a non-issue for what is important is the use to which the profit is put – whether it is used for the continued personal aggrandizement of a few, as is usually the case in a private enterprise system, or used in the overall interest of the general public as a whole, as is usually the case in a socialist economic system. To this extent, then, socialism does not abhor profit. In addition, the profitable operation of an enterprise may merely mean that 'the costs of acquiring and organising factors of production, raw materials and other inputs to produce final investment or consumer goods can be met from the revenues from sales, leaving a surplus which is available for further investment in the enterprise, for the payment of taxes, or for any other desired uses.'[15]

We do not want to leave the impression that profits are always put to good use in socialist countries, i.e. in the best interests of the public. Far from it. In some respects it has been less than satisfactory. Thus Milovan Dijilas points out that even though attempts at giving workers a share in the profits have been made in both Yugoslavia and other East European countries,

> . . . these quickly result in the retention of 'excess profits'
> in the hands of the bureaucracy who justify this action by

saying that they are checking inflation and investing money wisely. All that remains for the worker are small, nominal sums and the 'right' to suggest how they should be invested through the party and trade union organization – through the bureaucracy. Without the right to strike and to decide on who owns what, the workers have not had much chance to obtain a real share of profits. It has become clear that all these rights are mutually interwoven with various forms of political freedom. They cannot be attained in isolation from each other.[16]

Nevertheless, it cannot be overemphasized tthat too often 'the question of the objectives of an enterprise is usually put in the form of the emphasis that should be given to profitability which is also usually contrasted with social objectives and often assumed to be inconsistent with such objectives'[17] – and by implication inconsistent with socialism.

The NDC and Industrial Development

With the Arusha Declaration the NDC and parastatals in general assumed a far greater role and responsibility in the management of the economy. They became identified as the critical instruments in Tanzania's efforts towards socialist transformation of the economy in general, and the industrial sector in particular,[18] in spite of the ambiguous relationship between nationalization and socialism. The rapid expansion of the NDC's role in the national economy can be seen from the following. By 1967, the NDC controlled 21 firms and held approximately 50 per cent of the shares of 17 others. But by 1972, it had come to control about 50 associated and subsidiary companies in addition to a few other investments.[19] Another indication of the scope of the expanded public sector is borne out by the fact that the NDC's total fixed investment rose from shs.123 million in 1965 to about shs.243 million by the end of 1967. The NDC thus became by far the largest and oldest of all investment parastatal organizations in Tanzania. Little wonder then that with the creation of the NDC it was thought that the basic ingredients of the public corporation were firmly established – ownership and operations by and on behalf of the public to whom a separate and commercially expert management were to be responsible, through the medium of the national government and under the watchful eye of the party. We shall see later how far this was to be the case.

Given the dominance of the NDC in Tanzania's industrialization efforts and the fact that the attempt to industrialize will determine, in part, the success of the country's overall development strategy, the performance of the NDC becomes critical. We therefore devote the rest of this chapter to a discussion of major issue areas in the 'strategy of industrialization' under the NDC in our attempt to evaluate its role in building a socialist and self-reliant economy for Tanzania. These will include, first, the problems related to the objectives and goals of the enterprises under the management of the NDC. An examination of the objectives will, of course, afford us a useful criterion at the same time, against which we can judge the performance. Secondly, the issues related to the investment policies of the NDC – which at once raises the critical question of the kinds of new industrial investments which should be made, to contribute to a more balanced integrated national economy capable of attaining increased productivity and higher levels of living throughout the country. The attainment of this, in turn, largely depends on the ability of the government to formulate the appropriate industrial strategy for the NDC to implement. And thirdly, the problems of management and decentralization.

The Problem of Objectives

We noted earlier that the question of objectives or goals is usually viewed from the rather narrow perspective of profitability, and almost always contrasted with the social objectives of socialism for which it is 'often assumed to be inconsistent.'[20] But as we have argued and has been pointed out by Nyerere regarding Tanzania, 'profit is necessary whether an enterprise is privately or publicly owned. Public ownership affects what happens to the profits, not the necessity for them.'[21] It never meant, of course, that the NDC could only look at profitability when considering whether to initiate or maintain an enterprise. It certainly has to consider the 'development of Tanzania as a whole.' The debate over profit is therefore misplaced and above all trivializes the seriousness of the problem of objectives on which the NDC could predicate the operations of the enterprises under its control. It is not the least surprising therefore that Amin's advice to the Third World to reject profitability as a criterion for economic decisions was roundly described as 'utopian and wrong as his call for "a break with the world market." '[22]

Having said that, we will quickly add that no clear-cut objectives were formulated for the NDC either at its inception in 1965 or at any time during the period of our study.[23] The NDC at its inception was simply called 'our instrument for socialist development'. Equally, we recall the fact that nationalizations were seen merely as economic expressions of nationalism. The NDC was thus to live with the ambiguous relation of nationalization to socialism.

This should not be surprising for we contend that in the absence of a clear-cut national industrial development strategy, it is virtually impossible to lay down broad objectives or goals to guide the activities of the NDC. What comes closest to objectives are put in the form of tasks for the NDC: 'for its task is not only to organize the production of high quality goods at reasonable prices, and to save imports, or earn foreign exchange by exports. It also has the task of increasing wage employment and of diversifying economic activity in the rural areas.'[24]

The uncertainty that reigned in the boardrooms of the NDC as a result, in part at least, of the lack of an industrial strategy and hence objectives is underscored by the statement of the chairman, Ndugu Kahama, when he said:

> If you put together all the industrial investment figures of the plan where NDC's name is mentioned, you will come up with an astonishing figure of shs.1,300 million. You may say that these 93 industrial projects contained in the plan constitute a marvellous action programme for the NDC. Unfortunately, apparently no one was seriously aware of the critical deficiencies in the plan which made it manifestly inadequate as an action programme . . . the

> plan as a whole is overestimated by about 30% as far as
> financial resources are concerned and also overestimated
> by about 30% as far as market capacity is concerned.
> Without details as to which projects are affected by these
> overestimations of financial resources and market capacity,
> the individual industrial projects listed become surrounded
> by a veil of uncertainty . . . what should be taken now,
> therefore, as an official guideline in the formulation of our
> industrialization policies?[25]

One of the more serious consequences of the government's
failure to formulate broad national objectives for the NDC and
parastatals is that the NDC and its organizations virtually had a
monopoly of the decision-making process. It was a common
practice (and it is still to a very large extent today) of the
management of the NDC to express quite often their resentment
of what they considered to be 'outside' interference in the running
of their firms. In the absence of clear-cut national objectives and
plans to follow, given the strategic vacuum, they were able for a
considerable period of time to withstand pressures from, for
example, the planning machinery. They sought to maintain an
organizational autarchy with the result that the operation of their
enterprises remained virtually the same as it had been before the
Arusha Declaration and the subsequent nationalizations. The
tendency towards organizational autarchy can be explained, at least
in part, by the fact that coming mainly from the civil service, the
managers of the NDC were still imbued with the administrative
practices of the relatively autonomous and conservative civil
service. They had yet to be sensitized to the socialist goals of
post-Arusha Tanzania. Even though the 'institutional framework
for parastatal enterprises can be characterized as public
ownership, there was little or no effective control by Government
over NDC and in general parastatal enterprises.'[26] Edmund Clark,
for instance, noted in his study that too often parastatals adopted a
very narrow definition of socialism and often acted as if socialism
only meant government control.

It could be argued (and perhaps with some justification) that the
dizzy speed of the post-Arusha nationalizations afforded very little
time for the government to draw up an industrial strategy consistent with the country's socialist objectives, with which to guide the

operations of the NDC enterprises.[27] It is more difficult to argue convincingly (as attempted by Shivji, for example) that the absence of an industrial strategy in the wake of the Arusha Declaration was due to the inevitable capitulation of the 'bureaucratic bourgeoisie' to their international cohorts – the 'international bourgeoisie'. To say this, is not to deride the importance of the relationship between the 'bureaucratic bourgeoisie', on the one hand, and the 'international bourgeoisie' on the other hand. We are only saying that given the temporal considerations, the relationship between the two strata could not be considered the prime contradiction. This may explain why others, like Mapolu and Cliffe, are simply satisfied to stress the fact that there has been an 'insufficiently forceful emphasis on the contradictions which continue to characterize the relationship between "privileged domestic classes" and the "workers and peasants" and hence the failure of the leaders to confront adequately the realities of class struggle, as yet another manifestation of the leadership's ideological weakness.'[28]

While there may be greater justification for the latter point of view, we agree with Saul that the political leadership stratum under the leadership of Nyerere and the party has 'managed both to exemplify unity and to link its destinies to the needs of the masses in ways almost unknown elsewhere on the continent. It is Tanzania's progressive constellation of "organization and ideology" which has pushed imperialism and the locally privileged as far as they have had to go in order to accommodate to the imperatives of Tanzanian socialism.'[29] To this extent Shivji's root-and-branch manner of criticism, in which he lumps together the political leadership and the bureaucratic bourgeoisie strata as belonging to the same odious gang of petty-bourgeoisie, borders on dogma or at best a demonstration of 'effusive enthusiasm' by an erudite scholar, more so as he had earlier in his *Silent Class Struggle* described the relationship between the 'top political leadership' and the bureaucracy in these terms:

> . . . Tanzania does not definitely fall under the heading of bureaucratic capitalism . . . because the bureaucracy does not appear to have an upperhand and certainly does not hold political power. This may be due to the fact that the *top leadership of the Party is dedicated to socialism.*[30]

The lack of an industrial strategy and hence national objectives will, of course, be reflected not only in the investment policies of the NDC but also in the areas of management and decentralization. In the absence of an appropriate strategy for industrial development, it is, to say the least, highly unlikely that the NDC would adopt the kinds of investment and management policies best suited to ensuring the government's control of the 'commanding heights' of the economy.

The Problem of Investment Policies

In the wake of the Arusha Declaration, three main sectors of investment in Tanzania were delineated:[31]

1 Wholly-owned state enterprise which included banking, insurance, major import-export houses, and major grain mills and fire-arm industries.
2 State controlled enterprises. This sector included those industries classified as the major means of production in the country, namely, the land, forests, mineral resources; water, oil and electricity; communications and transport; steel, machine tool, motor car, cement and fertilizer factories; the textile industry and any other big industry upon which a large section of the population depends for its living or which provides essential components for other industries; and large plantations, especially those which produce essential raw materials. The primary concern of the NDC was in this sector of industrial and agricultural undertakings.
3 Other enterprises not covered by 1 and 2 above and open to investment by the private sector, either on its own or in partnership with government. And although the NDC was concerned with promoting the second sector, it was also prepared to participate with private enterprise, or rather, investors in the third sector.

The NDC or its subsidiaries could also develop the industrial and agricultural undertakings of the second sector on their own or in partnership with private firms. Furthermore, the partnerships permit foreign or lcoal investment of up to 50 per cent of the equity by the firms concerned, as well as provision of expatriate management and know-how. There is no doubt that these provisions have had significant implications for the country's claim to self-reliance, as we shall see later. We shall therefore consider the NDC's pattern of investment and the role foreign partnerships play in influencing and structuring the pattern of investment.

In the absence of a clearly defined industrial strategy consistent with the post-Arusha socialist objectives of Tanzania, no rational criteria could evolve for assessing the NDC, parastatal investment and other policy decisions. Under these circumstances, individual parastatals have had to resort to drawing up their own criteria for investment and appraisal of projects. The NDC was able to draw up its own criteria for the first time in its 1971/72 Plan. This means that up until 1971 the NDC operated in more or less the same manner as its private enterprise forerunners. This state of affairs prompted the Planning Ministry to publicly admit that parastatals 'remain so far largely outside attempts at socialist planning of the economy; investment decisions are made in essentially the same way as in the private sector of an unplanned economy.'[32] While it is true that the NDC and its subsidiaries, and parastatals in general, have involved the creation of a large number of new firms (see Table 1), and the extension of government involvement with sectors in which it was previously not involved, it is no exaggeration to say that there has not been a dramatic break with the past.

In fact, the NDC's eight criteria for project selection (three primary, five secondary) are revealing for its appalling lack of criteria relating to the broad socialist objectives of post-Arusha Tanzania.[33] If anything, the criteria are largely technical. Besides, the operational utility of the criteria is very marginal given the indistinct categories. How do we, for example, differentiate category (a) of the primary criteria from category (e) of the secondary criteria? Can we establish the fact that category (a) under the secondary criteria is more important than category (c)? Furthermore, if they are to be useful for project appraisal then these criteria must, of course, be readily amenable to weighting. But how do we weight the various categories to reflect the order of importance? Is it in terms of money or social welfare? Even if this were possible, how useful will it be at the macro-level if the NDC

Table 1 *Share of New Investment in Total Parastatal Investment*
(per cent shares)

	1964	1965	1966	1967	1968	1969	1970	1971	Total
Manufacturing	–	64	84	72	63	55	73	66	68
Non-Majority Manufacturing	100	100	91	96	98	77	–	–	90
Mining	–	–	–	–	–	–	–	–	–
Construction	–	–	–	–	–	–	–	–	–
Electricity	–	–	–	–	–	–	–	–	–
Transport	–	–	–	100	100	100	–	–	78
Tourism	93	92	25	51	78	95	97	84	90
Non-Majority Tourism	–	–	–	–	–	100	100	100	100
Commerce	–	–	–	–	–	–	7	–	1
Non-Majority Commerce	–	–	–	–	–	100	100	–	18
Agriculture	–	–	–	–	–	30	37	–	26
Non-Majority Agriculture	–	–	–	–	–	44	54	–	24
Finance	–	–	–	35	65	36	–	–	20
Non-Majority Finance	–	–	–	–	–	–	–	–	–
Total Majority	19	34	33	70	61	35	48	29	45
Total Non-Majority	100	96	90	95	92	71	51	11	82
Total	22	56	41	73	66	41	48	28	48

Source: Clark, Table IV–IV, p. 174.

criteria is unco-ordinated with those of other public corporations. In this respect, Penrose's observation becomes pertinent: 'In weighing these criteria in any given case the difficulty of course lies in the nature of the trade-off; how much to sacrifice employment to improve industrial linkages, or location to increase investible surplus, etc.'[34]

Significantly, however, the NDC criteria gave greater decision-making powers to her foreign partners since they were weighted heavily in favour of technology for which the foreign partners had a convincing monopoly. In fact, in the early years of its existence, the NDC saw its role as far as project preparation was concerned as essentially a passive one. It viewed itself as an organization designed to attract foreign firms which had projects to build. There was little input from the NDC in the actual design of the project. And quite often (as noted by many researchers on Tanzania, e.g., Loxley, Saul, Seidman) the area of investment chosen was in response to foreign initiatives, rather than the result of the NDC's desire to operate a certain sector or in accordance with its investment criteria. Little wonder then that the NDC remained largely incapable of changing its approach to investment in response to the changed ideology of the government.

Some observers, like Clark, have attributed the failure of the NDC to develop significantly different parastatal organizations to the role played by nationalization itself. They argue that these firms have not been significantly altered since their acquisition, and operate as essentially private firms under government ownership, because the parastatal assets acquired before 1964 were mostly private firms in which the government acquired equity control.[35] Surely, the argument is tautological and has failed to explain why the NDC failed to significantly alter its mode of operations. Clark's other observation is, however, more significant:

> The use of nationalizations as a means of creating much of the parastatal sector was a two-edged sword. On the one hand, it allowed the government to move easily into the productive sector. By acquiring established firms the government minimized the degree of difficulty it would have operating the firms. On the other hand, the government acquired a large number of companies whose

basic structure and orientation was that of private firms. If the Arusha Declaration was to mean the establishment of a radically different investment strategy, these companies would not be a good basis for such a change.[36]

Not least significant is the fact that other related phenomena, at least in part attributable to the influential role of the foreign partners, become evident in the investment pattern of the NDC and parastatals in general. These include the fact that investment by the NDC and other parastatals is characteristically capital intensive,[37] import intensive; it has tended to be oriented towards import substitution (though there are a number of investments which have yielded some exports, about 19 per cent, especially to other East Africa Community countries before its dissolution). It has concentrated not only on the manufacturing sector, especially after the decentralization of the NDC in 1969, but also on a few large firms located in Dar es Salaam and other urban centres to the detriment of the rural sectors.

The capital-intensive nature of its investments can be gleaned from Table 2 which compares the average wage and value added per worker in each parastatal sector to the economy as a whole. According to Clark's findings, parastatals 'consistently pay higher wages' which reflects both 'the policy of the government and the more capital intensive nature of the parastatal sector.'[38] Arrighi has argued that foreign partners or multinational corporations are greatly biased against labour-intensive investments and capital-goods industry.[39]

A classic example of the role played by foreign partners in the choice of projects which are capital intensive is illustrated by the NDC's decision to build the friendship Textile Mill and the Mwanza Textile Mill. The Peoples' Republic of China built the former at a cost of £2.5 million with an interest-free loan; it is now fully owned by the Tanzanian government. The latter was built at a cost of £4 million, is 40 per cent owned by NDC, 40 per cent by the Nyanza Co-operative Union and 20 per cent by Amerital, a French company representing the consultants and managing agents. In contrast to the Chinese, the cost for the Mwanza Mill is not interest free and 75 per cent of the capital cost was financed by loans from two French banks. More significantly, unlike the Friendship Mill which employs 3,000, the Mwanza Mill employs

Table 2 *Some Basic Ratios for Majority Parastatals*

	Capital/ Value Added Shs.	Capital/ Labour Shs.'000	Wages/ Labour Shs.'000	Wages/ Value Added %	Return to Capital %	Profit Rate %	Value Added/ Labour Shs.'000
Manufacturing	2.5	38	6.5	43	23	13	15.2
Mining	2.9	103	10.4	29	25	20	35.8
Construction	3.0	23	5.7	75	8	1	7.6
Electricity	5.7	134	5.3	23	14	8	23.6
Finance	0.9	41	12.1	25	87	56	47.7
Transport	3.5	119	12.0	35	19	13	34.5
Tourism	9.3	56	5.5	92	1	–6	6.0
Commerce	0.9	30	8.8	27	80	60	33.2
Agriculture	5.5	12	1.6	75	5	–	2.1
Average	2.4	40	5.9	35	27	17	16.8

Source: Clark, Table IV–XIV, p. 190.

only 1,000 local people, though they both produce the same quantity of square yards – 24 million.[40] The primary reason for the difference is that the Mwanza Mill is more capital intensive. Equally, whereas the Friendship Mill was fully turned over to local manpower, trained by the Chinese, the Mwanza Mill was only beginning to initiate a programme for training by 1970.[41] Indeed, the Sixth NDC Annual Report conceded that whereas the Friendship Mill has been making profits, the Mwanza Mill has been making losses due to heavy loan and interest payments.[42] We are not suggesting that only labour-intensive projects are appropriate for the industrial development of Tanzania during this phase of transition to socialism. All we are saying is that the decision about what projects to invest in must lie primarily with the NDC, not foreign partners, bearing in mind the developmental imperatives (already referred to) of a nationally integrated economy. If this had been the case, the decision to build the Mwanza Textile Mill would have been seen for what it really is – a bad investment decision (seen in the context of Tanzania's overall socialist objectives) foisted on the NDC by her foreign partners solely in their interest.

Closely allied with the above is the fact that investments have also been import intensive. Table 3, for example, gives us the percentage of parastatal investment which has gone each year into firms where more than 25 per cent of the raw materials used are imported.* Clark, for instance, finds that the average import intensity of parastatal firms is 45 per cent while the average for non-parastatals is 28 per cent. The difference, he argues, reflects the type of industries in which the parastatal sector is located, but it also reflects the particular approach used to develop the industry.[43] A classic case in point is the fertilizer plant at Tanga. Under the influence of the NDC's powerful foreign partners for the project – Kloeckners of Germany – it used entirely imported raw materials for its development, despite the fact that there was an abundance of locally available raw materials such as phosphates, etc.[44] In this respect, Coulson's conclusions following his study of Tanzania's fertilizer factory are pertinent and we shall quote him in full:

* We are greatly indebted to Edmund Clark for the discussion here on the problems of investments by the NDC and parastatals in general.

146

Table 3 *Import Intensity of Parastatal Investments (%)*

	64/65	65/66	66/67	67/68	68/69	FFYP	69/70	70/71	71/72	72/73	73/74
% Share of Firms with Import Intensity Above 25%	31	70	58	65	47	56	57	53	41	21	45

Source: Adapted from Clark, Table IV–XIX, p. 198.

There is evidence that both the NDC and the Government are today more careful about the small print in the agreements they sign with foreign companies. But there are some further implications for Tanzania and other African countries that can be learnt from this study. The first is that a factory producing for a local market cannot be allowed to depend on imported inputs, especially if these form a high proportion of total costs. The people's needs must be met, as far as possible, from local resources. In the case of fertilisers, this might mean making more use of natural manure, and local raw materials . . . More broadly every country must have an industrial strategy, and the following are just some of the factors which would have been clear if the production of fertilisers had been part of such an overall plan in Tanzania:

   – The factory would have been put near the oil refinery so that it could use the waste gases and steam.

   – The production of cement would have been developed at Kilwa so that sulphuric acid could have been produced there too.

   – The manufacture of sulphuric acid would have been on a sufficient scale to supply all other users of this basic industrial chemical, including, for example, the tanneries and paper-making mills.

   – The mining of local phosphate would have been recognized as essential.

   – The importance of transport would have been realised, and the siting of the petro-chemical complex would have taken this into account.

   – The development of industry and agriculture would have been planned together so that locally available natural fertilisers would have been used where possible. Artificial products to meet real (and not imagined) local needs should have been identified by the farmers themselves, rather than by research stations.

In short, industrial projects have to fit together so that the sum is more than the part, and without an overall plan this cannot happen. The fertiliser factory in Tanzania illustrates what can go wrong.[45]

Table 4 *Important Ratios for Parastatal Manufacturing Firms*

	Capital/ Value Added (shs)	Capital/ Labour (shs)	Average Size of Firm	Wages/ Labour (shs)	Wages/ Value Added (%)	Return to Capital	Profit Rate (%)	Value Added/ Labour (shs)
Local Materials Based								
1. Agriculture	2.151	23347	21795	5116	47	25.4	15.2	10852
2. Mining	3.236	65272	27167	7387	36	19.7	12.3	20309
3. Forestry	1.521	15228	8014	4267	43	37.7	11.2	10009
Sub-Total	2.210	25030	20295	5165	46	25.3	14.5	11325
Immported Materials Based								
4. Metals	2.841	32204	7257	8655	76	8.3	0	11332
5. Plastics/Chem./								
Fuels	4.397	168094	62783	15436	40	13.6	1.5	38227
6. Food/Fiber/Paper	1.288	39904	13214	7981	26	57.6	14.3	30980
Sub-Total	2.675	81417	20300	10564	35	24.4	4.7	30433
Total	2.379	34908	20297	6109	42	24.9	10.5	14671

Source: Clark, Table Vb–IV, p. 213.

Other examples include the tyre and shoe factories which could have used local rubber and hides respectively – although both industries started using more of local inputs later. Table 4 shows the different ratios for firms based upon local materials (import intensity less than 50 per cent) and firms based upon imported materials (import intensity over 50 per cent). Based on this Clark estimates that the 'capital/labour ratio of import oriented firms is more than three times that of local materials based firms. The capital/value added ratio, is, as well, 10 per cent higher, and the return on capital marginally lower. Only 0.2 per cent of the assets of imported materials based firms are located outside of Dar es Salaam, Tanga, Arusha and Moshi, while 30 per cent of the assets of local materials based firms are located outside the cities.'[46]

Closely related to the above is the fact that import-intensive firms tend to be more capital intensive; have a higher capital/value added ratio, and tend to be larger. Moreover, because they rely upon imported raw materials, such industries must be located on the coast or in towns with a relatively adequate transportation system; as far as the foreign partners are concerned, this is the only rational thing to do. The result is that these industries tend to be located in the towns and regions which are already more 'developed', adding again to the pangs of the urban, rural dichotomy (See Tables 5, 6 and 7).

Lastly, the emphasis on manufacturing as well as on a few large firms has meant the failure to establish an industrial policy which will complement agricultural development. There has been an absence, in several instances, of backward and forward linkages with agriculture.*

We conclude this section by noting that the high external orientation of much of the NDC and other parastatal investment

---

* In all fairness, it must be pointed out that attempts are being made, albeit haphazardly, in this regard. Thus the Ubongo Farm Implement Factory, for example, is an attempt at fashioning a previously non-existent kind of integration between the rural and urban sectors. But it cannot be overemphasized that 'genuine industrial development in poorer countries should generate considerable linkages to indigenous resources.' See, for example, S. Langdon, 'MNCs, Taste Transfer and Underdevelopment: A Case Study from Kenya,' *RAPE*, No. 2 (1975), p. 13.

Table 5 *Regional Location of Parastatals*

Region	Dar es Salaam	Kilimanjaro	Arusha	Tanga	Mwanza	Other
Assets (shs million) (1970)	402	27	47	128	85	203
% of Total	45%	3%	5%	14%	10%	25%
Value Added (shs million)						
(1971)	151	54	13	7	25	166
% of Total	41%	1%	4%	2%	7%	45%
Employment (1971)	125%	238	840	430	1730	9840
% of Total	49%	1%	3%	2%	7%	32%

Source: *Survey of Industrial Production 1970*, p. 72, unpublished data.

Table 6 *Regional Location of all Industries, 1970*

Region	Coast	Kilimanjaro	Arusha	Tanga	Mwanza	Other
Value Added (shs million)	365	24	26	33	57	56
% of Total	65%	4%	5%	6%	10%	10%
Employment	22016	2537	3020	4427	4964	11735
% of Total	45%	5%	6%	9%	10%	25%
Population as % of Total	7%	6%	5%	6%	9%	27%

Source: *Survey of Industrial Production 1970*, p. 72, unpublished data.

Table 7 *Urban Location of Parastatal Investment*

	First F.Y.P. shs million	%	Second F.Y.P. shs million	%
Dar es Salaam	350	58	603	35
Tanga	11	2	209	12
Arusha	5	1	80	5
Moshii	12	2	84	5
Mwanza	52	8	80	5
Sub-Total	430	71	1056	62
Other towns	178	29	645	38
Total Towns	608	100	1701	100
Towns as Share of total		57		64

Source: Clark, Table IV–XXI, p. 201.

indicates that they have failed to be, or even seem to be, self-reliant and are developing the economy in a way which makes it quite externally dependent. Its investment pattern has led to a situation where quite often industries are developed by foreign firms, drawing heavily upon foreign personnel and dependent upon foreign technology.

The Problem of Management

The problem of management in the context of Tanzania is intrinsically linked with the investment decisions, or rather, policies of the NDC and parastatals in general. One of the more common criticisms of public corporations and public enterprises in Tanzania has been about the unhealthy pattern of linkages between the public corporations and the foreign private firms through partnership agreements and management contracts.[47]

One major consequence of the post-Arusha rapid expansion of the NDC's role in the national economy was that it led not only to a reorganization of parastatal institutions in 1969* but, perhaps more importantly, it created an acute shortage of local business managers in the country. While we concede that management contracts are in part attributable to the dearth of indigenous business managers in Tanzania,** we would argue that the NDC's overwhelming reliance on management agents from countries whose economic system is diametrically opposed to the socialist objectives of Tanzania, is, to say the least, inconsistent with the overall national objectives of Tanzania. Can we really expect management consultants like McKinsey and Co. or Dr. David E. Emery (who was on secondment to NDC from the IBM Corporation!), for example, steeped as they are in the ethics of capitalism, to train suitable indigenous managerial cadres to run the affairs of the NDC and parastatals in general? On the question of Dr. Emery, Shivji expresses his amazement and concern thus: 'so here is a man coming from one the world's largest corporations, sponsored by an American foundation, to train Tanzanian managers to run a socialist economy!'[48] The NDC's apparent uncritical

* Based on the recommendations of the management consultancy firm of McKinsey and Co. of the United States, the NDC was decentralized in 1969 to streamline its operational base. Under the new arrangements the NDC was to confine its activities primarily to the manufacturing, processing and mining sectors. Both the Tanzania Tourist Corporation and the National Agricultural and Food Corporation were created to take care of the management of tourist hotel and other related activities and ranching respectively. It also entailed a sharper delineation of duties between the NDC and its other various subsidiaries. It was also designed to ensure closer co-ordination between each public corporation and its corresponding parent ministry in the areas of government policy and development strategy. As a further measure of decentralization the Tanzania Wood Industries Corporation was created in 1971 to take over the NDC timber industry, and in 1973 the State Mining Corporation was established to take over the mining activities of the NDC. See *Jenga* (NDC Publication), No, 14 (1973), p. 40.

** Shivji's attempt to ignore this important factor, to our mind, may have weakened his case in the eyes of his detractors. On the other hand, Rweyemamu's uncritical acknowledgement of this factor trivializes the serious implications. See A. H. Rweyemamu, 'The Predicament of Managers of Public Enterprises in Tanzania,' *African Review*, Vol. 5, No. 2 (1975), p. 122.

reliance on foreign management consultants regardless of their places of origin, is premised partly on 'the mistaken belief in the neutrality of management and that these management systems are therefore capable of universal application regardless of the socio-political and the ideological basis of the economic system.'[49] It is in part a legacy of the British parliamentary system which views the civil service as a neutral agent. This is particularly pertinent when one realizes, as Packard does, that 'for the most part, the members of boards are civil servants.'* 'Their experience, together with their attitudes, militates against too detailed questioning or under-standing of management . . . the most likely result is that review of management actions by the board of directors will be perfunctory, so that the board in effect abdicates any responsibility for shaping the operations and development of the enterprise.'[50]

Perhaps it was in recognition of the subservient role played by the indigenous managers of public corporations and the inherent threat to the continued progress towards socialism posed by the dominant role of management agents (foreign consultants) that prompted the Presidential directives in Circular No. 1 of 1970[51] and the publication of the Party Guidelines (Mwongozo) in 1971. Thus the presidential directive, for example, ordered the establish-ment of workers' participation in the management of public enterprises in 1970. It emphasized the need for management to pay heed to workers and to include workers' interests in decision-making by the management. It directed that workers' councils be set up in all public enterprises to advise on wages and production targets as well as other matters of concern to workers. In short, it urged the democratization of the decision-making process of the public corporations.

The Mwongozo was even more far-reaching in its implications for industrial relations in public enterprise. It demanded that:

> the conduct and activities of the parastatals must be looked into to ensure that they help further our policy of socialism

---

* It is well to be reminded that we have established in this study the lingering conservative civil service mentality of the 'bureaucratic bourgeoisie' in Tanzania – including the new university graduates from Dar es Salaam.

and self-reliance. Those activities of the parastatals should be a source of satisfaction and not discontent. The party must ensure that the parastatals do not spend money extravagantly on items which do not contribute to the development of the national economy as a whole.[52]

Together then, both the Presidential directives and the Party Guidelines were designed to check the excesses of the management agents in the face of what may best be described as an impotent indigenous managerial sector – the bureaucratic bourgeoisie. Writes Neerso, 'the companies with foreign management are largely run according to the wishes of the foreign managers, irrespective of the distribution of ownership. The members of the companies' boards appointed by the parastatal holding corporations tend to be passive and to agree to the proposals made by the foreign managers because they lack managerial and especially technical knowledge. Furthermore the parastatals have only to a limited extent elaborated socialist business principles. This is not helped by the *lack of clear guidelines by the Party and Government on key policy issues.*'[53] These two documents were designed to establish effective political control of the public corporations by the party and government.* The consequences of these policy

---

* As a result of the directives, the General Manager of the NDC is now appointed by the President. Political and trade union leaders are also appointed to the boards of companies including senior government officials from the parent ministries. More importantly, the directives and the Mwongozo suggest that the Party has come to recognize the fact that ownership and control are two different things: that it is one thing to take over foreign enterprises and another thing to be able to maintain effective control over them. The simple legal ownership of a given corporation in whatever shared ratios (50:50, 80:20 etc.) between national and expatriate interests tells us nothing about the relative control exercised by each of the parties. This is not only because modern corporations tend to divorce ownership from management but, in the case of Tanzania, also because the foreign partners exert a disproportionate influence on the firms of which they are co-owners, given their overwhelming technical expertise and the absence of clear national objectives for national industrial development. It follows that, given the fact that expatriate advisers or investors owe primary loyalty to their multinational firms in the metropole, the policies followed by national enterprises may tend to further interests of the metropolitan

documents have been fully described elsewhere.[54] Suffice it to say that 'despite the directives and the formation of workers' councils in industrial enterprises, not much progress has been made in developing socialist management techniques that are consistent with industrial discipline.'[55]

All this is not to deny that the NDC has played a pivotal role in establishing the base for Tanzania's industrial activity. Based on some relevant indicators such as employment, wages, salaries, taxes, sales, net investment, etc., NDC's contribution to Tanzania's development shows an impressive rate of growth (in purely economic terms) between 1966 and 1972. Table 8 shows that between 1966 and 1972 NDC's employment level increased by 100 per cent, the wage bill by over 170 per cent, sales by over 350 per cent, taxes by over 790 per cent, and net investment by over 180 per cent – an impressive performance from a temporal standpoint.

Table 8 *Some Relevant NDC Growth Indicators Between 1966 and 1972*

	Employment	Wage Bill	Sales	Taxes	Net Investment
		(in million shillings)			
1966	11,360	53.0	311.5	20.2	117.0
1967	17,460	89.3	805.7	145.9	211.0
1968	22,030	104.9	724.3	176.6	311.1
1969	16,170	94.8	710.6	179.9	260.7
1970	18,030	99.7	968.6	194.2	333.5
1971	18,640	109.7	1,062.1	156.4	429.7
1972	22,960	144.4	1,422.8	181.4	450.8

Source: *NDC Annual Report (1973)*, p. 40.

When these statistics are examined more closely, we find that

foreign firms supplying the consultants more than they further the interests of Tanzania itself. This is in spite of the rather simplistic suggestion by Mramba and Mwansasu that 'the recommendations of consultants are not imposed on their principal.'

156

these indicators reveal quite an important aspect of NDC's role in Tanzania's development. Table 9 shows that compared to the millions of shillings spent for net investment each year, the number of new jobs created is 'startlingly small.'[56] In 1967, for example, shs.35,000 of net investment were needed to create one job, while by 1972 the same job needed shs.111,000 of net investment.* The implications are obvious. It means that most of the investment carried out by NDC is unnecessarily capital intensive or that it goes into luxurious office buildings, etc. It could also mean, as Nyerere took pains to point out in his *Ten Years After Arusha*, that:

> Management and administrative costs are often much too high in relation to output. In every parastatal we have a whole series of managers for different functions, and a general manager on top. Each manager has a secretary, an office of his own, and often a car . . . We employ some 'sales managers' who sit in their offices and wait for customers to search them out, without making any attempt to find out what needs the factory could be fulfilling and is not, or what change in their product could make it more useful to their customers, etc. We employ some 'production managers' who do not order spare parts or the necessary raw materials on time, or having done so just sit and complain instead of going after them if the goods are not delivered. We have 'maintenance managers' in our transport enterprise** who apparently find it acceptable to

---

* This, no doubt, was in the mind of the President in his assessment of ten years after Arusha, when he said:
'The problem has not been a failure to make investments in new factories or farms. In the four years 1967–1970, Shs.1,555 million was invested in new productive facilities by the parastatals alone . . . [the problem is that] we are not using our investments as efficiently as we should. Almost all our industrial plants are running well below capacity. Sometimes less than 50% of what could be produced with established machinery is actually being manufactured and put on to the market!'
See Nyerere, *Ten Years After Arusha*, p. 21.

** Incidentally, the Transport Corporation of Tanzania went bankrupt in 1977.

have as many as 40% of their vehicles off the road at any one time waiting for repairs or service.[57]

Table 9 *NDC Net Investments in Relation to New Jobs Created Between 1966 and 1972*

	Net Investment (million Shillings)	Changes in Employment
1966	117.0	–
1967	211.0	6,100
1968	311.1	4,570
1969	260.7	–5,860
1970	333.5	1,860
1971	429.7	610
1972	450.8	4,320

Source: *Ibid.*

What clearly emerges from the above is whether, given the internal organizational deficiencies of the NDC so poignantly described by the President, the NDC can continue to play its leading role in expanding the base for industrial activity in Tanzania. But even more crucial is whether, in fact, its role has been in the overall interest of a national development strategy consistent with the socialist objectives and goals of post-Arusha Tanzania.

In summary then, we have argued that the lack of a clearly defined strategy for industrial development has left policy directives ambiguous enough for the NDC's managerial sector to interpret widely. More importantly, this has led to the dominant role being played by foreign consultants or management agents (not ideologically sympathetic) in directing the affairs of the national economy, plus the fact that they command a disproportionate managerial expertise within the partnerships. A more serious consequence of this master/servant relationship is that the indigenous managerial sector (the bureaucratic bourgeoisie) is drawn more closely to the international bourgeoisie – willy-nilly – through the intermediary of the management agents who are the representatives of the multinational corporations in the metropole.* Indeed, it is this latter aspect that has usually received the more acid criticism. Although we agree with the significance of that criticism, we argue (and have tried to show in the preceding chapters) that the lack of a clear national strategy for industrial development precedes the problem of the bureaucratic bourgeoisie/international bourgeoisie linkages. Until that basic problem is resolved (quickly, one hopes)** the relationship of the duo may continue to grow in strength (with all the attendant implications), in spite of the rather severe but welcome circumscription of the avenues for personal aggrandisement imposed on the bureaucratic bourgeoisie by the leadership code.

* We might add that no serious attempts are being made by the indigenous management of the NDC to escape from the strait-jacket in which it now finds itself as a result of its relationship with foreign partners and management consultants.

** Indeed, the United Nations Research Institute for Social Development captured the essence of the urgency when it observed: 'A style of development once established tends to persist because it involves an array of interrelated activities and interests (political, economic and social, domestic and foreign) which tend to support and maintain or at least accommodate each other, to the exclusion of other arrangements. Thus industrialization in the form of domestic manufacture of expensive durable goods, once introduced (perhaps for import substitution reasons and often by mnc's), demands an income distribution that will maintain and expand the market – a market that must depend on high-income receivers with consumption interests similar to those found in the rich countries. Dependency on various imported inputs will be established and pressures will mount for certain kinds of infrastructure that will be favourable to the growth of the industry. This would contrast with forms of industrialization that concentrate on basic consumption items, on products of use to small farmers (fertilizers, sprays, water pumps, cement etc.), on means of mass transportation, on cheap hand and power tools for artisan and repair work, and other products that will serve to raise the level of skills, output and welfare of the ordinary workers.'
See *UNRISD*, No. 4 (June 1974).

Chapter 5   The Role of the National Development Corporation in Building a Socialist and Self-Reliant Tanzania

1.   It is generally acknowledged and has recently been noted by the *World Bank Report of 1977* that until the early 1970s the Government of Tanzania 'did not have a well-articulated long-term industrial strategy.' A basic industrial strategy was adopted by 1974. More importantly, the lack of a conceptually integrated strategy for the creation of a nationally integrated economy consonant with the objectives of socialism must not be mistaken for that of a systematic and coherent theoretical framework. The former is a problem of implementation. We maintain, as we have argued all along, that Tanzania under Nyerere has laid the foundations for the continued development, refinement, and clarification of a systematic and coherent theoretical framework on which to base its actual programmes of action consistent with its socialist goals.

2.   T. Szentes, *Economic Policy and Implementation: Problems in Tanzania* (Budapest: Center for Afro-Asian Research, 1970), p.6.

3.   The term 'parastatals' is used to describe those governmental organizations which fall outside the mainstream of the departmental and ministerial hierarchies. Thus they have a considerable degree of autonomy in their day-to-day operations even though they remain tied ultimately into the centralized decision-making process. They have, by and large, been established since the Arusha Declaration and the attendant nationalization measures of 1967. The Central Bureau of Statistics defines a 'parastatal' as an organization in which the government holds at least 50% of the equity. Initially there were a number of firms in which the government did not hold 50% of the equity.

4.   The central role of the NDC in the industrialization process can be readily deduced from Nyerere's statement, 'To plan is to choose,' in May of 1969:

    '. . . In 1964, we had not worked out at all clearly the implications of our socialist belief. As a result, we were simply trying to attract investment of any type, and the role of public enterprise appeared to be that of filling in gaps left by private investment. Indeed, it is worth remembering that the NDC was not created until 1965, and its function as a promoter of socialist large-scale production was spelt out even later.'

Julius K. Nyerere, 'To plan is to choose' in *Freedom and Development* (London: Oxford University Press, 1973), p. 82.

5.   Julius K. Nyerere, 'The Arusha Declaration' in *Ujamaa: Essays on Socialism* (Dar es Salaam: Oxford University Press, 1968), p. 15.

6.   See *Background to the Budget 1968–69* (Dar es Salaam: Govern-

ment Printer, 1968), p. 3.

7. Fanon argues in his *Wretched of the Earth*, that the mentality of the emergent 'national bourgeoisie' in the post-independence era in Africa is not that of a captain of an industry but essentially that of a merchant.

> '. . . immediately after independence, it will want to take over the middlemen's activities for the paltry economic benefits they offer. That is why it is obsessed with the question of "economic sabotage" by foreign minorities which have dominated these activities from the colonial times but it does not tackle the question of imperialism and the liquidation of underdevelopment. This is by no means typical of the whole of Black Africa especially in areas where there was no real settler problem, but it does capture the essence of the attitude towards nationalizations by many of the national leaders in Africa.'

8. Quoted in I. G. Shivji, 'The Silent Class Struggle' in *Socialism in Tanzania*, edited by Cliffe and Saul, Vol. 2, *Policies* (Nairobi: East African Publishing House, 1972), p. 309.

9. *Ibid.*

10. Julius K. Nyerere, *Freedom and Socialism* (London: Oxford University Press, 1968), pp. 262–3.

11. P. C. Packard, 'Management and Control of Parastatal Organizations' in *Towards Socialist Planning*, edited by Rweyemamu and J. Loxley (Dar es Salaam: Tanzania Publishing House, 1974), p. 74.

12. We have already pointed out the fact that various scholars have remarked on the absence of a clear-cut industrial strategy in Tanzania as a serious problem during the period of transition. Thus Loxley sums it up when he said in effect that the major defect in the industrialization efforts in Tanzania is the failure to define in clear terms the direction in which the economy should be moving; to spell out the long-term strategies that financial planning, for example, is designed to serve.

13. *The Tanganyika Development Corporation (Amendment) Act, 1964* (Dar es Salaam: Government Printer, 1964).

14. In their discussion of the National Development Corporation of Tanzania, Mramba amd Mwasansu, for example, agonized over the fact that:

> 'The NDC is expected to operate on a commercial basis and at the same time serve other socialist objectives. . . . Socialist management implies structural changes of the existing management system as well as heavier emphasis on social as opposed to economic criteria of performance . . . The National Development Corporation has attempted to marry the two, simply because our social economic position is too weak to allow for the pursuance of only one of the possible alternatives . . . Exclusive emphasis on the social criteria would imply heavy government subsidies of unprofitable enterprises which is not

    possible now and which may, in fact, encourage laxity among workers and managers and impose unnecessary strains on an economy with limited results. On the other hand, maximisation of profit alone would give no sense to the Arusha Declaration and socialist development.'

See B. P. Mramba and B. U. Mwansasu, 'Management for Socialist Development in Tanzania: The Case of the National Development Corporation,' *African Review*, Vol. 1, No. 3 (1972), pp. 41–2.

15.   E. Penrose, 'Some Problems of Policy in the Management of the Parastatal Sector in Tanzania: A Comment,' *African Review*, Vol. 1, No. 3 (1972), 49.

16.   M. Djilas, *The New Class: An Analysis of the Communist System* (New York: Frederick A. Praeger, 1957), pp. 108–9.

17.   *Ibid.*

18.   The fact that the NDC has been particularly concerned with industrialization in Tanzania is borne out by the fact that by and large investments by the NDC and other parastatals have been capital intensive as well as import intensive. This, no doubt, has wide implications for self-reliance in the economy. Although initially the promotion of agriculture was considered important by the NDC, by 1967 its importance quickly diminished. Consequently, both the NDC and parastatals in general have not played a large part in agricultural production. Up to 1971 (i.e., 1964–71) agriculture has accounted for only 4% of total investment of the parastatal sector. See Edmund Clark, 'Socialist Development and Public Investment in Tanzania 1964–73,' (Ph.D. dissertation, Harvard University, 1974), p. 239.

19.   Nyerere, *Freedom and Socialism*, p. 254.

20.   Sometimes such viewpoints merely become an expression of utter confusion or at best a lack of analytical clarity on the part of the individual holding such views, as we can see in the case of Neerso, when he said:

    'But in spite of the Arusha Declaration and the subsequent nationalizations foreign companies have continued to invest in Tanzania and to cooperate with the parastatal corporations through joint ventures and management contracts. Part of the reason is the fact that the socialist principles enshrined in the Arusha Declaration have as yet only been carried out to a limited extent. The Tanzanian economy is still more of a market economy than a centrally planned economy, and the private profitability criterion as opposed to the social profitability criterion has until now been dominant in economic decision.'

P. Neerso, 'Tanzania's Policies on Private Foreign 'Investment,' *The African Review*, Vol. 4, No. 1 (1974), 63.

21.   Julius K. Nyerere, *The Arusha Declaration: Ten Years After* (Dar es Salaam: Government Printer, 1977), p. 22.

22.   G, Rubinstein, G. Smirnov and V. Solodovnikov, 'On Some

Statements by Samir Amin,' *RAPE*, No. 5 (January-April, 1976), p. 105.

23. We recognize the fact that the Minister of Commerce and Industries did in fact define his Ministry's 'industrial development strategy' in 1969. This aimed to:[1]
    (a) Increase per capita income;
    (b) increase the rate of industrial income;
    (c) increase the rate of growth of industrial development
    (d) increase technical knowledge;
    (e) increase capital investment in the rural areas and in Ujamaa Vijijini;
    (f) increase import substitution;
    (g) increase export of our manufactured goods;
    (h) increase employment;
    (i) increase the quality of the labour force;
    (j) increase the industrial contribution to regional development and decrease the disparity between incomes in different regions;
    (k) increase the efficiency of firms;
    (l) increase the utlization of domestic raw materials;
    (m) lay the foundation for the development of heavy industry – especially coal, iron and steel.

    With specific reference to the NDC the Minister defined its policy in his 1971/72 budget speech as follows:

    (i) continuation of its import substitution industries based on the home market;
    (ii) large-scale manufacturing to take advantage of the economies of scale which should aim at both the domestic and home markets;
    (iv) small-scale industries in rural areas;
    (v) investment to be spread in the regional centres designated in the Second Five Year Plan, to avoid regional imbalances and the overconcentration of industries in Dar es Salaam.

    Surely, this pot-pourri of aims (apart from its sectoral nature) can hardly be described as an 'industrial development strategy.' It is clear, writes Saul, that 'such a crude but comprehensive listing of objectives could be used to justify almost any conceivable project but is useless in terms of specifying in concrete terms, what the Tanzanian industrial sector should look like in several years' time and what its contribution to the economy and to the socialist aspirations generally should be. It is therefore not surprising that a shopping list approach to planning ensued and it says little for NDC that it "has attempted to formulate its investment strategy within the framework of the plan (i.e., Second Five Year Plan) and the above Ministerial policies."'[2]

    [1] See B. P. Mramba and B. U. Mwansasu, 'Management

      for Socialist Development in Tanzania: The Case of the National Development Corporation,' *The African Review*, Vol. 1, No. 3 (January 1972), p. 36.

      [2] John Saul and John Loxley, 'Multinationals, Workers and the Parastatals in Tanzania,' *RAPE*, No. 2 (January-April 1975), p. 67.

24. Julius K. Nyerere, 'Ten Years After Independence' in *Freedom and Development* (London: Oxford University Press, 1973), p. 311.

25. N. Kahama, in an interview with 'Face the People,' *Sunday News* (20 January, 1972).

26. Philip C. Packard, 'Management and Control of Parastatal Organizations' in *Towards Socialist Planning*, edited by Rweyemamu and Loxley (Dar es Salaam: Tanzania Publishing House, 1974), p. 75. In this regard, the later attempts by both Devplan and the Ministry of Commerce and Industry to oversee the functions of the NDC in order to move it along the lines of socialism become very instructive indeed.

27. The significance of the time factor is noted by the President in his Presidential Circular, No. 1 of 1970 when he said:

> '. . . when we first began to own industrial and agricultural enterprises as a community, and especially when we expanded public ownership so rapidly after the Arusha Declaration, we inevitably – and rightly – concentrated first on the sheer mechanics of setting up, or taking over, economic concerns. We therefore followed in our public enterprises the same work customs as we had learned from the traditional capitalist enterprises . . .'

Similarly, it is implied by Saul when he writes: 'There was insufficient time after the Arusha Declaration to achieve any fundamental improvements in public sector planning which could be embodied in the Second Five Year Plan' – (1964–69); see John Saul and John Loxley, 'Multinationals, Workers and the Parastatals in Tanzania,' *The Review of African Political Economy*, No. 2 (January-April, 1975), p. 63.

More importantly, as we can see from Lange's exposition, the question of which method of nationalization is more apporpriate for socialist transformation (either the speedy or the gradual approach) is very much unresolved. While the economist would argue for a speedy takeover, both the 'right-wing' and 'left-wing', 'socialists and communists' opt for a gradual take-over if considered purely on economic grounds, though politically they would consider the speedy take-over to be more desirable. Lange writes:

> 'The first question is whether the transfer into public property and management of the means of production and enterprises to be socialized should be the first or the last stage of the policy of transition. In our opinion it should be the first stage. The

socialist government must start its policy of transition immediately with the socialization of the industries and banks in question . . . If the socialist government attempted to control or supervise them while leaving them in private hands, there would emerge all the difficulties of forcing a private entrepreneur or capitalist to act differently than the pursuit of profit commands. At best the constant friction between the supervising government agencies and the entrepreneurs and capitalists would paralyze business. After such an unsuccessful attempt the socialist government would have either to give up its socialist aims or to proceed to socialization.

The opinion is almost generally accepted that the process of socialization must be as gradual as possible in order to avoid grave economic disturbances. Not only right-wing socialists but also left-wing socialists and communists hold this theory of economic gradualism. While the latter two regard a speedy socialization as necessary on grounds of political strategy, they nevertheless usually admit that, concerning economic considerations alone, a gradual socialization is much the preferable course. Unfortunately, the economist cannot share this theory of economic gradualism.'
O. Lange, *On the Economic Theory of Socialism* (New York: McGraw-Hill, 1964), pp. 122–3.

28. Loxley and Saul, 'Multinationals, Workers . . .' *op. cit.*, p. 62.
29. *Ibid.*, p. 61.
30. Shivji, 'The Silent Class Struggle' in *Socialism in Tanzania, op. cit.*, p. 313. Emphasis is mine.
31. National Development Corporation, *Annual Report*, (Dar es Salaam, 1970), p. 9.
32. See *The Economic Survey and Annual Plan 1970–71* (Dar es Salaam: Government Printer, 1970), p. 90.
33. These criteria are grouped into two broad categories – primary and secondary. The primary criteria were designed to be satisfied by all projects 'due to their importance to the viability of the projects or the national economy,' and include:
(a) profitability
(b) national cost/benefit
(c) foreign exchange effects.
The secondary criteria were required to be considered for all projects in the following 'order of importance':
(a) employment
(b) location
(c) industrial linkages
(d) budgetary impact
(e) investable surplus.
See B. Mramba and B. Mwansasu, 'Management for Socialist Development in Tanzania: The Case of the NDC in Tanzania,' *African Review*, Vol. 1, No. 3 (January 1972), p.37.
34. E. Penrose, 'Some Problems of Policy . . .' p. 50.

35. Clark, *op. cit.*, p. 185.
36. *Ibid.*, p. 186.
37. It must be pointed out that many of the firms nationalized were in fact not very capital intensive and, indeed, are often the most 'profitable and have the best capital/value added ratio' to date.
38. Clark, *op. cit.*, p. 191.
39. G. Arrighi, 'International Corporations, Labour Aristocracies, and Economic Development in Tropical Africa' in *Imperialism and Revolution* edited by I. Rhodes, (New York: Monthly Review Press, 1970).
40. A. Seidman, *Comparative Development Strategies in East Africa* (Nairobi: East African Publishing House, 1972), p. 166.
41. See *Sixth NDC Annual Report (1970)*.
42. *Ibid.*, p. 60.
43. Clark, *op. cit.*, p. 211.
44. Indeed, the contract for the project contained the clause that 'Kloeckner will select the most modern process corresponding with the latest technical development in the chemical industry taking into consideration the objective conditions in Tanzania'! Clearly, this 'turn-key' offer arrogates many decision-making powers to the foreign partners. It has been rightly pointed to as one more example of the NDC and parastatals in general giving powers to her foreign partners to supply virtually any equipment they liked. Coulson concluded that the NDC considered the project entirely from the corporation's point of view, rather than the nation as a whole. For a comprehensive account of the fiasco in Tanzania's fertiliser factory, see Andrew C. Coulson, 'Tanzania's Fertiliser Factory,' *Journal of Modern African Studies*, Vol. 15, No. 1 (1977).
45. *Ibid.*, p. 125.
46. Clark, *op. cit.*, p. 212.
47. It has often been pointed out, and rightly too, that through such agreements and management contracts surpluses, for example from the joint enterprises, have been flowing to the metropolitian countries. The drain is usually procured through such mechanisms as share acquisition, exhorbitant salaries and management fees for the expatriate staff, royalties, patent rights, annual dividends and over-invoicing of capital funds imported by the management. For a comprehensive analysis of the role of management contracts, see I. Shivji, 'Capitalism Unlimited: Public Corporations in Partnership with MNCs' *African Reivew*, Vol. 3, No. 3 (1973), pp. 359–81.
48. Isa G. Shivji, 'Capitalism Unlimited,' p. 379. It is significant that the Chinese, Cubans and North Koreans have all relied on technical expertise by and large from the socialist bloc.
49. Conclude Saul and Loxley: 'Management systems are not, therefore, ideologically neutral and hence the wholesale importation of western capitalist management systems in Tanzania

166

should be viewed with concern. The extensive use of the purveyors of these systems – western management consultants and in particular the American company McKinsey – is an even more bewildering aspect of Tanzania's policy in the public sector.' See Saul and Loxley, 'Multinationals, Workers and the Parastatals in Tanzania,' pp. 71–2.

Ann Crittenden wrote in the *New York Times* in 1975 that U.S. consultants such as McKinsey and Co., Krebes, etc. maintain that: 'even when a study has no tangible impact, the client is still left with a valuable research document . . .' Krebes is, in fact, quoted as saying that: 'Keeping other countries in ignorance is never to the national advantage. It can only be to our advantage when another government can see that an *American firm is free to offer objective, unbiased advice, unconstrained by the national policies of the moment.*' She concluded her piece with reference specifically to a Tanzanian 'client' who, when asked why he turned to a team of capitalists to organize his government, reportedly replied '*we are more interested in the development of our country than in the ideology of our advisers; we want the best talent and we'll go where we can get it.*' Surely, the consultants cannot agree more! See Ann Crittenden, 'Apolitical American Consultants: Third World Uses Firms' Expertise,' *New York Times* (1975), p. 5. Emphasis mine.

50. P. C. Packard, 'Corporate Structure and Socialist Development in Tanzania' (Dar es Salaam, 1971), mimeo.

51. See Presidential Circular No. 1 of 1970, The Establishment of Workers' Councils, Executive Boards and Boards of Directors (Dar es Salaam: The State House, 1970).

52. See the *TANU Guidelines* (Mwongozo), (Dar es Salaam: Government Printer, 1971), Clause 33.

53. P. Neerso, 'Tanzania's Policies on Private Foreign Investment,' *African Review*,Vol. 4, No. 1 (1974), p. 63. Emphasis mine.

54. For a critical analysis of the consequences of the Presidential directives and Mwongozo see Henry Mapolu, 'The Organization and Participation of Workers in Tanzania,' *African Review*, vol. 2, No. 3 (1972), pp. 381–415.

55. *Ibid.*, p. 383.

56. Indeed, this aspect of Tanzania's economy is confirmed by the World Bank's 1977 Report on Tanzania, when it states:
    'The difficulties with devising an appropriate framework for industrial activities has been reflected in the overall performance of the manufacturing sector. Between 1967 and 1973 manufacturing value added increased at 7.6% per year. But this growth was not commensurate with the increase in productive factors allocated this sector.'
    See the *World Bank Report on Tanzania (1977)*, p. 28.

57. *Ibid.*, p. 22.

Chapter 6

Socialism and Self-Reliance: An International Dimension – Foreign Aid and a Comparative Experience Between China (1950–60) and Tanzania

I am going to argue that the whole concept of aid is wrong. I am saying it is not right that the vast majority of the world's people should be forced into the position of beggars, without dignity.

Julius K. Nyerere

One of the consequences of the dependence of developing countries on the more industrialized nations for the supply of technical know-how, patents, management and finance is the power that rests in the latter countries to influence trade policy in the former. This can, for example, take the form of an agreement by the developing country not to export certain products utilizing specific know-how, or a requirement to import machinery and other goods from some specified enterprise. This asymmetry of trade bondage may put a developing country at a considerable disadvantage in the utilization of modern technology and in making use of the best available exchange opportunities.

UNCTAD Secretariat,
Nairobi, 1975.

168

The first section of this chapter examines the role of foreign aid in building a socialist and self-reliant Tanzania. We shall argue that while foreign aid in post-Arusha Tanzania may not have influenced to any considerable degree the foreign policy of Tanzania – especially with reference to Africa and, in particular, South Africa – it has not contributed in any appreciable way to the development of a self-reliant national economy in Tanzania. If anything, it has made Tanzania more dependent economically on international capitalism. In the second section we look briefly at a comparative experience in development between China (1950–60) and post-Arusha Tanzania in the four areas covered in this study, to provide a broader perspective on the international dimension of the developmental process in Tanzania.

SECTION I: FOREIGN AID

In the preceding chapter we established that the absence of a national strategy for industrial development was in large part responsible for the NDC's failure to provide for Tanzania the basis for an integrated national economy with the socialist objectives of post-Arusha Tanzania. To the extent that foreign aid formed a significant portion of the NDC's industrialization efforts, it becomes crucial to understand its role in light of the NDC's failure to fulfil its role as the 'medium of socialist economic development'. We begin with a broad overview of the concept of foreign aid in general, and its application to Tanzania.

The concept of foreign aid has elicited a considerable amount of controversy among scholars and observers alike. There is hardly any consensus as to its meaning, let alone the objectives and motives of both the 'donor' and 'recipient' countries. Part of the conceptual and definitional problem, to our mind, lies in the fact that the objectives (national security, humanitarianism, economic development, etc.) are essentially political questions which must largely be decided on the basis of political strategies. Social scientists among others have attemptd to categorize and provide a more precise definition of public policy objectives in the field of foreign aid. These attempts have so far failed to dispel the confusion in the donor countries, for example, over the ultimate national objectives of aid or in relating specific economic and social targets to these ultimate objectives.

The scope of the study does not permit us to clarify the conceptual and definitional problems of foreign aid.[1] Suffice it to say, however, that public or official foreign aid involves 'a transfer of real resources or immediate claims on resources (e.g., foreign exchange) from one country or group of countries to another which would not have taken place . . . in the absence of specific official action designed to promote the transfer by the donor country.[2] This definition requires that the specific forms of transfers be development-oriented, i.e., that they represent direct economic aid. We are thus concerned with official or public (including internationaal organizations) direct economic aid. This means the exclusion of such items as private aid (e.g., donations by foundations, technical assistance through private organizations, societies etc.) It also excludes military assistance and famine relief, while not denying their quantitative importance, and even their substantial capacity for indirectly influencing the rate and pattern of the receiving country's economic development. Our main reason for excluding these items lies in the difficulty of obtaining reliable data on private aid within the context of Tanzania. On the other hand, official direct economic aid will include such items as grants and loans, in cash or kind, made by a government or international organization, plus technical assistance.* Foreign aid therefore simply means grants and loans and technical assistance available on an intergovernmental basis primarily for economic development. It is 'neither a gift nor does it necesssarily have to involve an imperialist plot.'[3] That foreign aid is not a gift is demonstrated by the fact that in the US national security objectives have been overtly emphasized by three successive Presidents – Eisenhower (throughout much of the 1950s), Kennedy and Johnson. In his Annual Report to Congress on aid, Eeisenhower wrote: 'We have had as our goal the promotion of peaceful change for millions of peoples in Latin America, Asia and the Middle East

---

* While the notion of the country granting assistance to another is as old as the history of nation-states, the role of economic aid as now understood dates back only to the Second World War and especially to the Marshall Plan.

who are seeking domestic tranquility and a better way of life. We have responded to the hope of these millions . . . through well-conceived programmes of economic and technical assistance . . . our common safety has been of equal concern and it has been our purpose to unite the free people of the world in a sustained common defense against overt attack or suppression of liberty . . .'[4]

Similarly, in his message on foreign aid, President Kennedy said in 1961 that: 'Foreign aid is a method by which the US maintains a position of influence and control around the world, and sustains a good many countries which would definitely collapse or pass into the communist block.'[5] But in another instance Kennedy is reported to have said: 'We pledge our efforts to help them help themselves, for whatever period is required – not because the communists may be doing it, not because we seek their votes, but because it is right.'[6]

And finally, President Johnson in his foreign aid message to Congress of January 14, 1961, said: 'For our own security and well-being and as responsible free men, we must seek to share our capacity for growth, and the promise of the better life, with our fellow men around the world. That is what foreign aid is all about.'[7] What emerges from the above official statements on US foreign aid objectives is that they at least connote the element of 'enlightened self-interest' in the recognition and identification of both short- and long-term national security objectives, as well as there being elements of humanitarianism.

That aid does not necessarily involve an imperialist plot is demonstrated by the continued demand by the recipient countries for increased economic assistance (although this demand is now more often coupled with a call for aid without any strings). It is possible, to our mind, to extend economic and technical aid without necessarily achieving a high degreee of control over the recipient country.*

---

* It seems fair to say that the objectives of foreign aid have centred around two poles. On the one hand are those who regard aid as a relatively disinterested attempt to assist the poor countries of the world toward economic development, and on the other hand, those who see aid as an instrument of economic control of the recipient countries by

There has been a growing disillusionment with aid in both donor and recipient countries (perhaps more with the latter). The Pearson Report of the Commission on International Development said: 'The climate surrounding foreign aid programmes is heavy with disillusionment and distrust . . . it is not only among the developed countries that the climate has deteriorated. On the developing side too there are signs of frustration and impatience. In much of the developing world there is a sense of disillusion about the very nature of the aid relationship.'[8] While part of the public disillusionment can be traced to a failure to educate public opinion about the nature and purpose of aid, it is nevertheless true that in many cases the economic results of aid have neither been very dramatic nor is it possible to foresee an early end to the burdens it entails for both parties. Echoing a somewhat similar viewpoint, the Pearson Report remarks: 'Some of this [disillusionment] is due to the fact that attitudes in donor countries often have been affected by misconceptions and unrealistic expectations of "instant development" when we should have known that development was a long-term process. There has also been strong criticism of waste in the use of aid in the developing countries and complaints that aid activities lead inevitably to entanglement in political conflict and military hostilities in which recipient countries may become engaged.'[9]

On the other hand, in the recipient countries both the political and economic elements underlying the aid programme are often regarded by critics as menacing and irrelevant to the real needs of the recipient countries. Aid in its different forms is seen as an instrument of control over the recipient country – a tool of neo-colonialism. In the words of Teresa Hayter, it is 'merely the smooth face of imperialism.'[10] In a more subdued tone, the Pearson Report described the aid programmes of the 1950s thus:

> A good deal of bilateral aid has indeed been dispensed in order to achieve short-term political favours, gain strategic advantages, or promote exports from the donor. Much foreign aid was granted in the 1950's to enable some

the donor countries. In other words, aid contributes to the 'development of underdevelopment' and thus perpetuates the dependency relations that already exist between the two parties.

countries to maintain large armed forces rather than to promote economic growth. In none of these cases was the promotion of long-term development a dominant objective of the aid given . . .[11]

Against this background the report concluded: 'International support for development is now flagging. In some of the rich countries its feasibility, even its very purpose, is in question. The climate surrounding foreign aid programmes is heavy with disillusion and distrust. This is not true everywhere. Indeed, there are some countries in which the opposite is true. Nevertheless, we have reached a point of crisis.[12] Any study of the impact of foreign aid on the development process in Tanzania will have to take into consideration this broad context. In other words, any systematic approach to the study of foreign aid (even when it is a partial study) must be placed in broad analytical perspective. Little has been done in this direction. Even more striking is that very little intensive effort has been devoted to defining the central problems of foreign aid, such as determining its complementary and competitive effects on domestic investment, deriving meaningful criteria for appraising foreign aid results, analysing the aid-giving process, and judging the economic impact on Tanzania or recipient countries in general.[13] We cannot embark on such a project in this study, but merely mention the task that has to be done. We shall be satisfied with examining how far foreign aid has affected Tanzania's industrial performance in spite of the limitations imposed by the conceptual and definitional problems noted above. No attempt will be made to particularize the evaluation of the costs and benefits of foreign aid projects, but we shall provide a general evaluation of foreign projects in relation to the economy as a whole.

It now remains for us to identify the major types of foreign aid, bearing in mind our definition of foreign aid as essentially grants and loans available on an intergovernmental (including international organizations) basis primarily for economic development. One vital point to stress at this point and in the context of Tanzania is that foreign assistance bears a close reciprocal relationship to economic transformation. Thus Meier writes: 'At any given time, aid is effective to the degree that it acts as a catalyst in the development process; while over time, the economic change induced by aid, among other inputs, will determine whether and how fast the need for aid can disappear.'[14]

Returning to the question of types of foreign aid, at least two functional categories of foreign aid become readily discernible. There is project aid and there is programme aid; technical assistance is usually subsumed under both types of aid.

The Project Approach

Apart from being tied to purchases in the donor countries, most aid is given on condition that it be spent for a particular defined purpose. It has been estimated that about half of the bilateral, and practically all multilateral, aid commitments are for specific projects, as either technical or capital assistance.[15]

The project type or approach, predominant in the 1960s, is normally provided for specific projects forming part of a development programme, after a determination of economic and technical feasibility by the donor country for each project submitted by the recipient country. It usually falls into two classes* – capital and technical assistance. The former covers the cost of equipment for projects, while the latter includes expert advisory service in the field, training facilities in donor countries, and equipment for instruction and demonstration.

One of the characteristics of the project approach is that it began with those schemes which were relatively large. It was presumed that the project approach works best in such circumstances and that it is least satisfactory in those sectors where projects are not large in relation to the whole pattern of development expenditure (this may be the case for most of industry). This might explain why in the case of Tanzania the NDC virtually neglected the development of cottage industries, particularly in

---

* We say 'usually' because not all technical assistance is linked to a specific project. Thus expatriate teachers, for example, may serve on a more flexible basis to help implement the recipient country's educational programme.

rural Tanzania as noted earlier, even though the NDC had hoped to develop cottage industries. It has been suggested that the basic attractiveness of the project approach, from the donor's standpoint, lies in the fact that it enables an account to be kept of what the money obtained from abroad has been used for; it relates means to an end. And this, it is argued, helps to indicate the final purposes for which resources are being transferred. Consequently, some general features of projects become discernible in any aid involving the project approach. There must be, for example, a specific aim which can be agreed upon and it must be possible to specify how that aim can be reached. The project approach usually calls for technical details of the project, thus exposing it to critical examination by the appropriate experts. It usually includes details on management requirements as well as attempts to relate the new objectives being sought to past activities. Finally, it indicates the way in which plans for the future link with other possible developments in the same or neighbouring fields.

It has been suggested that the donor is interested in such details in order to ensure that the recipient country is able to repay and service the loan, where lending is involved. This, it is argued, is the long-standing traditional interest of the banker in the activities of the borrower. It may also mean, of course, a desire to make sure that every step involved in the new enterprise is soundly based. There may also be other reasons peculiar to particular suppliers of funds; international agencies, for instance, have their own reasons, which may not necessarily be connected with the nature of particular projects, for insisting on a fairly detailed plan of action. These reasons may be purely institutional in form. Whether the aid is bilateral or multilateral could make all the difference for 'it is well known that bilateral aid is highly affected by non-developmental considerations. The donor's interest in furthering his own exports, or promoting his political and military objectives, is likely to make the aid programme less development-oriented, and consequently of less value to the recipient . . . This is one important aspect in favour of multilateral aid.'[16]

All in all however, the main reason for wishing to relate ends and means in a particular project from the point of view of the donor country is to see whether proper use is made of the resources involved.[17] The attractiveness of the project approach to aid donors lies primarily in the accountability aspects. However, one cannot discount the fact that both profitability, and the possibility of immediate returns on investment, motivate and to a large degree determine the concern with means and ends. Furthermore, the possibility of selecting projects which have multiplier effects for the donor, i.e., providing outlets for a lot of different projects, as well as export markets for the donor countries, is also an important consideration.

However, the project approach is not without its disadvantages. Perhaps chief among these is that too strict an adherence to the method tends to ignore the links that exist between projects. By concentrating on specific details of the economy, the project designer may be led into thinking that this is the optimum use of the resources available. It thus discounts the links that may exist with other projects and with other plans for the economy as a whole. Much of the criticism of the project approach stems from the possibility that those concerned with the details of the projects and their own objectives will fail to see or take into account the wider implications of what they are doing. It is argued that in the last resort only national governments, in most of the developing countries, able to set the political and social aims behind a certain rate of economic development, can really assess the cost and benefits attached to good project design and implementation. In short, the project appproach, if carried on regardless of its implications for the rest of the economy, may very well result in the 'excellent being the enemy of the good.'[19]

The Programme Approach

Unlike the project approach (which largely takes a single plant or other unit of investment as the basis for analysis and aid decisions), the programme approach is based, at least in theory, on the needs of the whole economy. It provides capital either to governments or institutions who need not spell out in detail what they propose to do with it. It rests on the argument that it is more easily related to the benefits of overall planning for development purposes, as well as an awareness of the inherent problems of the project approach. It is a method necessarily limited to the consideration of broad objectives, often measured in terms of target rates of growth of national income or in per capita incomes.

176

The programme approach also has its critics. It is perhaps instructive that international agencies, especially the World Bank group, have continued to adopt the project approach, and that by and large the programme approach, though it has continued to exist, is less often the route adopted by donor countries. It is often argued that the project approach seems better for most of the countries of the Third World whose governments 'have not yet acquired the ability to fomulate and execute national development plans.'[20] Similarly, the project approach is more flexible and therefore more suitable in cases where the donor, for example, is not satisfied with the general thrust of the recipient country's development programme, and wants to ensure that the resources provided by him are used only for ends which he can support.

Before leaving this discussion it must be pointed out that the choice of approach (and it is not unusual for countries to combine the two approaches) rests with individual recipient countries, and it would therefore be incorrect to state generally that programme aid is superior to project aid, or vice versa. Against this background, we can now examine the role of aid in building a socialist and self-reliant Tanzania.

The Setting

For largely historical reasons, the bulk of official foreign aid to the newly independent countries of Black Africa has come primarily from their former colonial powers. It is therefore not surprising that both the British and the French, for example, have sought to concentrate their aid programmes in their former colonies, as shown in Tables 1, 2 and 3. Pre-Arusha Tanzania is no exception. Tanzania's heavy dependence on British foreign aid including technical assistance* is amply demonstrated in Tables 4 and 5.

---

* Official British bilateral economic aid to Tanzania was and is still in the form of grants, loans and technical assistance. However, it is worth noting here that much of her aid to Africa in general is tied. Thus of British bilateral aid to African countries in 1967, for example, 17% was wholly tied to British goods and services, rising up to a total of 43% if partly tied aid is included. See Paul Streten, *Aid to Africa* (New York: Praeger, 1972), p. 15.

Table 1 *British Government Bilateral Disbursements of Economic Aid to Africa, 1957–58 to 1965–66 (million $)*

	1957–58			1964–65				1965–86			
	Grants	Loans	Total	Grants	Loans	Technical Assistance	Total	Grants	Loans	T.A.	Total
Africa	52.3	10.0	62.3	95.7	83.9	50.2	209.8	76.9	97.2	35.6	209.7
Commonwealth	39.5	10.0	49.5	84.6	79.1	49.4	213.1	76.6	91.5	54.2	222.3
Others	12.8	–	12.8	11.1	4.8	0.8	16.7	0.3	5.7	1.4	7.4

Source: Ministry of Overseas Development, *Overseas Development: The Work in Hand* (August, 1965; January, 1967).

Table 2 *British Bilateral Aid Program Disbursements to Africa 1967 and 1968 (gross and net of amortization; million £)*

	1967		1968	
	Gross	Net	Gross	Net
Commonwealth Africa	57.67	54.08	63.17	59.09
Non-Commonwealth Africa	1.237	1.227	1.237	0.804

Bilateral Technical Assistance Disbursements

	1967	1968
Commonwealth Africa	17.6	20.8
Non-Commonwealth Africa	0.56	0.87

Source: Ministry of Overseas Development, *British Aid Statistics* (1964–68).

Furthermore, betweeen 1962 and 1966, out of a total of 674 expatriate officers recruited by the Ministry of Establishment, 549 were from the United Kingdom.[21]

Though our focus is not on Tanzania's foreign policy, it is worthwhile noting that there was a corresponding development in the field of foreign relations during this period. Just as Tanzania's major source of aid came from Britain and other Western countries, the bulk of her other links – political, cultural, etc. – were also with the Western world. This is not to suggest that Tanzania's foreign policy was determined by the source of her foreign aid. If this were so, how do we explain the change in the nature of her foreign relations with the West, which was accentuated by the crisis in foreign policy between 1964 and 1966; for Western aid was just as substantial (see Table 4) as it had been before 1964. Indeed, in his study of 'Aid and Foreign Policy in Tanzania,'* Niblock

* Niblock's study 'Aid and Foreign Policy in Tanzania 1961–1968 (Ph.D. dissertation, University of Sussex, 1971) has so far been the most comprehensive analysis in this field.

179

Table 3 *French Official Bilateral Aid Flows to Traditionally French Areas 1962–67
(net of amortization; million $)*

Area	1962	1963	1964	1965	1966	1967
Franc Zone, Africa[1]	728.9	648.4	607.9	516.6	471.0	497.2
Cambodia, Laos, Vietnam	8.1	8.0	9.1	16.0	16.3	19.2
French Overseas Territories and Department, Latin America	64.5	87.2	118.6	94.4	138.5	145.7
French Overseas Territories Oceania[2]	18.9	18.1	24.2	31.0	30.6	26.7
Total Traditionally French Areas	820.4	761.7	759.8	658.0	656.4	688.8
Other Countries[3]	40.0	59.7	50.6	66.5	59.8	98.4
Total Official Bilateral Aid	860.8	821.4	810.4	724.5	716.2	787.2
Aid to Traditionally French Areas as Percentage of total	95.3	92.8	93.7	90.8	91.6	87.5

[1] French franc area, south of the Sahara (African and Malagasy States, French overseas territories and departments), Algeria, Morocco, Tunisia.

[2] Data on aid to French overseas territories in Oceansia are not available separately for the period 1962–64 and are included in 'unallocated' flows to Oceania. However, the other components of this 'unallocated' flow are unlikely to be significant.

[3] Includes unallocated flows.

Source: OECD, *Geographical Distribution of Financial Flows to Less Developed Countries 1960–64, 1965,* and 1966–67.

Table 4 *Tanzania Government: Sources of External Development Fund 1961–5*
(In thousands of shillings)

	1961/2	1962/3	1963/4	1964/5	1961/2–1964/5
Governments					
United Kingdom	61,620	93,720	22,680	23,900	201,920
USA	2,220	5,020	5,440	19,960	32,640
Federal Republic of Germany		2,540	16,400	7,220	26,160
Israel			700	8,460	9,160
China				5,980	5,980
Multilateral					
IDA			3,260	12,980	16,240

Source: Adapted from: *Budget Survey 1965–66* (Dar es Salaam, 1966) and in the *Background to the Budget, An Economic Survey, 1966–67* and . . . *1967–68* (Dar es Salaam, 1966, 1967).

Table 5 *Expatriates Recruited by the Establishment Division January 1962 – December 1965*

United Kingdom	516	Czechoslovakia	4
India	19	UAR	3
USA	6	Netherlands	3
Yugoslavia	8	West Germany	1
Bulgaria	6	Jamaica	1
USSR	5	Malaysia	1

Source: C. Pratt, Table 6, p. 132.

concluded that Tanzania's eventual aid pattern was 'determined by Tanzania's foreign policy, rather than the foreign policy being determined by the aid pattern.'[22] He argued that aid given did not affect foreign policy because of the 'clear priorities held by the President and the principal policy makers. In spite of their country's need for aid they clearly saw domestic political interest and political principles as more important than aid.'[23]

Foreign aid, contrary to the lead quote of this chapter, was seen as an important component of Tanzania's pre-Arusha development programme by the country's leadership. In his address to the National Assembly, President Nyerere clearly stated that the financing of the First Five Year Plan was heavily dependent on help from overseas – foreign aid, including the recruitment of large numbers of skilled expatriate personnel from abroad.[24] As shown in Table 6, nearly all of the capital budget came from external sources (shs. 143 millions out of a total of shs. 147 millions in capital revenue). The total amount of capital revenue from external sources for development purposes dropped somewhat from 1962–66. But this came about not primarily as a result of increased mobilization of local resources, as suggested by government officials at the time [25] as well as observers such as Pratt,[26] but largely as a result of the fact that between 1964–66 many of the assumptions on which the Plan was based proved to be unrealistic. For example, Britain froze £7.5 million earmarked for aid to Tanzania as a result of the diplomatic break between the two countries following the Unilateral Declaration of Independence (UDI) by Ian Smith in Rhodesia in 1965. Both West Germany and the United States took similar actions during the foreign policy crisis of this period. Furthermore, the level of foreign aid planned was not forthcoming because aid projects took longer to negotiate than had been allowed for in the Plan.

Post-Arusha Foreign Aid

One of the consequences of the foreign policy crisis of the mid 1960s is that it markedly strained the relationship between Tanzania and the Western world, particularly Britain, the United States and West Germany, for the first time since her independence. On the other hand, Tanzania's contacts with the communist bloc countries, and particularly with China, increased with the loosening of the economic, political and cultural links with the Western world. Moreover, the threat posed by the UDI in

Table 6 *Tanzania Government Capital Budget Sources of Funds*
(in millions of shillings)

	1961/2	1962/3	1963/4	1964/5	1965/6	1966/7	1967/8	1968/9
External (loans and grants)	143.0	104.3	51.5	78.5	83.5	127.3	84.0	122.8
Internal (borrowing contrib-ution for recurrent revenues, etc.)	3.8	9.1	93.8	125.3	146.4	167.1	260.1	337.7
Total	146.8	113.4	145.3	203.8	229.9	294.4	344.1	460.5

Sources: Tanzania, *Budget Survey 1965–66*, table 35; *Background to the Budget 1967–68*, table 67; *Economic Survey and Second Annual Plan 1970–71*, table 68.

Rhodesia, the growing intensity of the armed struggle waged by various national liberation movements of Southern Africa (and resolutely backed by Tanzania's political leadership) and in the former Portuguese colonies, the 'intrusion of the cold war' into Tanzania following the union of Tanganyika and Zanzibar in 1964,* posed a formidable array of policy options for the Tanzanian leadership.

Not only was the level of foreign aid planned not forthcoming; perhaps even more crucial was the realization that foreign aid as offered did not always fit in well with the development plan. For one thing, donors often had strong ideas of their own about the kind of projects they wanted to support.[27] Of particular interest and significance for our purposes is the fact that virtually all aid for Tanzania, both bilateral and multilateral (including the communist countries and the UN agencies), was of the project type even though Tanzania had produced two Five Year Plans during this period (see, for example, the pattern of aid by the UNDP in Table 7).

We have already noted the high-level manpower requirements of the project approach (see also Table 13). Needless to say, there were not enough skilled personnel (not to talk of socialist cadres) in the Tanzanian ministries for the planning and implementation of projects. The result was that these projects came to depend largely on the expatriate managerial staff (most of whom were unsympathetic to socialism) for their survival. There was also a crucial lack of local currency to cover the local costs of projects,** given the fact that so much of the aid was import-tied.[28]

*The two opposing parties in Zanzibar – the Arab-led Zanzibar Nationalist party (ZNP) and the Afro-Shirazi Party led by Karume – were supported by the West on the one hand, by China and Cuba on the other.

**It has been suggested by Niblock in his study (based on information given to him by an official of the Soviet Economic Mission in Dar es Salaam) that the reason why Tanzania refused to sign the agreement with the Soviet Union on aid, that had been negotiated in 1965, was partly due to the fact that they were experiencing severe difficulties in raising local currency to cover local costs. They eventually agreed to the terms only after the Soviet Union had promised to cover at least part of the local costs of projects. See Niblock, 'Aid and Foreign Policy . . .' p. 90.

Table 7 *Preinvestment projects supported by UNDP, as of June 30, 1969*

Project	Agency	Approved by Governing Council	Project duration (years)	Project Costs (US dollar equivalent)		
				Total	Governing Council earmarkings	Government counterpart contribution
TANZANIA, UNITED REPUBLIC OF						
Survey and Plan for Irrigation Development in the Pangani and Wami River Basins	FAO	Jan. 1964	3	2,146,300	1,225,300	921,000
Mineral Exploration of the Lake Victoria Goldfield	UN	June 1964	3	1,010,500	625,500	385,000
College of African Wildlife Management, Mweka	FAO	June 1964	5	1,038,100	502,100	536,000
Kitulo Sheep-Raising Project	FAO	Jan. 1965	5	1,951,400	964,400	987,000
Training of Secondary School Science Teachers at the Faculty of Science of the University College, Dar es Salaam	UNESCO	Jan. 1965	5½	3,978,600	978,600	3,000,000
Industrial Studies and Development Center, Dar es Salaam	UNIDO	Jan. 1965	5	1,290,000	1,000,000	290,000
National Institute for Productivity, Dar es Salaam	ILO	Jan. 1965	5	1,185,500	860,500	325,000
Work-Oriented Adult Literacy Pilot Project	UNESCO	June 1966	5	6,397,900	1,181,900	5,216,000
Forest Industries Development Planning	FAO	Jan. 1967	3	1,269,900	769,900	500,000
National Industrial Apprenticeship Scheme	ILO	June 1967	5	1,030,100	820,100	210,000
Livestock Development in Masailand, Gogoland and Sukumaland	FAO	June 1968	5	2,464,800	1,409,800	1,055,000
Improvements of Tick Control Methods, Mwanza	FAO	Jan. 1969	4	872,100	531,100	341,000

Source : *UN Documents DP/SF/REPORTS, Series B, No. 8*, as of 30 June, 1969.

It has been suggested by most observers of Tanzanian politics that the cumulative effect of all this was partly responsible for the Arusha Declaration and the subsequent policy document on self-reliance. The major thrust of the Declaration in terms of foreign aid is that aid as a major source for development purposes was to be de-emphasized because 'it was stupid for us to imagine that we shall rid ourselves of our poverty through foreign financial assistance rather than our own financial resources.'[29] Furthermore, 'independence cannot be real if a nation depends upon gifts and loans from another for its development.'[30] However, in spite of the desired intentions to reduce the amount of foreign aid, Tanzania's share of foreign aid in the post-Arusha period actually increased, as shown in Tables 8 and 9. To some extent, given the very limited local resources available to finance the necessary development programmes, the rise in foreign aid is understandable. However, most senior government officials, the management of the NDC and parastatals in general do not seem to see it in quite the same way. They have often tended to justify the continued dependence on foreign aid and do not see a threat to self-reliance or, for that matter, any contradiction. As Mbioni expresssed it:

> . . . it is neither a serious analysis of our history nor that of other socialist countries to claim that a self-reliant socialist economy cannot at times use foreign resources to augment domestic resources without losing control of its own development. On the contrary, it is self-reliance and commitment alone which provide a framework within which it is safe to use some foreign finance, personnel and knowledge. To call for total avoidance of such use is not only to call for much slower advance of our productive forces and our mass standards of life [sic] but to proclaim a frightening lack of confidence in our goals and to deal with the world beyond our frontiers.[31]

Given this attitude of the managerial sector, it is not surprising that very little recognition is usually given to the dependency problems posed by a heavy reliance on foreign aid for development, especially when it involves aid from a donor country whose ideological and economic orientation is at variance with

186

Table 8 *Foreign Aid 1962–67*
(Million shs.)

Pre-Arusha Period

	1961–62	1962–63	1963–64	1964–65	1965–66	1966–67
External loans	79.4	5.8	27.8	59.1	75.7	119.9
External grants	63.6	98.6	23.6	19.5	7.8	7.4
TOTAL FOREIGN AID	143.0	104.4	51.4	78.6	83.5	127.3

Total foreign aid in the Pre-Arusha period (6 years), 588.2

Table 9 *Foreign Aid 1967–72*
(Million shs.)

Post-Arusha Period

	1967–68	1968–69	1969–70	1970–71	1971–72	1972–73*
External loans	81.5	122.7	121.5	269.7	347.4	635.9
External grants	2.5	0.1	0.4	0.1	37.8	110.7
TOTAL FOREIGN AID	84.0	122.8	121.9	269.8	385.2	746.6

Total foreign aid in the Post-Arusha period (6 years), 1730.3

* Estimates. (Excluding TAZARA).
Source for Tables 8 and 9: *The Annual Economic Surveys*

that of the recipient country. (The question of congruency, to our mind, is, or should be, the more crucial deciding factor in any aid programme.) It is usually not readily acknowledged that aid could affect drastically the type of society which exists within a recipient society; that in providing assistance for a university, for example, a donor may successfully mould the institution in such a way as to encourage the growth of elitist attitudes among the students and faculty alike in a country that has committed itself to building an egalitarian society.* Furthermore, in the case of Tanzania, the separation of elite attitudes from mass attitudes would affect the domestic policies of the government and party. While accepting the continued need for foreign aid in post-Arusha Tanzania, the political leadership seems to demonstrate a more critical understanding of the potential dangers of a heavy dependence on foreign aid. In his *Ten Years after Arusha* Nyerere expresses his concern over the rising trend in foreign aid:

> . . . we have sought for and welcome a great increase in foreign assistance in recent years. It is now a high percentage of our development budget – in the current financial year it is likely to constitute something like 59% of the total! This rate of dependence upon external aid is much too high.[32]

What clearly emerges from the above quote, however, is that the political leadership has failed to show any critical appreciation of, or enough sensitivity to, the inherent problems likely to arise as a result of the undifferentiated acceptance of aid by Tanzania – regardless of the source. Observes Cranford Pratt:

---

* Even technical experts from some socialist countries have been known to exhibit elitist attitudes in the recipient countries. The difference in attitude between Soviet and Chinese experts in the recipient countries of the Third World is a classic case in point. It is generally acknowledged that the former are more elitist in their attitudes towards the indigenous population that the latter. However, in general, East European countries have contributed no significant aid to Tanzania. Even if personnel were counted, their aid would be insignificant as shown in Tables 10 and 13. Chinese aid is dominated by Tazara.

> . . . whatever discount one wishes to place upon the face value of the foreign capital assistance to Tanzania, it remains true that foreign capital assistance to the government of Tanzania throughout the period under review was substantial. The Tanzanian government itself was never in doubt that it was of real value. Nyerere did not hold the radical position that Tanzania should not accept Western capital assistance. Where the integrity of his foreign policy demanded it, as in the crises with Britain and with Germany, he was ready to sacrifice their aid. But these sacrifices were specific to the individual dispute. There was no blanket rejection of Western aid. Rather,
> . . . with each new crisis with a Western country, more care than ever was taken to minimize its wider consequences and to involve other Western states in Tanzania's developmental efforts.[33]

Although there appears to be some diversification of aid sources in post-Arusha Tanzania, as shown in Table 10, the change is more apparent than real. The fact remains, as shown in Table 11, that the bulk of foreign aid for Tanzania still came from capitalist sources.[34]

The initial reluctance of both Tanzania and Zambia to accept Chinese aid for the Tazara Railroad demonstrates that the Tanzanian government accepted the offer as a last resort and only when all attempts to secure assistance from the West had failed.* This is borne out by the series of negotiations with Western aid sources that preceded the approach to China – now one of the more significant sources of aid for Tanzania. For instance, the rail-link proposal was rejected by the World Bank Mission in 1963 on the grounds that the likely economic benefits would be negligible; that the existing rail lines were sufficient to handle the traffic; and that development in Tanzania and Zambia would be better served by other projects.[35] Similarly, the Seers Report (made under the auspices of the UN in 1964) also rejected the idea

---

* It has been suggested that the apparent reluctance was more of Zambian making than Tanzanian. There is, however, no convincing evidence yet on this score.

Table 10 *Tanzania Treasury: External Sources of Development Funds 1965–9
(in thousands of shillings)*

	1961/2–1964/5 total	1965/6	1966/7	1967/8	1968/9	1965/6–1968/9 total*
Governments						
United Kingdom	201,920	17,517	8,201	8,314		34,032
USA	32,640	29,956	17,395	24,841	55,278	127,479
Federal Republic of						
Germany	26,160	4,318	6,092	258	642	11,310
Israel	9,160	6,349	194			6,543
Sweden		1,593	3,361	7,943	20,803	33,691
Netherlands				753	1,949	2,702
China	5,980	19,091	51,279	3,796	1,725	75,891
Canada			665	2,283	10,458	13,406
Denmark					3,320	3,320
USSR			46	494	*	530
Zambia			3,969	5,163		9,132
Multilateral						
IDA	16,240	18,699	30,213	30,091	42,453	121,456
UNESCO		4,020	500			4,520
Unidentified	180	210	1,400	1,947	11,429	14.986

* Receipts from a number of sources including the USSR and American foundations were recorded differently in the 1968–9 appropriation accounts and so were no longer separately identifiable.

Source: Adapted from the statements of development revenues and of unfunded debt for the year (revenue head 137) in Tanzania, *Appropriation Accounts of Tanzania for the Year 1965–6, . . . 1966–7, . . . 1967–8 and . . . 1968–9. These record funds received. The 1961/2–1964/5 figures are from Table 7 above, p. 185.*

Table 11 *Source of External loans 1962–72*

Area	1962		1968		1972*	
	Million shs	%	Million shs	%	Million shs	%
Developed capitalist world (including US dominated world agencies)	105.6	100	380.9	81.5	991.9	81.5
Socialist countries of which China is the major donor	–	–	76.3 (75.1)	16.3	207.5 (207.5)	17.0
Others	–	–	10.0	2.1	17.9	1.5
TOTAL	105.6	100	467.2	100	1217.3	100

* As at 31st March. (Excluding TAZARA.)

Source: *The Annual Economic Survey, 1971–72*, p. 31 and *1966–67, p. 66.*

of the rail link. The report argued that the reasons put forward for the railway were speculative, that the existing rail systems in the area had space capacity, and that the likely development benefits, measured in terms of stimulating Zambian agricultural growth, were invalid.[36] An appeal to the Soviet Union in 1964 also failed to elicit any favourable response. More significant is that the Anglo-Canadian Consortium (The Maxwell Stamp Survey), after a detailed study, concluded that the project would be feasible and that it would be more profitable than originally thought; but it too failed to respond to the appeals of Tanzania and Zambia.

Table 12 *Destination of Exports 1962–71*
(Per cent of total value of exports) (Excluding East Africa)

Area	1962	1968	1971
Developed capitalist countries	88	64	61
Socialist countries	–	6	7
'Third World' countries	10	27	25
Others	2	3	7
Total	100	100	100

Source: E.A. Customs & Excise, *Annual Trade Reports*.

Closely allied with the above is the fact that the bulk of technical assistance, especially in the form of technical know-how (see Table 13), has also come from Western capitalist sources. We noted earlier that this situation is brought about partly as a result of the requirements of the project approach, which favours large projects over medium and small industries* and is both capital- and import-intensive.

* That foreign aid has tended to reinforce the Tanzanian emphasis on large infrastructural projects can be seen from the fact that in 1961/70, 72% of aid went to roads, aerodromes and electricity. Thus aid has the potential to distort investment by drawing off local resources in areas not considered to be the main priorities.

Table 13 *Technical and Educational Assistance (Excluding Military Assistance) From Selected Donor Countries*

SOVIET UNION

Technical Experts
    8   veterinary doctors
    4   experts in the operation of trade ships

Teachers
    3   secondary school teachers
    1   co-operative college teacher, 1967
  20   secondary school teachers by end of 1968

    In addition, by mid-1968 350 Tanzanian students were to be trained in the Soviet Union. By 1967, 70 Tanzanians received Soviet qualifications.

WEST GERMANY
Technical Experts
    1   adviser in the Ministry of Commerce and Industries 1963–65.
    1   agricultural adviser in the Ministry of Development Planning 1963–65.
    1   adviser in the Ministry of Finance 1963–65.
    1   teacher for Kivukoni College 1964–67.
    7   teachers (and some equipment) for the College of Business Education 1964–69.

    About 30 Tanzanian students a year since 1962 to be trained in institutions of higher learning in W. Germany.

    There were by early 1968, 65 volunteers including teachers and nurses.

It must be noted that 'a number of experts and advisers provided held positions of considerable influence in Tanzania.'

DENMARK
Technical Experts
    a small number of experts, mostly concerned with the development of co-operatives.
  146   Tanzanian students for institutions of higher learning in Denmark 1961–68.

    80   Danish volunteers 1964–68

FRANCE
    25   teachers and experts mainly teachers of French. A small number of Tanzanian students to France.

HOLLAND
    10   Dutch experts 1965–68

ITALY
    4   experts
    3   Tanzanian students in Italy in July 1968.

NORWAY
    10   experts 1967–68

CANADA
1961–62
    1   teacher
    2   professors
    2   Tanzanians being trained in Canada

1962–63
    8   teachers
    2   professors
    2   Tanzanians being trained

1963–64
    15   teachers
    5   Tanzanians being trained

1964–65
    25   teachers
    5   experts
    31   Tanzanians being trained

1965–66
    36   teachers
    13   experts
    44   Tanzanians being trained

1966–67
- 36 teachers
- 15 experts
- 1 university lecturer
- 60 Tanzanians being trained

About 100 Canadian volunteers by mid-1968.

ISRAEL
1962–68

About 30 experts distributed as follows:
- 6 on the National Service 1965–68
- 3 in the Medical Service 1966–68
- 1 in the Ministry of Economic Affairs and Development Planning 1966–68
- 10 in settlement schemes 1962–66
- 4 in the Police
- 1 in the TANU Youth League 1965–67
- 1 in the National Lottery
- 1 in the National Housing Corporation
- 5 in Cosata (Tanzania Cooperative Society) 1964–66
- 500 Tanzanian students for Israel 1962–68

JAPAN
- 4 experts 1967–68
- 4 Tanzanian students in Japan 1966
- 30 Japanese volunteers in 1967

SWEDEN

1968
- 7 Swedish experts
- 40 fellowships were provided for Tanzanians to study in Sweden.
- 20 Tanzanian civil servants for 6-months training course in Sweden 1967.
- 26 volunteers 1968

SWITZERLAND
A few medical and biological experts by 1968.

YUGOSLAVIA
- 16 experts by 1968
- 60 Tanzanian students in Yugoslavia at the beginning of 1968.

BRITAIN

At the beginning of 1968 British expatriate officers under OSAS were divided among the Tanzanian Ministries as follows:

155	Ministry of Agriculture
16	Commerce
85	Communications, Labour and Works
6	Ministry of Development Planning
276	Education
14	Finance
45	Health and Housing
1	Information and Tourism
10	Home Affairs
49	Land Settlement and Water Development
7	Local Government and Rural Development
6	President's Office
10	Justice
850	Students between 1961–68

USA

About 40% of all qualified teachers in Tanzania were Peace Corps Volunteers. They were obviously playing 'an important role in the educational system.' But by the beginning of 1967 there was a decline in the Peace Corps programme following criticism in the National Assembly, the TANU Youth League and NUTA. By 1968 Peace Corps volunteers fell to a mere 8.

CHINA

No reliable figures were available but generally Chinese experts worked in their various aid projects such as the Friendship Textile Mill in Dar es Salaam, Agricultural Implements Factory, RUVU State farm mainly for rice cultivation, a radio transmitting station and the Tazara Railroad.

Source: Compiled from Niblock's study, 'Aid and Foreign Policy in Tanzania,' (unpublished Ph.D. thesis, University of Sussex, 1971).

Capital-intensive projects often involve among other things higher local costs absorbed by the Tanzanians.[37] And they require highly skilled personnel. We have also noted that these requirements, as well as the lack of an industrial strategy and the subsequent dominant managerial role played by the foreign consultants/ managers (who are in many cases representatives of multi-national companies), tend to undermine the development of an integrated national economy. The technical assistance received by Tanzania through foreign aid has, in its heavy reliance on capitalist donor countries for these highly skilled personnel,* also tended to reinforce dependency relations by at least fostering the continued symbiotic relationship between the indigenous bureaucratic bourgeoisie and international capitalism. It therefore seriously questions the claim to self-reliance by the government of Tanzania.[38]

To conclude this section we would reiterate that the thrust of our argument is not that foreign aid is inherently bad and therefore unnecessary for Tanzania. On the contrary, real aid remains a vital component of the developmental process for most of the developing countries. In spite of the crushing debt-burden that has now become a familiar component of foreign aid, as shown in Table 14, in the case of Tanzania aid terms have in many cases been

---

* This is not to suggest that there is an inexhaustible pool of highly skilled personnel from which the donor countries can continue to supply the recipient countries. Perhaps too little consideration has been given to this dimension of the aid equation by the recipient countries. In fact, the Pearson Report concluded with reference to highly skilled expatriate staff that, 'the supply of competent people from the donor countries for overseas work is limited and there is heavy competition for their services in their own countries. It is not surprising therefore that the average quality of personnel who offer their service has tended to deteriorate as the demand has risen . . .' See L.B. Pearson, *Partners in Development . . .* p. 184.

In more dramatic language, Little writes: '. . . the bottom of the world's barrel has been scraped for suitable fairly high level people willing to serve in underdeveloped countries.' See I.M.D. Little, *Aid to Africa* (New York: Pergamon Press, 1964), p. 56. However, as Clark suggests: 'Because foreign aid usually involves the importation of a large number of technical personnel, the country is swamped with people who are generally, in the case of capitalist aid, suspicious of socialism. Aid donors are often skeptical of the Ujamaa Village programme, and try to undermine it. Aid also has an important demonstration effect. The presence of highly paid Western oriented technical personnel makes it difficult for a value shift in the urban elite to occur.' Clarke, p. 306.

Table 14 *Tanzania's Foreign Aid Debt as of March 15, 1974 (in shillings) To be repaid by 2023*

Donor Country	Aid Debt
PRC	1,949,319,625
World Bank	821,266,042
Canada	413,348,338
USA	357,709,044
Sweden	337,425,060
W. Germany	175,605,880
USSR	172,334,800
UK	105,009,685
Denmark	98,560,000
Italy	91,621,276
Holland	54,864,100
India	46,725,000
Bulgaria	21,000,000
Zambia	20,629,328
Romania	7,349,300*
Finland	39,487,140
East Africa Power & Lighting Co	50,657,269
CDC	37,984,800
Soleh Boneh Co	5,621,911
UNDP	1,750,000
TOTAL =	4,818,268,598

* Yet to be disbursed.

Source: *Daily News*, March 15, 1974, p. 3.

relatively favourable to Tanzania.** However, aid is more than that. If we agree that the ultimate objective of aid programmes should be to help developing countries reach a position where, while still benefiting from co-operative exchanges, they would no longer be dependent on outside help, then this study has shown that Tanzania is far from reaching that goal. For, in general, the aid pattern in Tanzania has tended to reinforce the dependency features of the Tanzanian economy and thus undermine her claim to self-reliance – this in spite of the apparent shift to the more peripheral Nordic countries, for example, which have stronger social-democratic traditions.

SECTION II: A COMPARATIVE EXPERIENCE

Let us now turn to the comparative experiences of Tanzania and China (1949–60) in the four key areas we have been examining. The juxtaposition of this section with the first is justified on the grounds that foreign aid formed a critical component of China's economic development during this period. It is not uncommon for analysts of socialist development in Tanzania to compare it to the experience of other more advanced socialist countries. Bienen, for instance, maintains that because Tanzania still is at a low level of economic development, it cannot sustain a Leninist Vanguard Party which he argues is a prerequisite for radical and purposeful change.[39] However, Bienen's position is difficult to maintain as there is no logical relationship necessarily between the level of economic development and a Leninist Vanguard Party, on the one hand, and radical and purposeful change, on the other. Surely,

** For example, most donor countries extend low interest rates to Tanzania with generally long repayment periods. Interest rates range from 0–6% (see below).

Donor Country	Interest Rate	Repayment Period	Grace Period
USSR	2½ %	12 yrs.	No Grace
W. Germany	3 %	20 yrs.	5 yrs.
Israel	6 %	8 yra.	No Grace
Sweden	2 %	Over 15 yrs.	5 yrs.
Japan	5.75 %	Over 18 yrs.	5 yrs.
IDA	0 %	Over 50 yrs.	10 yrs.
IBRD	3–6 %	Over 23 yrs.	3 yrs.
China	0 %	20 yrs.	10 yrs.
USA	1–2 %	40 yrs.	10 yrs.

Source: Compiled from Niblock, 'Aid and Foreign Policy.'

there can develop, at least in theory, a Vanguard Party capable of initiating radical and purposeful change in a country with a 'low level of economic development'. We suggest (without running the risk of over-simplification) that Cuba, with a low level of economic development at the time (in the absence of a precise definition by Bienen of what a 'low level of economic development' means), was able to develop a Leninist Vanguard Party, under Fidel Castro, that has largely been able to initiate radical and purposeful changes in Cuba. In a review of Bienen's work Lionel Cliffe questions the validity of the analysis of Tanzania which is premised on the Soviet model, because he argues that Tanzania's emerging socialism is rural, therefore the country has more to learn from the Chinese experience.[40] Interestingly enough, the prescriptions of observers of Tanzania's socialist development are invariably a reflection of the Chinese model. Cliffe also suggests that, as in China, reliance on people and local cadres rather than a state bureaucracy must be Tanzania's strategy for a revolutionary transformation of the society.[41]

Similar views are expressed by John Saul. He urges the need to consider the socio-political context of planning and maintains that the latter is not exclusively a matter of economic calculation or simply a case of improved co-ordination. In offering prescriptions as to how the contextual variables can be changed, the experience of revolutionary transformations in socialist societies like China becomes the yardstick.[42] This position is perhaps strengthened by the fact that official statements (especially following the visits by Nyerere and Chou to China and Tanzania, respectively) from both countries are quick to emphasize the fact that the two countries belong to the 'world's countryside' and as such have much in common.

While we concede that there is some substance to the above points and they should therefore be taken into account in any comparative analysis of 'transition to socialism,' there is the danger of overstretching the comparative experience of other socialist countries at the expense of local objective conditions. Indeed, this tendency has led one observer to comment that the focus on the comparative experience is usually limited to economic factors rather than socio-political factors,[43] the implication being, of course, that socio-political factors reveal more of the differences in objective conditions within the socialist countries. This cautionary note, however, should not be allowed to mask many similar problems and choices confronting various countries in the period of transition to socialism, in spite of the diversity of the inherited economic, political and social systems. If nothing else, these different experiences may serve as useful sources from which some valuable lessons can be learnt, just as the Soviet Union's pioneering experiences provided a reservoir of knowledge and often resources on which later socialist countries could tap – either selectively or wholly, and in accordance with the countries' objective conditions. In other words, there are valuable lessons to be learnt from the experience of other socialist countries for developing countries seriously attempting to build socialism. But any slavish attempt to copy their methods and strategy is likely to be counter-productive, just as the failure to learn the lessons of the socialist experience, to differentiate the common ingredients from the particular conditions, will likely increase the problems encountered on the road to socialism.

Before discussing the comparative experiences between China and Tanzania in the four areas covered in the study, we shall outline briefly the major differences in objective conditions between the two.* Whereas the establishment of the Peoples' Republic of China in October 1949 was preceded by a protracted revolutionary struggle – conducted to a large extent under guerilla warfare conditions – the 'revolutionary basis' of Tanzania was not laid through a protracted struggle but by political means through organizations, notably TANU. This difference is very significant in that the protracted struggle in China enforced new attitudes on the people affected. Participation, self-discipline and self-criticism became the products of these revolutionary activities in China even before the final communist victory in 1949.[44] They at least in part facilitated the communists' consolidation of power within a relatively short period of time in a hitherto highly fractionalized society. In contrast, because Tanzania has been unable to build its socialism from a revolutionary base, its concern with building up a

---

* The differences in objective conditions between the Soviet Union and China had a lot to do with the revolutionary strategies of these two countries.

socialist polity based on a wide network of followers loyal to the centre has been a major issue since 1967.

This has been conditioned in part by the other difference between the two countries – that is, the specific conditions imposed by colonial rule in the case of Tanzania.* Another significant difference lies in the fact that the degree of perceived deprivation amongst the peasantry was very much higher in China than in Tanzania, though it is difficult to measure this variable. At the risk of sounding tautological we would argue that the revolution itself, in the case of China, is in part a reflection of the relative degree of deprivation. The claim by Nyerere and other African socialists that there were no classes in traditional African societies (and including the colonial period) is in part premised on this very factor. Finally, another major difference lies in the fact that the level of productive forces, as we shall see later, was more developed in China than in Tanzania. There were, for example, 141 enterprises that were to be rehabilitated in the wake of the communist victory in China. Although this number appears small relative to the size of the country, the importance lies in the fact that the bulk of these enterprises were in the field of electric power generation, mining, chemicals, and producers' goods industries, particularly metals and engineering as well as fertilizer and textile plant that were very highly developed.[45] Against this background of differences in objective conditions – anchored in differing historical experiences – we now examine the comparative experience in socialist development between the two countries in the areas of industry, collectivization, education and foreign aid. We shall examine questions relevant to both cases, for example, the choice of initial emphasis on industry or agriculture and the related question of the choice of labour- or capital-intensive methods of production; the method of rural socialism, i.e., agricultural collectivization; the pattern of foreign aid and the methods of peasant and worker mobilization, especially through the medium of education.

* We agree with Mao that China was not a colony but a 'semi-colony'.

Industry Versus Agriculture

Although there was hardly any significant industrial base to speak of in Tanzania in the wake of independence, the debate over which sector to emphasize (agriculture or industry) came to the forefront after the Arusha Declaration in 1967. The decision to emphasize agriculture over industrial development in post-Arusha Tanzania came as a result of Tanzania's commitment to Ujamaa Villages in the rural areas (which was seen at the time as a necessary preliminary to mobilizing the surplus from agriculture to finance industrialization, and perhaps the realization that Tanzania's socialism can only be built on the basis of a rural transformation policy). It was recognized that it had been a mistake to have 'put too much emphasis on industries' in the early years of independence.[46] So the strategy of building up an industrial capacity to make the producer goods for increased agricultural productivity was rejected as unrealistic, at least in the initial stages of development. It was unrealistic, it was argued, because for one thing Tanzania did 'not have the means to establish many modern industries . . . we do not have either the necessary finances or the technical know-how'[47] to start the many modern industries that are essential for this strategy option.

In the process of debating whether to emphasize one sector or the other, the essential question of the inter-dependency of agriculture and industry was often forgotten in the wake of the pressures to develop rural socialism through the Ujamaa Village programme. We have already noted the general lack of backward and forward linkages between the two sectors in the preceding chapter.

The decision to emphasize agriculture over industrialization in post-Arusha Tanzania departs from the experience of other socialist countries including China. It is readily discernible from the history of the socialist countries that each one recognized the basic need to industrialize first, not only because it was thought to be the way out of a dependency relationship with capitalism, or because this route was historically proved to be the more rapid means of developing the productive forces, but also because of industry's essential interaction with agriculture. The development, therefore, of an industrial capacity alongside the development of rural areas became a logical extension of the recognition of the essential relationship between the two sectors. It is worth noting that collectivization in the Soviet Union just slightly preceded in time the greatly accelerated rate of industrialization in the 1930s. The Chinese also emphasized at the onset the interdependency of agriculture and industry – the Maoist philosophy of 'walking on two legs' is a clear testimony. In the early post-revolutionary period (up to 1960), Communist China imitated the Soviet model, with the aid of Soviet advisers, of course. This emphasized rapid industrialization while at the same time allowing the rural areas, unaffected by the communist reforms during the war period, to undergo the social and economic transformation which had begun in the liberated areas in the war years.

In noting the difference in emphasis between China and Tanzania it must be pointed out that the choice of emphasizing agricultural development over and above industrialization in the wake of the Arusha Declaration, may simply have been a recognition by Tanzania that rapid industrialization requires massive investment in the form of plant and machinery which was beyond the capabilities of Tanzania.

It is interesting to note as a corollary the close link between a strategy in which industrial development dovetails into agricultural development and the nature of the industries which are built. For instance, a capital goods sector which supplies the rural areas with tractors and electricity, presupposes a basic heavy goods industry, manufacturing domestic or imported iron and steel or coal. It is therefore not surprising that China followed in the 1950s the Soviet Union's pattern of massive expansion of coal, electricity, machine tools and steel production when the decision to emphasize industrialization had been taken.[48] We would point out however, that there was an apparent switch in this area following the withdrawal of Soviet aid in 1960.* The point we are making is that Tanzania, in the wake of the Arusha Declaration, abandoned

* The emphasis in post-1960 China was on those industries which could supply the agricultural sector – transport, tractors, fertilizers and construction of dams and flood control works. However, as Wheelwright points out, the ground for the necessary expansion of these industries had been laid down by the development of heavy industry in the 1950s. *Ibid.*

the 'traditional' socialist emphasis on industrialization over agriculture, and the emphasis on heavy industrial development over light industrial development.[49]

Closely allied with the above is the question of the choice of technique, i.e., the problem of the use of capital- versus labour-intensive techniques of production. Interestingly, the debate among socialists and non-socialists alike has invariably been carried on with reference to the differences in approach between the Soviet Union and China. It has generally been argued that whereas the Soviet Union had adopted the capital-intensive approach, the Chinese had opted for the labour-intensive approach in keeping partly with the Maoist philosophy that the worker and peasant must be able to retain control of technological developments – the 'technical expert' must be held in check if only to thwart the development of an elitist position through his specialized knowledge. Based on this postulate, socialist observers in many Third World countries have suggested the adoption of the Chinese model for these countries, although not always for the same reasons.

The discussion of techniques in Tanzania has more or less followed similar lines. While there is some substance in the labour-intensive approach, there is a tendency to over-simplify the Chinese model by presenting the Chinese level of technological development as 'intermediate rather than advanced, labour rather than capital intensive.' But Wheelwright and Macfarlane point out that Chinese industry 'covered a whole spectrum'; sophisticated technology exists side by side with the 'backyard furnaces,' often in the same factory. Where there is a real choice of technique, which does not require a specific industrial process, the choice is often low-level technology. This is done apparently because it is less expensive, and hence more suitable for industries in the rural areas since the processes are more easily learnt, which in turn helps to overcome the shortage of skilled manpower. Workers can dismantle these machines, rebuild them again. This, it is suggested, not only aids in the search for a low-cost method of industrial expansion through a release of popular energy, but lessens the degree of 'worker alienation'.[50] Given the rather diverse 'spectrum' of Chinese industry, any mechanical adoption of the Chinese technique by Tanzania without a full understanding of the historical context, therefore, will likely be counter-productive. In any case, for reasons already given in the preceding chapter, Tanzania has so far not demonstrated any serious attempt to implement a labour-intensive technique in its developmental strategy, though it remains a policy preference of the political leadership.

On Agricultural Collectivization or Villagization

There are several common features found in nearly all socialist countries engaged in the task of rural transformation, particularly in the area of agricultural collectivization. Some of these common features include: a) a far-reaching land-reform programme which invariably involves the redistribution of large landholdings to the poor and landless peasants; b) the implementation of the programme through various stages; and c) a counter-attack on the tendencies to rural capitalism, depending, of course, on the stage of development in the rural sector.

To the extent that there are these common features, there is some substance to the suggestion that the socialist learning process has been most apparent in rural development. Thus, the Chinese learnt from the failure of the Soviet Union's forced collectivization programme (failure in the limited sense that it did not raise agricultural output*) that force mainly accomplished negative results. It did so by alienating the peasant from socialism and from the land; the rural population first had to be convinced of the benefits of collective work and living. Forced collectivization, along Soviet lines, was therefore largely rejected by not only China but other socialist countries as well. While they may have conceded that forced collectivization was perhaps a necessary

---

* It was not uncommon, for example, for the 'kulaks' in the Soviet Union to have carried out large-scale destruction of their property, including livestock, in the post-revolutionary collectivization programme of the Soviet Union. For a comprehensive analysis of the process of collectivization in the Soviet Union, see M. Lewin, *The Russian peasant and Soviet Power* (London: Allen and Unwin, 1968).

method for the first socialist country at the critical juncture in her socialist construction, they nevertheless saw it as being counter-productive, especially when seen in the all-important context of the need to maintain mass support for the leadership.

The rejection was also a recognition of the fact that the social structure of the peasantry and historical conditions were not the same in all socialist countries, which meant that different socio-economic relations would prevail. Thus in China the collectiviz-ation programmes progressed through various stages – from mutual aid teams, to Lower Producer Co-operatives, to Higher Producer Co-operatives, and through to the communes by 1958. Moreover, the emphasis, at least in theory (and in concert with the method used for the liberated areas during the war) was on persuasion rather than force,* though the use of force was not entirely ruled out.[51] Indeed, Mao's argument that co-operation had to be seen to result in higher production and living standards.[52] may have been predictably taken to heart by the cadres in the villages.

Some parallels can be drawn between Tanzania and China's first decade of socialist construction. The view of the party and political leadership of post-Arusha Tanzania was that collectivization should be gradual and voluntary. The credibility of the principle of voluntary participation was virtually destroyed in China during the various campaigns to spread mutual aid co-operatives (1952 and 1954) and the collectivization campaigns of 1955–56 in which about 60 per cent of Chinese peasant households became members of collectives within a 12-month period.** Similarly, Tanzania's 'Operation Planned Villages' of 1974 and onwards seems to have

---

* In this regard, Huberman and Sweezy reported that in both Cuba and North Korea the 'Leninist voluntary principle' was followed. See Leo Huberman and Paul M. Sweezy, *Socialism in Cuba* (New York: Modern Reader Paperbacks 1970), Chapter 7.

** Tanzania also witnessed successive waves of high and low activity in the villagization programme. Thus in 1967, after the Arusha Declaration, there was a noticeable proliferation of Ujamaa villages followed by an apparent retreat and lull in late 1968 and part of 1969 when local administrators were being criticized for high-handedness in the implementation of Ujamaa villages. In 1970–71, another wave of enthusiasm and expansion began.

largely destroyed the principle of voluntarism and persuasion – and perhaps not only because of a few overzealous cadres, as is often claimed. There were, however, differences in some of the salient features of the collectivization programmes of the two countries. For instance, Tanzania had no land reform anywhere near the scale and size of that in China.* Its cadres are just beginning to form, though Mao's argument (that cadres can only become trained by trying) is sometimes also voiced in Tanzania. The argument was used by Mao against those who had tried to hold back the rapid progress of collectivization on the grounds that there were not enough trained cadres.

On Education

The potential of education as a powerful tool for re-socialization is recognized by all socialist countries well before taking power, and educational reforms usually form part of the early changes initiated in a post-revolutionary socialist society. The kind of educational system which makes political education the basis of the curriculum and links the various disciplines to it becomes the goal of educational reforms. Equally important is concern for the kind of education which entails learning by doing – for most of the school population is expected to return to their family farms. This means practical agricultural education. Closely allied with the above is an interest in a curriculum related to educational needs that demand more specialized training, including on-the-job training for various professions, e.g. the bare-foot doctors of China.

The wide-ranging educational reforms in post-revolutionary China, such as agricultural farms and production units in schools, study groups in schools and factories, thought reform programmes, wide-ranging curriculum changes, etc., were designed to

* Of course, the need for land reform in Tanzania was practically non-existent compared to that of China since there were hardly any large-scale private landowners in Tanzania.

achieve the above objectives. More importantly, it is seen as an ongoing process, as the reforms of the Cultural Revolution demonstrate. In the case of Tanzania, although the policy document 'Education for Self-Reliance' spells out almost identical goals in the educational system, its execution, as we have tried to show earlier, has been rather effectively obstructed by educators whose educational background has been unsuitable for the kinds of objectives expected from the educational system, during the period of this study. We noted, however, that the schools are slowly changing while curriculum reforms and other reorganizations continue. In all, however, some of the reforms initiated so far, such as *shambas* in schools, and the abolition of direct entry into universities from high school, suggest that Tanzania is not likely to ignore the experience of other socialist countries in its attempt to tailor the educational system to its overall socialist objectives.

The Use of Foreign Aid

Socialist development strategy clearly calls for structural transformation. A socialist aid strategy is required to select donors according to the degree to which structural change is likely to result from the implementation of aided projects. Thus the aid strategy for China (as with, for example, Cuba and North Korea) has meant relying on aid primarily from the socialist countries, and the Soviet Union in particular in the case of China. Following a series of protracted negotiations in the wake of the communist victory, the Soviet Union is reported to have granted, over a period of five years, US $300 million in aid to China. Eckstein has estimated the level of Soviet aid to China for the 1954–59 period as of US $117 million.[53] Such an aid strategy is designed to encourage the total transformation of the Chinese economy from a dependency relationship with its former capitalist trading powers to a 'self-reliant' relationship with other socialist countries; and such an aid strategy would fit into a coherent industrial strategy. But we have pointed out that, for one thing, Tanzania did not have a coherent industrial strategy during the period covered in this study; and its bulk of foreign aid has come largely from non-socialist sources even though the political leadership has in various cases shown some concern about the dependency implications of such a relationship. The political leadership recognizes to some extent the fact that there are lessons, for a foreign-aid policy based on socialism and self-reliance, which can be learnt from both capitalist and socialist transfers. The fundamental nature of capitalist transfers is the strengthening of the existing dependency ties of the recipient countries to the donor – economically, technologically and therefore politically. Thus Nyerere observes:

> How can we depend upon gifts, loans and investments
> from foreign countries and foreign companies without
> endangering our independence? . . . How can we depend
> upon foreign governments and companies for the major
> part of our development, without giving to those govern-
> ments and countries a great part of our freedom to act as
> we please. The truth is that we cannot.[54]

An interesting point is that in none of his observations on this has there been any mention of the difference the source of aid can make. The implication is that for him there is little or no concrete relation between capitalist aid and continuing dependency, or that the source does not really matter since any foreign aid nibbles away at any claim to self-reliance. For instance, is Cuba today a self-reliant country or a satellite of the Soviet Union? Do large socialist countries attempt to utilize smaller ones to their own ends? How can we characterize China–Albania relationships, at least before the rupture? Was the sudden withdrawal of aid to China by the Soviet Union prompted by China as a way of breaking loose from a perceived threat to her independence? While these are not questions to be easily brushed aside, they are beyond the scope of this study. For our purposes, the point at issue here is whether there are parallels in the pattern of aid between China (1950–60) and Tanzania (1967–72). Moreover, since Tanzania has declared her commitment to the goal of socialism, then the test of the usefulness of a specific aid package lies in the extent to which it contributes to both long- and short-run socialist economic and social goals, particularly those related to making a structural change in the economy and a break with dependency on the capitalist centre. Viewed from this perspective, the fact that China relied almost entirely on the Soviet Union for foreign aid ('leaning to one side'),* and Tanzania on both capitalist and socialist sources – with the bulk of it coming from the former – makes for a significant difference in the experiences of the two countries. In all, however, contrary to the view usually expressed by some African academicians, politicians, civil servants, etc., which suggests that there is little to learn from either the Chinese or Soviet experiences, it cannot be overemphasized, that while Tanzania cannot ignore the experience of other socialist countries, the differences in historical experiences do inform Tanzania's path to socialism.

Chapter 6   Socialism and Self-Reliance: An International Dimension

1. For some of the more comprehensive works representing the various aspects of foreign aid, see: Raymond F. Mikesell, *The Economics of Foreign Aid* (Chicago: Aldine Publishing Co: 1968); I. M. Little and J. M. Clifford, *International Aid* (Chicago: Aldine Publishing Co., 1966); L. B. Pearson, *Partners in Development: Report of the Commission on International Development* (New York: Praeger, 1969); and Teresa Hayter, *Aid as Imperialism* (Harmondsworth: Penguin Books, 1971).
2. R. F. Mikesell, *The Economics of Foreign Aid* (Chicago: Aldine Publishing Co., 1968), p. 194.
3. D.L. Johnson, 'Dependence and the International System' in *Dependence and Underdevelopment*, edited by J. D. Cockcroft, A. G. Frank and D. L. Johnson (New York: Anchor Books, 1972), p. 100.
4. Quoted in Mikesell, *The Economics of Foreign Aid*, p. 6.

* We cannot overemphasize the point made earlier. That is, the policy of 'leaning to one side' for foreign aid also carries with it some serious limitations. In this regard, the rather extensive disruptions reported (e.g., the bridge over the Yangtse River was left half completed) in the Chinese industrialization process in the wake of the sudden withdrawal of Soviet aid in 1960 serves as a pertinent reminder.

5. Quoted in Teresa Hayter, *Aid as Imperialism*, p. 5.
6. See S.O. Adebo, 'Why Aid' in *International Cooperation in Aid*, edited by R. Robinson (Cambridge: Cambridge University Press, 1966), p. 57.
7. *New York Times*, January 15, 1965, p. 12.
8. L. B. Pearson, *Partners in Development: Report of The Commission on International Development* (New York: Praeger, 1969), pp. 4 and 5.
9. *Ibid.*
10. Teresa Hayter, *Aid as Imperialism, p.* 7.
11. Pearson, *Partners in Development . . .,* p. 4.
12. *Ibid.*
13. See, for example, S. H. Robcock, *Brazil's Developing Northeast: A Study of Regional Planning and Foreign Aid* (Washington, D.C.: Brookings Institution, 1963).
14. See G. M. Meier, *The International Economics of Development Theory and Policy* (New York: Harper and Row, 1968), p. 190.
15. See, for example, *The Development Assistance Committee (of OECD) 1969 Review*, p. 313.
16. M. Radetzki, *Aid and Development* (New York: Frederick A. Praeger, 1973), p. 26.
17. It must be pointed out that although many projects are of a commercial nature, others may not be entirely e.g., water supply and health centre projects.
18. In fact, as we shall soon see in the case of Tanzania, given the rigorous management and technical expertise requirements of the projects as demanded by the donor country, most projects, at least initially, almost always come under the control and management of the donor country, given the dearth of such personnel in the Third World.
19. See A. O. Hirschman and Richard M. Bird, *Foreign Aid: A Critique and a Proposal* (Princeton, New Jersey: Princeton University Press, 1968).
20. Radetzki, *Aid and Development*, p. 35.
21. See Cranford Pratt, *A Critical Phase in Tanzania 1945–1968: Nyerere and the Emergence of a Socialist Strategy* (Cambridge: Cambridge University Press, 1976), p. 132.
22. *Ibid.*, p. 367.
23. *Ibid.*
24. Address by President Nyerere to the Tanzanian National Assembly (Tanzania Parliamentary Debates, 1st Session, 12th Meeting, col. 37).
25. See, for example, *The Economic Survey: An Annual Plan 1970–71* (Dar es Salaam: Government Printer, 1970), pp. 73–74.
26. Cranford Pratt, *The Critical Phase . . .,* p. 166.
27. In a similar vein, Lars-Erik Birgegard, of the Econonic Research Institute of Stockholm, writes:
    'Most donors have openly made clear what their preferences are

regarding the kinds of development activities they wish to support, and they have often made clear to what extent they are prepared to give support by setting financial frames . . . The developing countries depending heavily upon external financing . . . will then be restricted in what kind of development projects she can present to a particular donor . . . This means that the financiers will exert influence on the project selection process already at its very early stage, when a choice is made as to what problem to attend, by reducing the number of alternatives considered. To the recipient country, needless to say, it appears useless to pursue project ideas if it is most unlikely that any donor is interested in financing them, if domestic resources are inadequate.'

See Lars-Erik Birgegard, *The Project Selection Process in Developing Countries: A Study of the Public Investment Project Selection Process in Kenya, Zambia and Tanzania* (Stockholm: The Economic Research Institute, 1975.).

28. For instance, 100% of Soviet Aid to Tanzania in 1966 was import-tied; about 50% from Denmark, France, Holland, Italy, Norway and Scandinavia; over 60% from Israel from 1962–63; 100% from Yugoslavia in 1963; 75% from Japan in 1966. But Swedish aid from 1963–67 and IDA aid from 1963–1964 were not import-tied. *Ibid.*, pp. 93–122.
29. Nyerere, 'The Arusha Declaration,' p. 22.
30. *Ibid.*
31. *Mbioni*, Vol. VII, No. 4 (1974), p. 42.
32. Nyerere, *Ten Years After Arusha*, p. 33.
33. Pratt, *The Critical Phase . . .* , pp. 169–70.
34. The fact that there was now no overwhelming dependency on any one country for aid, we would argue, may in large part be a reflection of the non-aligned foreign policy stance of the government, especially when it is realized that the important sources now included the 'middle power' countries like Sweden and Canada – by 1968 both West Germany and Great Britain were no longer providing significant capital assistance. It is also worth mentioning that there seems to be a strong correlation, as shown in Table 12, between the source of foreign aid and the destination of exports during the period under study.
35. See R. M. Bostock, 'Transport Sector' in *Constraints on the Economic Development of Zambia*, edited by Charles Elliot (Nairobi: East African Publishing House, 1971), p. 367.
36. R. Hall, *The High Price of Principle: Kaunda and the White South* (London: Hodder and Stoughton, 1969), p. 213.
37. For instance, in the case of the bakery unit built with Canadian aid, the Canadian loan was for only shs.25 million, the equipment portion of the project. But the equipment necessitated the construction of a shs. 10 million building; an extraordinarily expensive building for Tanzania. Thus 'even if the terms of the

Canadian loan are taken into account, the depreciated value of the project is about shs.8.5 million almost six times the private average for bakeries.' See Clark, 'Socialist Development and Public Investment . . .,' p. 305.

38. Expressing a similar viewpoint, Clark writes: 'the [aid] projects which require a turn-key approach are the very projects which use the least Tanzanian resources, and employ the most advanced techniques, and develop the most elite type of labour force. They are the exact opposite of projects which should come out of a philosophy of self-reliance.' Clark, p. 306.

39. See H. Bienen, *Tanzania: Party Transformation and Economic Development* (Princeton, N.J.: Princeton University Press, 1967).

40. See Lionel Cliffe, 'Tanzania: Socialist Transformation and Party Development,' *African Review*, Vol. 1 (1971).

41. *Ibid.*

42. See John Saul, 'Planning for Socialism in Tanzania: The Socio-Political Context' in *Towards Socialist Planning*, edited by Uchumi Editorial Board, (Dar es Salaam: Tanzania Publishing House, 1974), pp. 1–29.

43. See Clive Thomas, 'The Transition to Socialism: Issues of Economy Strategy in Tanzania-Type Economies,' (University of Dar es Salaam, 1972), (mimeo).

44. For a brilliant account of this process, see William Hinton, *Fanshen* (New York: Monthly Review Press, 1966). See also Frantz Fannon, *The Wretched of the Earth*.

45. New China News Agency, Peking, Sept. 15, 1953. Quoted in A. Eckstein, *China's Economic Development* (Ann Arbor: Michigan University Press, 1975), p. 232.

46. Nyerere, *Ujamaa: Essays on Socialism*, p. 26.

47. *Ibid.*

48. See E. L. Wheelwright and B. Macfarlane, *The Chinese Road to Socialism* (New York: Monthly Review Press, 1970), Chapter 3.

49. This also reflects the lack of a clear industrial strategy which made the job of the NDC as the main medium of socialist construction very difficult – a critical oversight that has continued to obstruct the progress towards socialist construction in Tanzania.

50. Wheelwright and Macfarlane, *The Chinese Road to Socialism*, Chapter 9.

51. See Jan Myrdall, *Report from a Chinese Village* (Harmondsworth: Penguin Books, 1967); and William Hinton, *Fanshen* (New York: Monthly Review Press, 1966).

52. Mao Tse-tung, *On the Question of Agricultural Cooperation* (Peking: Foreign Language Press, 1956).

53. A. Eckstein, *China's Economic Development* (Ann Arbor: Michigan University Press, 1975), p. 232.

We would like to point out that much as we would have liked to give more details of aid statistics for China, the absence or extreme dearth of official data on foreign aid has made it

imposssible for us to do more. Of course, this is a widely recognized fact and Eckstein – one of the foremost scholars on the economy of Communist China – takes pains to make the same point as late as 1975. See *ibid.*
54. Nyerere, *Unjamaa: Essays on Socialism*, p. 25.

Chapter 7

Conclusion

> The policy of inviting a chain of capitalists to
> come and establish industries in our country
> might succeed in giving us all the industries we
> need, but it would also succeed in preventing
> the establishment of socialism unless we believe
> that without first building capitalism, we cannot
> build socialism.

Julius K. Nyerere

The primary aim of this summary will be to pull all the strands together – to constitute a whole out of the various parts of the study – as well as to advance a reasoned prescription for a possible future course of action that will aid Tanzania to combat effectively the dependence syndrome.

Firstly, we would like to make a few observations about the main areas of our endeavour. We attempted to establish at the onset the extent to which 'socialist economic theory has neglected theoretical issues raised by the requirements of an economic strategy' for the period of transition to socialism. In our attempt to indicate the historical and social factors which account for this neglect, we did not mean to ignore the fundamental contributions made by the empirical and theoretical studies of classical Marxism and beyond. We were, rather, trying to point out the specific failure to develop any sort of theoretical apparatus to cope with the problems of transition in the new underdeveloped countries of the Third World.

In a related sense, we established the fact (though no novelty is

216

claimed) that the theory of socialism *qua* theory cannot lay claim to a monolithic interpretation. There is more or less a broad consensus on the primacy of the economic factor in the various interpretations of socialism as theory. But other components in the equation, perhaps no less important, such as the meaning of freedom, equality, democracy, etc., have made the search for greater clarity in the conceptualization of socialism, and thereby a more encompassing consensus, awfully difficult. Perhaps such a consensus is not necessary. We noted also that the conceptual or theoretical ambiguity has not found any clearer exposition in the writings and pronouncements of the politicians and the ideologues of 'African socialism' in Black Africa. If anything, by divesting from the classical theories of socialism the 'class' content – which was anchored in the relations of production and the productive forces – the African socialists have made the theory of socialism even more diffuse. They have done so by introducing what can best be described as a large dosage of 'conventional nationalism'. This goes far beyond the permissible limits of the recognition given by classical Marxism to the fact that local conditions will indeed shape one's perception and, by extension, the concretization of socialism in theory and practice. Observes Miliband:

> In regard to 'Third World' countries, it is clear that class relations are for most of them too central a determinant of their mode of being. But it is equally clear that the classes involved in these relations are in some major ways different or of different importance from those in advanced capitalist societies; and also that, in part because of this and in part for different reasons, the class conflicts engendered by their class relations assume other forms than those encountered in capitalist societies.
>
> The development of these countries has been exceedingly distorted by colonialism and external capitalist domination, direct and indirect; and this has been naturally reflected in their economic, social and political structures. But this also means that Marxism, primarily fashioned in and for a bourgeois/capitalist context has, to say the least, to be adapted to the very different circumstances subsumed under the notion of 'underdevelopment'.
>
> One of these different circumstances is that in a large

> number of these countries, there has existed no strong
> indigenous class of large-scale capitalists, since the major
> industrial, extractive, financial and commercial enterprises
> are likely to be mainly owned and controlled by foreign
> interests . . . this . . . means that class conflicts in these
> economies occur on a very different basis and assume a
> very different form from those encountered in advanced
> capitalist countries. This does not mean that Marxist
> 'guidelines' are inoperative in the analysis of these con-
> flicts. But it does very strongly emphasize the danger of a
> simple transposition of the Marxist mode of analysis of
> advanced capitalist societies to countries whose capitalism
> is of a very different nature.[1]

Indeed, the same point also applies to communist countries.

But we noted that although the general tendency of African socialists has been to describe traditional African society (including even the colonial period) as classless, even in the face of glaring empirical evidence to the contrary, Nyerere gives at least a token recognition of the embryonic existence of social classes – though as an adjunct of colonialism – and the potential for these social classes to congeal into antagonistic classes in Tanzania. This recognition, we argued, becomes even more discernible when one examines the evolution of socialism as a theory, in the writings of Nyerere. Thus socialism evolves in his writings from a concept denoting simply 'an attitude of mind' to the more usual con-cretized conceptualization of socialism as 'a way of life' in post-Arusha Tanzania and as a reflection of his recognition of the embryonic existence of social classes.

The importance of the evolutionary development of socialism as a theory in Tanzania, we have argued, marks the difference not only in theory but also in practice between Nyerere and his erstwhile African socialists such as Senghor and Kenyatta to name just a few. It is the underpinning of our thesis that the absence of a systematic and coherent theoretical basis or the appropriate ideological framework for practical programmes of action, *inter alia*, is largely responsible for the failure to transform funda-mentally most of the developing states in Africa along desired goals – which for many of them is socialism, albeit in various forms.

218

Again, while we accept the view that there are at least embry-onic social classes in Tanzania we have also demonstrated in this study the unsatisfactory efforts so far in the analysis of these social classes. There still remains the major task of producing a more rigorous analysis, for much of what is available has proved to be no more than pioneering efforts to map out the parameters of the task that still lies ahead. The analysis so far has been noticeably fuzzy – classifications have been characteristically indistinct. Notwith-standing these limitations, a fairly major argument of this study lies in our identification of two broad strata, among others, within the 'petty-bourgeoisie' – the political leadership stratum and the bureaucratic bourgeoisie stratum. This is contrary to the position taken more recently by such Marxist scholars as Shivji, Hirji, etc., (even though they had earlier also made this dichotomy, and in fact concurred with the general observation that the political leadership stratum had demonstrated their commitment to socialism in Tanzania). They lump the two strata together in an attempt to establish the external linkages between the petty-bourgeoisie and international capitalism (which they consider to be the decisive link). They see this as a vindication of their indictment of this stratum for having failed to bring about a structural transformation of Tanzanian society. This they attribute to the failure of the petty-bourgeoisie to grasp the all-important fact that the motive force behind such a structural transformation lies in class struggle itself. We have argued, perhaps in a rather impressionistic manner given the present state of research, that these two strata are separate both in their ideological orientation and, by extension, in the level of commitment to the cause of socialism – granted we need more evidence to establish the empirical validity of our postulate. The same is perhaps also true of the linkages we have tried to establish in this study. But the fact remains that the political leadership in Tanzania has often attacked the bureaucracy in rather strong terms, not unlike the attacks on the bureaucracy articulated by the Chinese during the Cultural Revolution. Thus, for example, following the President's policy statement on decentralization on May 1972, already referred to in this study, the President declares:

> There is, however, one danger which must be guarded against. The transfer of power to the Regions and the

> Districts must not also mean the transfer of a rigid and bureaucratic system from Dar es Salaam to the lower levels . . . It is essential that this should be understood by everyone, for those who cause the new system to become enmeshed in bureaucratic procedures, will, as they are discovered, be treated as what they will be – saboteurs.[2]

Therefore, notwithstanding the limitations noted above, we have provided a limited amount of evidence in this study from post-Arusha Tanzania that can be used to throw light on some general trends. In this regard, we should perhaps remind ourselves of Lucien Pye's modest but agonizing observations, albeit in a different context:

> . . . our awareness of the possibilities of sophisticated techniques of investigation has made us uncomfortable with loose and broad generalizations. Paradoxically however, with our methodological sophistication we have also come to appreciate fully the intellectual reasons why dynamic modes of analysis, so essential for understanding the development process, are inherently more difficult, and to some degree beyond our current capabilities, if the highest standards of rigor are to be maintained.[3]

This brings us to our other major observation. We have argued, contrary to the more conventional Marxist line both from within and without Tanzania, that the fundamental contradictions in Tanzanian society are first and foremost the internal contradictions (particularly the contradiction between the political leadership and the bureaucratic bourgeoisie strata which is conditioned by the ideological gap between the two strata), and not in the content and nature of the relationship of Tanzania's economy with international capitalism. Nevertheless, we are quick to point out that we do recognize the importance of the internal links – in spite of the fact that the links are usually judged by their external essence and very often without taking into account the total context in which they appear. The internal contradictions which aid and abet these links are usually left in the background, since they are not considered to be the decisive points in the causal chain. By establishing the primacy of the internal contradictions

220

we are able to show why progress towards socialist transformation has been haltingly slow. This is in spite of the fact that there has evolved over the years in post-Arusha Tanzania a relatively (i.e., when compared to other African countries) clear and coherent socialist framework on which to base the practical programmes of action. We do not mean to imply, by emphasizing the internal contradictions, that factors other than the ideological gap between the two strata play no important role. On the contrary, we noted throughout this study that such factors as shortage of skilled manpower (whether qualified teachers or technical experts), the impact of colonialism on indigenous productive forces and social relations (in short, the historical perspective), etc., act as powerful constraints on the possibility of a rapid progress towards economic independence and socialism in Tanzania. To emphasize the primacy of the internal contradictions is to postulate that a resolution of these internal contradictions and constraints will necessarily mean, at least in the long run (if not in the short run), first the loosening and then the breaking off of the dependency ties with international capitalism.

To the extent that there are other powerful constraints (besides the question of incongruency between political ideology and the practical programmes of action) that have vitiated against any rapid progress towards economic independence and socialism, our thesis appears only to be partly supported. However, this is more apparent than real. In the first place, it is highly unlikely, judging from the experience of many of the other non-revolutionary Black African states, that the little progress that there is in Tanzania's attempts to institutionalize socialism, would have occurred in the absence of what can best be described as a more clearly evolving theory of socialism in post-Arusha Tanzania. More importantly, the failure to rapidly institutionalize socialism lies more at the level of policy implementation, largely as a result of the confusion created by the lack of a clear ideological framework as well as national guidelines, than at either the theoretical or programme level which, needless to say, did not form part of our postulate. Nevertheless, what this does suggest is that the links between ideology and practice have perhaps not been made clear enough to the implementors. This means that the implementation of such a socialist strategy requires a further refinement and clarification to the nevertheless continually refined ideology. To be sure, a clearer statement of what socialism means, especially in relation to practical implementation, becomes imperative.

We established the need for a clearer ideological statement to guide policy implementors in the other areas of our study. We found, for instance, that there was neither a clear national industrial strategy nor any clear national guidelines on which the NDC, for example, could base the implementation of its task of socialist construction. This, in turn, gave the managerial sector (or the bureaucratic bourgeoisie) of the NDC the added impetus to implement the programmes under its jurisdiction not in accordance with socialist objectives, as defined by the political leadership, but rather to further entrench their relatively privileged positions. In the absence of a clear national guideline the NDC could absolve itself of any wrongdoings in such areas as the indiscriminate hiring of foreign consultants and teachers; defend its subservient role within the partnership arrangements; and justify uncritical approval of aid projects as well as the indiscriminate acceptance of aid regardless of its source, with all the attendant ramifications for the socialist objectives of Tanzania. Thus we established that one of the more important factors that tends to reinforce the economic dependence of Tanzania on the rich countries, particularly within the capitalist system (given the nature of its trade and aid pattern which has been so graphically illustrated), results from the partnership relationship between domestic (i.e., national) and foreign private enterprises. We showed, for example, that foreign enterprise has a distinct advantage *vis-à-vis* domestic enterprise with respect to technology, know-how, markets, finance, etc.; often their monopolistic control of nearly all of these factors accounts for their interest in investing in the poor countries of the Third World in general. Besides, it is within the interest of foreign private enterprise to maintain the conditions in which its activities or its aid are essential, for considerable monetary rewards accrue to its monopoly of productive techniques and expertise. Indeed, we noted that the incentives are often structured in such a way that it is usually not in the interest of a foreign partner or firm to want to impart to a domestic counterpart the knowledge, skills or advantages upon which its commercial success is based. Under such circumstances, domestic enterprise remains in a subordinate position and the indigenous managerial sector remains dependent upon the foreign partners, as indeed the NDC's management has now come to find itself. Consequently, the interests of the NDC are no longer in accordance with the socialist goals of Tanzania but, rather, become associated willy-nilly with that of their foreign partners.

Although some progress was made during the period of our study on various facets of the education system, following the educational reforms in post-Arusha Tanzania, it was not sufficient to contribute effectively towards finding solutions to some of the above problems – especially in the area of middle- and high-level manpower supply. Not only were the institutions of higher learning unable to produce enough socialist cadres but, more importantly, they were largely ill-prepared for the task. It was shown, for instance, that teachers and students alike saw education as a means to status and wealth, and that a large percentage of the expatriate teachers remained unsympathetic to socialism. It is pertinent to note that various researchers, including Lema and Mbilinyi, found that the most disturbing aspect of their findings was 'the evidence that the old attitudes which venerate academic education as a symbol of wealth and status are still held by a large number of school teachers themselves.'[4] This, of course, does not deny the fact that the post-Arusha educational reforms produced a measure of success. Even Lema was quick to point out that many teachers, pupils and parents expressed the feeling that education was now for the first time developing in the 'right direction for Tanzanian society.'[5] Nevertheless, given the strong evidence of the veneration of academic education as a symbol of wealth and status, the presence of a large number of non-sympathetic expatriate teaching staff (see especially Table 13, Chapter 6) cannot help but reinforce undesirable attitudes. More importantly, the fact still remains that the graduates who go through this kind of educational system find themselves in managerial positions not only in the NDC but in nearly all the other dominant sectors of the nation. Thus even with the limited evidence allowed us by the present state of data, it is fair to deduce that a significant number of the graduates of these institutions are more likely to form links with the bureaucratic bourgeoisie stratum than any other stratum of the society. Furthermore, we noted that this linkage is not limited only to the urban centres. Given the fact that they also occupy strategic positions (such as Regional and District Commissioners, etc.), linkages exist in the rural sector. There have been reports (though there has not been any documented evidence to this effect) of close relationships between these officers and the 'kulak' members of rural Tanzania in such areas as Ismani and parts of Bukoba.

While some may argue that the linkage role we ascribe to the unsympathetic expatriate teaching staff is based on very limited empirical evidence and hence the link is at best a tenuous one, we would like to suggest that the goal of institutionalizing socialism in Tanzania cannot begin with the appointment, for example, of the Harvard-based Development Advisory Service whose assumptions and methods are most likely to reflect their service to the inherited structures of colonialism and neo-colonialism.* The case of the non-socialist oriented expatriate teacher, we are inclined to think, is no different. They both are steeped in the same capitalist ethos and have both internalized the same. This is not intended as a criticism of capitalism but simply a restatement of a logical truism.

This leads us to our next observation – the Ujamaa Vijijini programme. We examined the Ujamaa village as a socio-economic institution and its place and role in the general task of socialist construction, particularly in rural Tanzania. This revealed that there is a long way to go to establish the credibility of the hitherto widely accepted view that the programme is intended to act as a lever in the transformation of the countryside along socialist lines (through the mobilization and institutionalization of popular forces) as expounded principally in the Arusha Declaration and in other policy documents of the party and its leadership. In many ways we found that the planning and implementation of the Ujamaa programme has tended to be overshadowed by the older 'improvement' and 'transformation' policies. Thus, despite the socialist thrust of the political leadership, a great deal of the agricultural effort and the major planned output increases, during this period, have been focused on the expansion and extension of primary export production, with the hope that it contains enough dynamic demand potential to transform agriculture. We have argued that the Ujamaa Village programme is designed to provide a social and institutional framework for building socialism. But

* Conversations this author had with some Tanzanians with links to the Development Advisory Service did confirm the general view that the services of the Harvard-based firm were of little use to the developmental problems of Tanzania.

success requires that the Ujamaa village must not only be the framework through which indigenous science and technology are developed and applied to economic activity (agricultural as well as non-agricultural), it must be the institution where the organic link between resource ownership, use and demand is forged.

Finally, consideration of the industrialization efforts in Tanzania led us to a discussion of the sensitive issue of the role of foreign aid during the period of transition to socialism. While conceding the fact that an augmentation of domestic resources by foreign resource inflows may speed up the domestic rate of economic development and thus the transformation process, we noted that the pattern of aid so far in Tanzania has vitiated this possibility because foreign resource inflows have tended to extend the role of foreign control, foreign techniques, and foreign decision-making in the national economy, and in many other ways to perpetuate underdevelopment. In the context of the transition to socialism the question arises of whether aid, irrespective of sources and the intentions of the donors, can avoid the manifestation of our malformations. This is less likely when the level of aid constitutes as high as 50 per cent of the government's development expenditure, even in recent years. Needless to say that even the government now finds the prevailing levels of actual dependence on foreign aid to be too high for comfort.

Another important matter was our consideration of the comparative experience between China (1950–60) and Tanzania (1967–72). This revealed that usually social scientists writing on the Tanzanian experience have portrayed the Chinese socialist model as coming closest to the objective ideal for Tanzania. Thus Marxists and non-Marxists alike have tended to assess Tanzania's efforts at planning for socialist development against this background. They have usually arrived at the conclusion that at best the Tanzanian model is a poor imitation of the Chinese model. However, this study has shown that while Tanzania cannot ignore to learn from the experience of other socialist countries, the differences of historical experiences between the two countries has been underplayed.

An Alternative Future Policy Option for Tanzania's Development Efforts

Tanzania does not suffer from a dearth of policy options in her development efforts. Two options have, however, featured most prominently. Thus, guided by the inherent logic of their kind of Marxist analysis, scholars like Shivji, Hirji, etc., have recommended a total disengagement for Tanzania in order to break away from the dependence relations she now finds herself in with international capitalism. However, in a world of increasing interdependence (though in many ways it is a non-symbiotic interdependence) it is difficult to see how such a policy can be maintained. We have therefore refused to accept this as a viable policy option.

This second option advanced by scholars like Szentes and Prebisch[6] calls for regional economic groupings or integration as a strategy to overcome the constraints imposed by national small markets and to take advantage of the economies of scale. To the extent that the level of national skilled manpower, the size of national markets, and the availability of other vital national resources constitute crucial constraints on the capacity for national development, the need for an economic grouping over a wider geographical area remains very appealing indeed. But appealing as this alternative may be, it assumes for one thing the existence of uniform historical conditions, so that such a collectivity would have equal or near equal bargaining powers with, for example, the multinational corporations. This would make collective exploitation of the collectivity by the multinationals virtually impossible. Above all, it assumes uniform ideological systems within the collectivity. It is, however, quite clear that those assumptions are at best very shaky. Thus 'it seems to us far more likely that many of the small underdeveloped areas will have to advance towards socialism in relative isolation from their neighbours, rather than in the context of a broad sweep of nations simultaneously moving in that direction . . . [Besides] in the process of socialist transformation integration can only play a meaningful role if it is based on simultaneous changes in the relations of production and the development of productive forces over contiguous areas. The prospect of this occurring seems very unlikely.'[7] It is instructive that the East African Community had to break up in the end.

It is against this backdrop that we offer an alternative. Our preferred policy option reflects a recognition of the primacy of the economic factor in any effective programme of socialist construction. Because foreign aid forms a critical component of development efforts in Tanzania, any corrective measures taken to change the present pattern of aid in Tanzania is more likely to advance the institutionalization of socialism. Against this background our policy option focus on foreign aid comes into clear relief. However, even though we seem to be emphasizing foreign aid in our policy option, our study suggests that the internal contradictions that exist between the political leadership and the bureaucratic bourgeoisie strata; the constraints that bear heavily on any planned implementation of a national integrated economy by such factors as the lack of an industrial strategy; the lack of clear national ideological guidelines; the dearth of skilled manpower, etc., must be tackled simultaneously with our policy prescription for foreign aid. In other words, a mere reversal of the foreign aid pattern without a parallel serious attempt at resolving the internal contradictions and constraints would prove futile. The emphasis on foreign aid stems, as already noted, from the fact that it forms a major part of the development efforts and hence there is prominent interplay between it and the internal contradictions.

Foreign aid does harm a critical component of the development efforts in Tanzania. It is found in all the major interstices of the developmental chain. But we have seen that the problem in Tanzania is not one of goal – the goal is socialism.

Now given that a socialist development strategy explicitly calls for structural transformation, a socialist aid strategy must also explicitly select its donors according to the degree to which structural change is likely to result from the implementation of aided projects. This, we believe, is commonsensical, too. Indeed, the results of such an aid strategy can be seen in the aid policies of other socialist countries like China, Cuba, North Korea, etc. The test of the usefulness of a specific aid package lies in the extent to which it contributes to both long- and short-term economic social goals, particularly those related to making a structural change in the economy and a break with dependency on the donor. Yet much of Tanzania's aid agreements during the period of our study and indeed beyond were concluded for projects which tended to reflect and buttress her dependence upon and integration into the orbits of the industrialized capitalist centres. Therefore, based on the above evidence, our policy option is to recommend that Tanzania's aid pattern be drastically revised to permit a decisive ideological shift from the present aid policy, which appears to give the impression of a non-aligned aid strategy of maintaining a fine balance between East and West. We will concede that our view is not without its limitations, particularly with reference to the question of dependence and self-reliance. It is quite probable that in the short run, at least, Tanzania may find herself equally dependent on her socialist aid donors, as both the experiences of China (before the rupture with the Soviet Union in 1960) and Cuba tend to show. Here, too, there will be limitations on the credibility of self-reliance. Nevertheless, in the long run such a decisive ideological shift will prove more compatible with the socialist goals of Tanzania, again as the examples of China and North Korea tend to show, provided of course (we would re-iterate) it is preceded or accompanied by the emergence and institutionalization of a more systematic, clear and coherent ideological framework than has been achieved so far. Therefore, in the words of the President himself, 'to plan is to choose', and it is high time Tanzania made the decisive choice.

Chapter 7 Conclusion

1. Ralph Miliband, *Marxism and Politics* (Oxford: Oxford University Press, 1977), pp. 29–30.
2. *Daily News*, Tanzania, May 14, 1972.
3. L. W. Pye, 'The Concept of Political Development,' *The Annals of the American Academy of Political and Social Science*, Vol. 358, March 1965, p. 4.
4. A. A. Lema, 'Education for Self-Reliance: A Brief Survey of Self-Reliant Activities in Some Tanzanian Schools and Colleges,' Institute of Education, University of Dar es Salaam, 1972, p. 51.
5. *Ibid.*
6. See for example, R. Prebisch, *Towards a Dynamic Development Policy for Latin America* (New York: United Nations, 1964).
7. C. Y. Thomas, *Dependence and Transformation* (New York: Monthly Review Press, 1974), pp. 276 and 284.

Appendix A

Scale   1:6,500,0000

Appendix B

Enrolments At Different Levels Of Education In Public Institutions 1963–72[1]

Level of Education	1963	1964	1965	1966	1967	1968	1969	1970	1971	1972 Estimate	1974 (Target)
A. PRIMARY EDUCATION:											
(i) Std. I Input	136,496	140,341	149,341	154,512	157,196	155,802	157,986	172,576	190,091	205,000	208,400
(ii) Std. VII Output	18,444	24,637	33,892	46,886	51,460	75,381	60,790	65,624	70,502	85,000	107,900
(iii) Std. I–VIII Population [2]	592,104	633,678	710,200	740,991	753,114	765,169	776,109	827,974	902,609	982,000	1,140,000
(iv) No. of Teachers all grades	11,100	12,044	13,576	14,809	15,271	16,787	16,577	17,790	20,819	23,400	25,400
B. SECONDARY AND TECHNICAL:											
(a) *Teacher Education:*											
(i) Form I Intake	4,972	5,302	5,942	6,377	5,635	6,989	7,149	7,372	7,570	7,740	8,160
(ii) Form IV Output	2,839	3,630	4,558	4,720	5,004	5,763	6,328	6,713	7,044	7,300	7,300
(iii) Form V Intake	297	604	780	828	895	1,214	1,410	1,506	1,608	1,670	1,870
(iv) Form VI Output	275	463	606	768	808	929	1,226	1,389	1,436	1,600	1,730
(v) Form I–VI Population	17,176	19,897	21,915	23,836	25,551	28,043	29,958	31,217	32,603	33,500	34,500
(vi) No. of Teachers all Grades	817	858	1,064	1,151	1,306	1,336	1,474	1,658	1,706	1,800	1,900
(b) *Technical Education:*											
Dar es Salaam Technical College	234	518	697	515	577	598	501	639	652	800	1,000
(c) *Teacher Training all Courses:*											
First Year	933	1,180	1,135	1,390	1,228	1,292	1,603	2,328	2,826	2,950	2,850
C. HIGHER EDUCATION[3]:–											
(i) Intake – Universities in East Africa	109	173	330	369	511	563	613	704	710	780	1,200

(ii) Output – Universities in East Africa	23	86	73	107	174	303	341	559	582	650	760
(iii) Intake – Overseas ...	335	303	246	137	190	108	139	472	479	350	273
(iv) Output – Overseas ...	200	335	274	368	330	143	104	120	444	570	100
U.E.A. Enrolment (all faculties)	305	407	642	740	1,313	1,498	1,975	2,028	2,090	2,230	2,790
At Universities Overseas ...	675	720	778	807	713	611	812	1,522[4]	1,561[4]	1,720[4]	1,200

Source:– Ministry of National Education, Directorate of Planning and Development.

[1] Excluding non-graduate courses except Universities overseas which include non-graduate courses.

[2] Standard VIII was discontinued from 1968 onwards.

[3] THIRD LEVEL (HIGHER EDUCATION):
The University of East Africa was split into three autonomous Universities in July, 1970. This institution of Higher Education in Tanzania is referred to as THE UNIVERSITY OF DAR ES SALAAM.

[4] Includes Diploma courses.

Appendix C

Value, Volume And Price Trends Of Six Major Agricultural Exports of Tanzania (Mainland), 1965–1975

	1965	1966	1967	1968	1969	1970	1971	1972	1973	1974	1975
Value (Millions of Shillings)											
Cotton	244.2	349.9	251.4	282.9	234.4	247.2	244.8	336.4	333.1	472.6	296.7
Coffee	171.8	301.0	237.0	265.0	257.0	312.0	227.0	383.0	495.3	375.1	483.0
Sisal	285.6	234.7	200.9	158.7	159.7	178.8	133.8	144.8	221.6	463.4	302.2
Cashewnuts (raw)	82.5	100.0	92.2	101.6	118.9	115.2	119.6	150.3	141.2	196.2	176.9
Tea	30.2	45.1	43.2	44.9	48.3	42.2	48.9	53.8	54.2	69.1	81.2
Tobacco, unmanufactured	22.6	23.4	39.2	40.2	38.7	59.5	60.3	64.8	67.7	133.6	117.6
Total	836.9	1,054.1	863.9	893.3	857.3	954.9	834.4	1,133.1	1,313.1	1,710.0	1,457.6
Percent Share of Mainland Exports	59.0	59.4	52.2	56.2	54.7	58.7	50.0	54.3	57.0	63.0	59.9
Volume (Thousands of Metric Tons)											
Cotton	56.2	86.2	60.8	62.9	56.7	60.7	54.8	64.5	60.0	49.1	38.0
Coffee	28.2	50.6	44.4	49.2	49.5	44.8	35.5	54.7	60.3	41.0	54.4
Sisal	213.6	198.9	204.4	189.1	171.9	217.2	160.8	153.1	113.4	93.4	101.6
Cashewnuts (raw)	64.6	72.2	70.9	79.7	82.2	77.4	95.9	112.9	109.9	114.0	97.3
Tea	4.3	6.3	6.1	6.7	7.6	6.9	8.3	9.2	9.5	9.6	10.4
Tobacco, unmanufactured	3.3	3.4	4.9	5.2	5.0	7.7	6.6	7.1	7.2	12.1	8.6
Unit Prices (Shillings per Ton)											
Cotton	4,345.2	4,059.2	4,134.9	4,497.6	4,139.3	4,072.5	4,467.2	5,215.5	5,551.7	9,625.2	7,807.9
Coffee	6,092.2	5,948.6	5,337.8	5,336.2	5,191.9	6,964.3	6,394.4	7,001.8	8,213.9	9,148.8	8,878.7
Sisal	1,337.1	1,180.0	982.9	839.2	929.0	823.2	832.1	945.8	1,954.1	4,961.5	2,974.4

Cashewnuts (raw)	1,227.1	1,385.0	1,300.4	1,274.8	1,446.5	1,488.4	1,247.1	1,331.3	1,284.8	1,721.1	1,818.1
Tea	7,023.3	7,158.7	7,082.0	6,701.5	6,355.3	6,115.9	5,891.6	5,847.8	5,705.3	7,197.9	7,807.7
Tobacco, unmanufactured	6,848.5	6,882.3	8,000.0	7,730.8	7,740.0	7,727.3	9,136.4	9,126.8	9,402.8	11,041.3	13,674.4

Source: East African Customs and Excise Department, *Annual Trade Reports of Tanzania, Uganda and Kenya*, and the *Economic Surveys*, various issues.

Appendix D

Gross Domestic Product By Industrial Origin, 1964–1975
(Shs. million at 1966 prices)

	1964	1965	1966	1967	1968	1969	1970	1971	1972	1973	Provisional 1974	Provisional 1975
Monetary Sector												
Agriculture, hunting, forestry & fishing	1,246	1,194	1,406	1,350	1,417	1,499	1,589	1,504	1,600	1,611	1,537	1,567
Mining and quarrying	141	163	186	192	136	135	97	134	97	74	70	60
Manufacturing and handicrafts	394	446	525	572	611	672	716	782	846	887	899	902
Electricity and water supply	51	53	62	66	72	82	92	96	98	114	123	133
Construction	142	148	173	238	256	236	270	322	329	363	357	320
Transport, storage & communication	301	400	482	536	618	644	729	814	852	889	944	956
Wholesale and retail trade & restaurants and hotels	670	710	825	816	912	914	984	996	990	1,068	1,096	1,110
Finance, insurance, real estate & business services	146	177	165	241	230	253	257	279	292	316	361	325
Public administration & other services	620	658	688	741	764	772	866	952	1,071	1,158	1,310	1,510
Less expected bank service charges	32	48	49	98	80	85	99	115	115	136	140	122
Monetary GDP at factor cost	3,765	3,901	4,463	4,654	4,936	5,122	5,501	5,764	6,060	6,344	6,557	6,761
Subsistence Production												
Agriculture, hunting, forestry & fishing	1,377	1,381	1,547	1,605	1,660	1,590	1,616	1,662	1,825	1,847	1,807	1,997
Construction	48	50	51	52	53	55	57	58	60	61	63	64
Owner-occupied dwellings	429	441	453	466	479	492	506	521	536	551	568	585
Total subsistence production	1,854	1,872	2,051	2,123	2,192	2,137	2,179	2,241	2,421	2,459	2,438	2,646
(?? at former cost (1966 prices)	5,619	5,773	6,514	6,777	7,128	7,259	7,680	8,005	8,481	8,803	8,995	9,407
(Annual rate of growth)	(. .)	(2.7)	(12.8)	(4.0)	(5.2)	(1.8)	(5.8)	(4.2)	(5.9)	(3.8)	(2.2)	(4.6)

Source: National Accounts of Tanzania, 1964–72 and The Economic Surveys

Appendix E

Disbursements of External Public and Publicly Guaranteed Debt, 1967–1975
(Thousands of US dollars)

					Disbursements				
	1967	*1968*	*1969*	*1970*	*1971*	*1972*	*1973*	*1974*	*1975*
Type of Creditor									
Suppliers' Credits	–	667	13971	3784	6676	–	–	–	–
Private Bank Credits	19804	6753	1202	171	–	2993	1207	–	–
Other Private Debt	6228	8505	16860	5194	833	–	–	–	–
Loans from International									
Organizations:	6545	5316	8702	10661	15323	18559	12580	22748	65226
African Development Bank	–	–	–	–	–	2474	505	1487	681
Arab Fund for Econ. & Social Dev.	–	–	–	–	–	–	–	7100	7100
IBRD	–	792	1685	1242	7245	13354	9021	8263	39715
IDA	6545	4524	7017	9419	8078	2731	3054	5895	17730
Loans from Governments:	10122	8845	15261	30043	32554	80401	84877	115269	164210
Bulgaria	–	–	–	–	–	–	–	–	1057
Canada	387	–	1503	681	704	1450	5596	25032	18902
China, People's Republic of	3140	972	2914	9681	6192	58453	53727	60414	74235
Czechoslovakia	–	–	–	–	–	–	–	–	–
Denmark	–	–	577	2225	1985	1373	1067	9356	14178
Finland	–	–	–	–	–	481	853	869	7212
Germany, Dem. Rep. of	–	–	77	–	–	2767	–	–	–
Germany, Fed. Rep. of	688	18	20	–	2407	1186	1729	2959	15426
India	–	–	–	–	–	–	–	–	–
Israel	–	–	67	–	–	–	–	–	–
Italy	–	–	–	5600	4441	–	–	–	–
Japan	–	625	942	344	217	484	1833	1731	17
Kuwait	–	–	–	–	–	–	–	–	–

Appendix E (cont)

Netherlands	–	–	–	–	629	905	3673	5023	10606
Sweden	715	358	5534	5585	8666	7628	11620	5520	2829
United Kingdom	898	–	–	–	–	751	–	–	–
United States	4077	6838	2292	4689	6999	4554	2023	2767	19277
USSR	217	34	139	1238	314	369	453	439	470
Zambia	–	–	1196	–	–	–	–	–	–
Multiple Lenders	–	–	–	–	–	–	2303	1159	–
Grand Total	42699	30086	55996	49853	55386	101953	98664	138017	229436

Source: IBRD, External Debt Division.

Appendix F

Commitments Of External Public Loans And Grants By Sources, 1967–75
(Thousands of US dollars)

	Commitments								
	1967	*1968*	*1969*	*1970*	*1971*	*1972*	*1973*	*1974*	*1975*
Type of Creditor									
Suppliers' Credits	–	14894	10140	3086	–	–	–	–	–
Private Bank Credits	15451	2400	1384	–	–	4200	–	–	–
Public Issued Bonds	–	–	–	–	–	–	–	–	–
Other Private Debt	6228	2973	16860	5194	833	–	–	–	–
Loans from International									
Organizations:	5200	4300	27500	39000	9800	14057	24389	133300	47100
African Development Bank	–	–	–	–	–	3257	1789	–	–
Arab Fund for Econ. & Social Dev.	–	–	–	–	–	–	–	7100	7100
IBRD	5200	–	7000	30000	–	–	–	65000	30000
IDA	–	4300	20500	9000	9800	10800	22600	61200	10000
Loans from Governments	17794	20404	48762	232530	25393	47117	82757	127136	91269
Bulgaria	–	–	–	–	–	3000	3000	–	–
Canada	416	–	925	2675	2079	7419	57606	–	4327
China, People's Republic of	–	799	1999	200811	–	1876	–	76458	–
Czechoslovakia	–	–	–	–	–	–	–	–	5428
Denmark	5677	–	–	–	5398	–	–	15612	17442
Finland	–	–	–	–	–	5285	–	2662	7611
Germany, Fed. Rep. of	–	38	–	–	3731	–	14534	17091	8148
India	–	–	–	–	–	6595	–	–	–
Israel	–	67	–	–	–	–	–	–	–
Italy	–	–	10000	–	–	10860	–	–	–
Japan	–	5600	–	–	–	–	–	–	–
Kuwait	–	–	–	–	–	–	–	–	15517
Netherlands	–	–	–	–	1028	5296	3955	14154	7927
Sweden	6572	–	17977	18944	6457	–	–	–	4829
United Kingdom	196	–	–	–	–	751	–	–	–

United States	1600	13900	–	10100	6700	4900	2600	–	20040
USSR	3333	–	16665	–	–	–	–	–	–
Zambia	–	–	1196	–	–	–	–	–	–
Multiple Lenders	–	–	–	–	–	1135	1062	1159	–
Loans – Total	44673	44971	104646	279810	36026	65374	107146	260436	138369
Source of Grants:									
Multilateral Agencies	2990	2990	3050	4480	3300	4490	5110	6600	10130
U.N. Development Program	–	–	–	–	–	–	–	2980	3740
U.N. Regular Program	2990	2990	3050	–	–	200	3030	520	410
U.N. Children's Fund	–	–	–	140	180	320	400	470	790
U.N. FAO World Food	–	–	–	450	280	410	190	340	1460
U.N. High Commission on Refugees	–	–	–	3400	2210	2780	1360	2290	3480
Other United Nations	–	–	–	490	630	780	100	–	250
European Development Fund	–	–	–	–	–	–	30	–	–
Governments	28180	17770	18010	19820	23560	25200	37350	55010	89870
Australia	120	90	100	100	80	80	80	150	790
Austria	20	30	10	20	10	30	20	–	–
Belgium	–	10	20	10	10	20	–	10	40
Canada	1430	1790	1670	1460	2340	3480	3910	3490	6130
Denmark	730	760	850	1280	1480	2680	4080	5520	5840
Finland	–	–	–	–	–	–	–	–	5800
Germany, Federal Republic of	5150	3220	3620	3540	4180	3620	5620	7790	10550
Italy	30	30	30	30	450	–	100	370	60
Japan	20	180	250	330	670	710	730	1020	1880
Netherlands	–	–	–	–	1130	900	2560	3360	5120
New Zealand	–	–	–	–	–	–	–	–	30
Norway	410	410	440	750	1390	2910	3480	6890	10760
Sweden	1630	1760	1560	2990	2110	3180	9110	17540	29500
Switzerland	20	60	220	180	410	170	210	470	310
United Kingdom	7620	2430	4240	4130	4300	3420	3450	3400	3060
United States	11000	7000	5000	5000	5000	4000	4000	5000	7000
Grants – Total	31170	20760	21060	24300	26860	29690	42460	61610	100000

Source: IBRD, External Debt Division.

Selected Bibliography

Books

Ake, Claude. 'The Congruence of Political Economies and Ideologies in Africa.' *The Political Economy of Contemporary Africa*. Edited by Gutkind and Wallerstein. Beverly Hills: Sage Publications, 1976.

Agger, Robert. *The Rulers and The Ruled*. New York: John Wiley & Sons, 1964.

Aiken, H. *The Age of Ideology*. New York: New American Library, 1956.

Almond, G., and Powell, G. *Politics: A Developmental Approach*. Boston: Little, Brown and Co., 1966.

Althusser, L. *For Marx*. New York: Vintage Books, 1970.

Amin, S. *Accumulation on a World Scale*. London: Monthly Review Press, 1974.

Andreski, S. *The African Predicament*. London: Michael Joseph, 1969.

Arrighi, G. 'Nationalism and Revolution in Tropical Africa.' *Socialist Registrar*. Edited by Miliband and Savile. London: Merlin Press, 1969.

———— 'International Corporations, Labour Aristocracies and Economic Development in Tropical Africa.' *Imperialism and Underdevelopment*. Edited by R. Rhodes. New York: Monthly Review Press, 1970.

———— and Saul, J. S. *The Political Economy of Africa*. New York: Monthly Review Press, 1973.

Avineri, S., ed. *Karl Marx on Colonialism and Modernization*. New York: Doubleday, 1969.

Bachrach, Peter. *The Theory of Democratic Elitism: A Critique*. Boston: Little, Brown and Co., 1967.

Baran, P. A. *The Political Economy of Growth*. New York: Modern Reader Paperbacks, 1968.

Barnet, Doak. *Chinese Communist Politics in Action.* Seattle: University of Washington Press, 1969.

Bauman, Z. *Socialism: The Active Utopia.* London: George Allen and Unwin, 1976.

Bell, D. *The End of Ideology.* New York: Free Press, 1962.

Bendix, R. *Nation-Building and Citizenship.* New York: John Wiley and Sons, 1964.

Benham, F. *Economic Aid to Underdeveloped Countries.* Oxford: Reprint, 1962.

Bernstein, E. ed. *Development and Underdevelopment.* London: Penguin, 1973.

Bernstein, E. ed. *Evolutionary Socialism.* New York: Schocken Books, 1961.

Bettelheim, C., and Sweezy, Paul. *On Transition to Socialism.* New York: Monthly Review Press, 1971.

Bienen, H. *Tanzania: Party Transformation and Economic Development.* Princeton: Princeton University Press, 1967.

Bottomore, T. B. *Elites and Society.* London: C. A. Watts and Co., 1964.

——— and Rubel, M. *Karl Marx: Selected Writings in Sociology and Social Philosophy.* Harmondsworth: Penguin Books, 1965.

Brett, E. A. *Colonialism and Underdevelopment in East Africa.* London: Heinemann, 1972.

Buber, M. *Paths in Utopia.* Boston: Beacon Press, 1949.

Cabral, A. *Revolution in Guinea.* London: Stage 1, 1969.

——— *National Liberation and Culture.* Syracuse: Syracuse University Press, 1970.

Cameron, John, and Dodd, W. A. *Society, Schools and Progress in Tanzania.* Oxford: Pergamon Press, 1970.

Carpenter, N. *Guild Socialism.* London: D. Appleton and Co., 1922.

Cliffe, L. 'Socialist Education in Tanzania.' *Education and Political Values.* Edited by K. Prewitt. Nairobi: East African Publishing House, 1971.

———; Saul, John; Lawrence, Peter; and Luttrell, W. *Rural Cooperation in Tanzania.* Dar es Salaam: Tanzania Publishing House, 1975.

——— and Cunningham, G. 'Ideology, Organisation and the Settlement Experience in Tanzania.' *Socialism in Tanzania.* 2 vols. Edited by Cliffe and Saul. Nairobi: East African Publishing House, 1973.

Coates, K. *Workers' Control.* London: Panther Modern Society, 1968.

Cockroft, J. D., and Frank, G. *Dependence and Underdevelopment: Latin America's Political Economy.* New York: Doubleday and Company, 1972.

Cohn-Bendit, D., and Cohn-Bendit, G. *Obsolete Communism: The Left-wing Alternative.* Translated by Arnold Pomerans. London: Andre Deutsch, 1968

Cole, G. D. H. *Case for Industrial Partnership.* London: Macmillan,

1957.
———— *Guild Socialism*. London: Fabian Society, 1920.
———— *Guild Socialism Restated*. London: L. Parson, 1920.
———— *A History of Socialist Thought*. 5 volumes. London: Macmillan, 1953.
———— *Self-Government in Industry*. London: D. Bell and Sons, 1918.
———— *Social Theory*. London: Methuen, 1923.
Coombs, P. H., and Manzoor, A. *Attacking Rural Poverty: New Informal Education Can Help*. The Johns Hopkins University Press, 1974.
Cox, I. *Socialist Ideas in Africa*. London: Lawrence and Wishart, 1966.
Cox, O. *Caste, Class and Race*. New York: Monthly Review Press, 1970.
———— *Capitalism as a System*. New York: Monthly Review Press, 1964.
Dahl, R. *After the Revolution*. New Haven: Yale University Press, 1970.
———— *A Preface to Democratic Theory*. Chicago: University of Chicago Press, 1965.
Dahrendorf, R. *Class and Class Conflict in Industrial Society*. Stanford: Stanford University Press, 1957.
Davidson, B. *The Liberation of Guinea*. Harmondsworth: Penguin, 1969.
———— *In the Eye of the Storm*. London: Longmans, 1972.
Davis, H. B. *Nationalism and Socialism*. New York: Monthly Review Press, 1967.
Dawson, Richard and Prewitt, K. *Political Socialization*. Boston: Little, Brown and Company, 1969.
Desfosses, H. and Levesque, J., eds. *Socialism in the Third World*. New York: Praeger Publishers, 1965.
Dodd, William A. *Education for Self-Reliance in Tanzania: A Study of Its Vocational Aspects*. New York: Teachers' College Press, 1969.
Dos Santos, Theotonio. 'The Structure of Dependence.' *Readings in U.S. Imperialism*. Edited by K. Fann and D. Hodges. Boston: Porter Sargent Publishers, 1971.
Drachkovitch, M. M., ed. *Marxist Ideology in the Contemporary World: Its Appeals and Paradoxes*. New York: Frederick A. Praeger, 1966.
Dreeben, R. *On What Is Learned In School*. Reading, Massachusetts: Addison Wesley, 1968.
Dumont, R. *Socialisms and Development*. London: Andre Deutsch, 1973.
Dupre, Louis. *The Philosophical Foundations of Marxism*. New York: Harcourt, Brace and World, 1966.
Durkheim, E. *Socialism*. New York: Collier Books, 1962.
Easton, Loyd and Guddat, Kurt. Edited and Translated. *Writings of the Young Marx on Philosophy and Society*. New York: Doubleday Anchor, 1967.

Eckstein, A. *China's Economic Development*. Ann Arbor: Michigan University Press, 1975.

Edward, Richard. *The Capitalist System: A Radical Analysis of American Society*. Englewood Cliffs: Prentice-Hall, 1972.

Emmanuel, A. *Unequal Exchange*. London: New-Left Books, 1972.

Engels, F. *Anti-Duhring*. Peking: Foreign Language Press, 1976.

Etzioni, A., ed. *Complex Organisations: A Sociological Reader*. New York: Holt, Rinehart and Winston, 1962.

Fann, K. T. and Hodges, D. C., eds. *Readings in U.S. Imperialism*. Boston: Porter Sargent Publishers, 1971.

Fanon, F. *Toward the African Revolution*. Harmondsworth: Penguin Books, 1970.

———— *The Wretched of the Earth*. Harmondsworth: Penguin Books, 1967.

———— *A Dying Colonialism*. Harmondsworth: Penguin Books, 1970.

Feuer, L., ed. *Marx and Engels: Basic Writings on Politics and Philosophy*. New York: Doubleday and Company, 1959.

Finucane, J. R. *Rural Development and Bureaucracy in Tanzania: The Case of Nwanza Region*. Uppsala: The Scandinavian Institute of African Studies, 1974.

Fitch, Bob and Oppenheimer, Mary, eds. *Ghana: End of an Illusion*. New York: Monthly Review Press, 1966.

Foster, P. 'Education for Self-Reliance: A Critical Evaluation.' *Education in Africa: Research and Action*. Edited by R. Jolly. Nairobi: East African Publishing House, 1969.

Frank, G. 'The Development of Underdevelopment.' *Imperialism and Revolution*. Edited by I. Rhodes. New York: Monthly Review Press, 1970.

Frank, Gundar. *Capitalism and Underdevelopment in Latin America*. New York: Modern Reader Paperbacks, 1969.

———— *Latin America: Underdevelopment or Revolution*. New York: Modern Reader Paperbacks, 1970.

Freire, Paulo. *Education for Critical Consciousness*. New York: Seabury Press, 1973.

———— *Pedagogy of the Oppressed*. New York: Herder, 1970.

———— *Cultural Action for Freedom*. Cambridge: Harvard Educational Review, 1970.

Fried, Albert. *Socialist Thought*. New York: Doubleday Anchor, 1964.

Friedland, H. and Rosberg, Carl G., eds. *African Socialism*. Stanford: Stanford University Press, 1964.

Fromm, E., ed. *Socialist Humanism*. New York: Doubleday Anchor, 1965.

Furtado, Celso. *Economic Development of Latin America*. Cambridge: Cambridge University Press, 1970.

Garaudy, R. *Marxism in the Twentieth Century*. New York: Charles Scribner's Sons, 1970.

Geertz, C. *Old Societies and New States*. New York: Free Press, 1963.

Ghai, D. P. 'An Economic Survey.' *Portrait of Minority: Asians in East*

Africa. Edited by Ghai. Nairobi: Oxford University Press, 1965.

Giddens, Anthony. *The Class Structure of the Advanced Societies*. London: Hutchinson University Library, 1973.

Gorz, Andre. *Socialism and Revolution*. Translated by Norman Denny. New York: Anchor Books, 1973.

Gramsci, Antonio. *Selections from the Prison Notebooks of Antonio Gramsci*. Edited and translated by Quintin Hoare and Geoffrey Smith. New York: International Publishers, 1971.

Gupta, R. C. *Socialism, Democracy and India*. Agra: Ram Prasad and Sons, 1965.

Gutkind, Peter and Wallerstein, Immanual, eds. *The Political Economy of Contemporary Africa*. Beverly Hills: Sage Publications, 1976.

Gutkind, P. and Waterman, eds. *African Social Studies: A Radical Reader*. London: Heinemann, 1975.

Hall, R. *The High Price of Principle: Kaunda and the White South*. London: Hodder & Stoughton, 1969.

Hatch, John. *Two African Statesmen. Kaunda of Zambia and Nyerere of Tanzania*. London: Secker and Warburg, 1976.

Hayter, T. *Aid as Imperialism*. Harmondsworth: Penguin, 1971.

Hegel, G. W. F. *The Phenomenology of Mind*. Translated by J. Baillie. New York: Harper and Row, 1967.

Hinton, William, *Fanshen*. New York: Monthly Review Press, 1966.

Hirschman, A. O. and Bird, R. M. *Foreign Aid: A Critique and a Proposal*. Princeton, New Jersey: Princeton University Press, 1968.

Holt, R. T. and Turner, J. E. *The Political Basis of Economic Development*. New York: Van Nostrand Co., 1966.

Horowitz, Irving. *The New Sociology*. New York: Oxford University Press, 1965.

Howe, Irving, ed. *The Basic Writings of Trotsky*. New York: Vintage Books, 1965.

——— *The Radical Papers*. New York: Doubleday Anchor, 1965.

Hume, David. *A Treatise of Human Nature*, ed. by L. A. Selby-Bigge. Oxford: The Clarendon Press, 1888.

Hyden, G. *Political Development in Rural Tanzania*, Nairobi: East Africa Publishing House, 1969.

Ilife, J. *Agricultural Change in Modern Tanganyika*. Nairobi: East Africa Publishing House, 1971.

Illich, I. *Deschooling Society*. New York: Harper, 1971.

——— *Education Without Schools*. New York: Harper, 1973.

——— *Celebration of Awareness: A Call for Institutional Revolution*. Garden City, New York: Doubleday, 1970.

Ingle, C. P. *From Village to State: The Politics of Rural Development*. Cornell University Press, 1972.

Jalee, P. *The Pillage of The Third World*. New York: Monthly Review Press, 1968.

Third World in World Economy. New York: Monthly Review Press, 1969.

James, R. W. *Land Tenure and Policy in Tanzania*. Nairobi: East African Literature Bureau, 1971.

Johnson, Chalmers, ed. *Ideology and Politics in Contemporary China*. Seattle: University of Washington Press, 1973.

Johnson, D. L. 'Dependence and the International System.' *Dependence and Underdevelopment*. Edited by Cockcroft, Frank and Johnson. New York: Anchor Books, 1972.

Johnson, Harry. *Economic Policies Towards Less-developed Countries*. New York: Frederick A. Praeger, 1967.

Jolly, R., ed. *Education in Africa: Research and Action*. Nairobi: East African Publishing House, 1969.

Kahl, J. *The Measurement of Modernization: A Study of Values in Brazil and Mexico*. Austin: University of Texas Press, 1968.

Kautsky, John. *Communism and the Politics of Development*. New York: John Wiley and Sons, 1968.

Kautsky, Karl. *The Dictatorship of the Proletariat*. Ann Arbor: University of Michigan Press, 1964.

Kemp, Tom. *Theories of Imperialism*. London: Dobson, 1967.

Kropotkin, Peter. *Mutual Aid*. Edited by P. Avrich. New York: New York University Press, 1972.

Laidler, Harry. *History of Socialism*. New York: Crowell, 1968.

Lane, Robert. *Political Ideology*. New York: Free Press, 1962.

Lang, Oskar and Taylor, Fred M. *On the Economic Theory of Socialism*. New York: McGraw-Hill Book Company, 1964.

Lefebvre, Henri. *The Explosion: Marxism and the French Upheaval*. New York: Modern Reader Paperbacks, 1969.

Legum, Colin. *Pan-Africanism: A Short Political Guide*. London: Pall Mall Press, 1962.

Lewin, M. *The Russian Peasant and Soviet Power*. London: Allen and Unwin, 1968.

Lewis, W. Arthur. *The Theory of Economic Growth*. London: Allen and Unwin, 1955.

—— *Development Planning: The Essentials of Economic Policy*. London: Allen and Unwin, 1969.

—— *The Principles of Economic Planning*. New York: Harper and Row, 1969.

Leys, C. *Underdevelopment in Kenya*. London: Heinemann, 1975.

Lichtheim, George. *Marxism: An Historical and Critical Study*. New York: Praeger, 1961.

—— *The Origins of Socialism*. New York, Praeger, 1969.

Lindbeck, J. M. *China: Management of Revolutionary Society*. Seattle: University of Washington Press, 1971.

Lipset, Seymour. *Union Democracy*. New York: Doubleday Anchor, 1956.

—— *The Political Man*. New York: Doubleday, 1963.

Little, I. M. D. *Aid to Africa*. Pergamon Press, 1964.

Loxley, J. 'Financial Planning and Control in Tanzania.' *Towards Socialist Planning*. Edited by Rweyemamu and Loxley. Dar es Salaam: Tanzania Publishing House, 1972.

Lukacs, George. *History and Class Consciousness*. Cambridge: M.I.T.

Press, 1968.

Luxemburg, Rosa. *The Russian Revolution*. Ann Arbor: University of Michigan Press, 1970.

————— *The Accumulation of Capital*. New York: Monthly Review Press, 1964.

MacPherson, C. B. *The Political Theory of Possessive Individualism: Hobbes to Locke*. Oxford: Oxford University Press, 1962.

Magdoff, H. *The Age of Imperialism*. New York: Monthly Review Press, 1969.

Mandel, E. *Marxist Economic Theory*. New York: Monthly Review Press, 1969.

Mannheim, K. *Ideology and Utopia*. New York: Harcourt, Brace and World, 1936.

Manuel, Frank, ed. *Utopias and Utopian Thought*. Boston: Houghton Mifflin, 1965.

Marcuse, H. *Reason and Revolution*. Boston: Beacon Press, 1960.

Marx, K. *Capital*. Edited by F. Engels. 3 vols. New York: International Publishers, 1970.

————— *The Communist Manifesto*. Edited by S. Beer. New York: Appleton-Century-Crofts, 1955.

————— *The Economic and Philosophic Manuscripts of 1844*. Edited by D. Stuik. New York: International Publishers, 1964.

————— *Grundrisse*. Translated by M. Nicolaus. Harmondsworth: Penguin Books, 1973.

Marx, K. and Engels, F. *The German Ideology*. Moscow: Progress Publishers, 1968.

Mbilinyi, M. *Education of Girls in Tanzania*. Dar es Salaam: Institute of Education, 1969.

McLellan, David. *Marx Before Marxism*. Harmondsworth: Penguin Books, 1970.

Meir, G. M. *The International Economics of Development Theory and Policy*. New York: Harper and Row, 1968.

Merhav, Meir. *Technological Dependence, Monopoly and Growth*. London: Pergamon Press, 1969.

Meyer, Alfred. *Marxism: The Unity of Theory and Practice*. Ann Arbor: University of Michigan Press, 1963.

Mikesell, R. F. *The Economics of Foreign Aid*. Chicago: Aldine Publishing Co., 1968.

Miliband, Ralph. *The State in Capitalist Society*. London: Quartet Books, 1969.

————— *Marxism and Politics*. Oxford: Oxford University Press, 1977.

Mills, C. W. *The Power Elite*. New York: Oxford University Press, 1956.

————— *Power, Politics and People*. Edited by Irving Horowitz. New York: Ballantine Books, 1963.

Moore, Barrington. *Social Origins of Dictatorship and Democracy*. Boston: Beacon Press, 1966.

Mosca, Gaetano. *The Ruling Class*. Edited by A. Livingston.

Translated by H. Kahn. New York: McGraw-Hill, 1939.

Muhl, G. 'Education, Citizenship and Social Revolution in Tanzania.' *Education and Political Values*. Edited by K. Prewitt. Nairobi: East African Publishing House, 1971.

Myrdall, Jan. *Report from a Chinese Village*. Harmondsworth: Penguin Books, 1967.

Nellis, John. *A Theory of Ideology*. Nairobi: Oxford University Press, 1972.

Nielsen, W. A. *The Great Powers and Africa*. New York: Frederick A. Praeger, 1969.

Nkrumah, K. *Neocolonialism: The Last Stage of Imperialism*. London: Heinemann Educational Books, 1968.

————— *Class Struggles in Africa*. London: Panaf Books, 1970.

Nurkse, Ragnar. *Problems of Capital Formation in Underdeveloped Countries*. New York: Oxford University Press, 1970.

Nyerere, Julius K. *Education for Self-Reliance*. Dar es Salaam: Government Printer, 1967.

————— *Ujamaa: Essays on Socialism*. Nairobi: Oxford University Press, 1968.

————— *Freedom and Socialism: A Selection from Writings and Speeches 1965–1967*. Oxford: Oxford University Press, 1968.

————— *Freedom and Development: A Selection from Writings and Speeches 1968–73*. Oxford: Oxford University Press, 1973.

————— *Freedom and Unity: A selection from Writings and Speeches 1952–65*. Dar es Salaam: Oxford University Press, 1966.

————— *Socialism and Rural Development*. Dar es Salaam: Government Printer, 1967.

————— *Democracy and The Party System*. Dar es Salaam: Government Printer, 1963.

Oksenberg, Michael, ed. *China's Developmental Experience*. New York: Praeger, 1973.

Owen, Roger and Sutcliffe, Bob, eds. *Studies in the Theory of Imperialism*. London: Longmans, 1972.

Oxaal, I.; Barnett, T.; and Booth, David. *Beyond the Sociology of Development*. London: Routledge and Kegan Paul, 1975.

Pareto, Vilfredo. *Selections from his Treatise*. Edited by J. Lopreato. New York: Crowell, 1965.

Parsons, Talcott, *The Structure of Social Action*. 2 vols. New York: Free Press, 1968.

Plamenatz, J. *Man and Society*. London: Longmans, 1963.

Polanyi, Karl. *The Great Transformation*. Boston: Beacon Press, 1957.

Popper, Karl. *The Poverty of Historicism*. London: Routledge and Kegan Paul, 1957.

Pratt, Cranford. *The Critical Phase in Tanzania 1945–1968: Nyerere and the Emergence of a Socialist Strategy*. Cambridge: Cambridge University Press, 1976.

Prebisch, R. *Towards a Dynamic Development Policy for Latin America*. New York: United Nations, 1964.

Prewitt, K. *Education and Political Values*. Nairobi: East African
  Publishing House, 1971.
———— *Political Socialization*. Boston: Little, Brown and Company,
  1968.
Pye, Lucien, ed. *Communications and Political Development*. Prince-
  ton: Princeton University Press, 1963.
———— 'Mass Participation in Communist China: Its Limitations and
  the Continuity of Culture.' *Management of a Revolutionary Society*.
  Edited by J. M. Lindbeck. Seattle: University of Washington Press,
  1971.
Radetzki, M. *Aid and Development*. New York: Praeger, 1973.
Resnick, I., ed. *Tanzania: Revolution by Education*. Arusha: Longmans
  of Tanzania, 1968.
Rice, Edward. *Mao's Way*. Berkley: University of California Press,
  1972.
Robcock, S. H. *Brazil's Developing Northeast: A Study of Regional
  Planning and Foreign Aid*. Washington, D.C.: Brookings Institute,
  1963.
Robinson, R., ed. *International Cooperation in Aid*. Cambridge:
  Cambridge University Press, 1966.
Rodney, W. *How Europe Underdeveloped Africa*. Dar es Salaam:
  Tanzania Publishing House, 1972.
Ruhumbuka, Gabriel, ed. *Towards Ujamaa: Twenty Years of Tanu
  Leadership*. Nairobi: East African Literature Bureau, 1974.
Russell, Bertrand. *Roads to Freedom: Socialism, Anarchism and
  Syndicalism*. London: Unwin Books, 1966.
———— *Meaning of Marxism*. New York: Farrar and Rinehart, 1934.
Rweyemamu, J. *Underdevelopment and Industrialization in Tanzania*.
  Nairobi: Oxford University Press, 1973.
————; Loxley, J.; Wicker, J.; and Nyirabu, C. *Towards Socialist
  Planning*. Dar es Salaam: Tanzania Publishing House, 1974.
Sargent, Lyman. *New Left Thought: An Introduction*. Homewood: The
  Dorsey Press, 1972.
Saul, John. 'The State in Post-colonial Societies: Tanzania.' *Socialist
  Registrar*. Edited by Miliband and Savile. London: Merlin Press,
  1974.
Saul, J. S. and Cliffe, L., eds. *Socialism in Tanzania*. 2 vols. Nairobi:
  East African Publishing House, 1973.
Saul, J. 'Planning for Socialism in Tanzania: The Socio-Political
  Context.' *Towards Socialist Planning*. Edited by Rweyemamu and
  Loxley. Dar es Salaam: Tanzania Publishing House, 1972.
Scheckele, R. 'National Policies for Rural Development.' *Rural
  Development in a Changing World*. Edited by R. Weitz. M.I.T.
  Press, 1971.
Schumpeter, Joseph. *Capitalism, Socialism and Democracy*. London:
  George Allen and Unwin, 1961.
———— *The Theory of Economic Development*. Cambridge, Mass.:
  Harvard University Press, 1934.

Schurmann, Franz. *Ideology and Organization in Communist China.* Berkeley: University of California Press, 1970.

Seidman, A. *Comparative Development Strategies in East Africa.* Nairobi: East African Publishing House, 1972.

Sen, Amartya. *Choice of Techniques.* Oxford: Basil Blackwell, 1962.

Senghor, L. S. *African Socialism.* New York: American Society of African Culture, 1959.

Shaw, L. E., ed. *Modern Competing Ideologies.* Lexington: D. C. Heath and Company, 1973.

Shepherd, G. W. *Non-aligned Black Africa.* Lexington: Heath Lexington Books, 1970.

Shinmoon, R. *Self-Reliance and Independent National Economic Construction.* Peking: Foreign Language Press, 1963.

Shivji, Issa. *The Silent Class Struggle.* Dar es Salaam: Tanzania Publishing House, 1973.

———— *Class Struggles in Tanzania.* Dar es Salaam: Tanzania Publishing House, 1975.

————, ed. *Tourism and Socialist Development.* Dar es Salaam: Tanzania Publishing House, 1975.

Smith, Adam. *An Inquiry into the Nature and Causes of the Wealth of Nations.* New York: Random House, 1937.

Socialism, Democracy and Secularism: A Symposium in Memory of Jawaharlal Nehru. New Delhi: National Book Trust, 1965.

Svendsen, K. E. and Teisen, M., eds. *Self-Reliant Tanzania.* Dar es Salaam: Tanzania Publishing House, 1969.

Sweezy, Paul. *Socialism.* New York: McGraw-Hill, 1949.

Szentes, T. *The Political Economy of Underdevelopment.* Budapest: Akademiai Kiado, 1971.

The Election Study Committee, University of Dar es Salaam. *Socialism and Participation: Tanzania's 1970 National Elections.* Dar es Salaam: Tanzania Publishing House, 1974.

The Socialist Union. *Socialism: A Statement of Principles.* London: Lincolns-Praeger Publishers, 1952.

Thomas, C. *Dependence and Transformation.* New York: Monthly Review Press, 1974.

Tishler, H. S. *Self-Reliance and Social Security 1879–1917.* New York: Kennikat Press, 1971.

Toennies, Ferdinand. *Community and Society.* New York: Harper Torchbooks, 1963.

Tordorff, W. *Tanzania: Government and Politics.* Nairobi: East African Publishing House, 1967.

Touraine, Alain. *The Post Industrial Society.* New York: Random House, 1971.

Toure, Sekou. *Guinean Revolution and Social Progress.* Cairo: S.O.P. Press, 1968.

Townsend, James. *Political Participation in Communist China.* Berkeley: University of California Press, 1969.

Weber, Max. *The Theory of Social and Economic Organization.*

Translated by A. M. Henderson and Talcott Parsons. New York: The Free Press of Glencoe, 1947.

Weitz, R., ed. *Rural Development in a Changing World*. M.I.T. Press, 1971.

Wilczynski, J. *The Economics of Socialism*. London: George Allen and Unwin, 1972.

Wodis, J. *Africa: The Roots of Revolt*. London: Lawrence and Wishart, 1960.

————. *An Introduction to Neo-colonialism in Africa*. London: Lawrence and Wishart, 1967.

Yaffrey, M. *Balance of Payments Problems of a Developing Country: Tanzania*. Munich: Weltforum Verlag, 1970.

Articles

Ake, Claude. 'Explanatory Notes on the Political Economy of Africa.' *Journal of Modern African Studies*, Vol. 14, No. 1 (1976), 1–23.

Alavi, H. 'The State in Post-colonial Societies.' *New Left Review*, (1974), 59–81.

Amin, S. A. 'Underdevelopment and Dependence in Black Africa – Origins and Contemporary Forms.' *Journal of Modern African Studies*, X, 4 (1972).

Amin, S. 'Underpopulated Africa.' *Maji Maji*, No. 6 (June 1972)

Barkan, Joel. 'What Makes the East African Students Run.' *Transition*, VII, 37 (1968), 26–31.

Bowles, Samuel. 'Class Structure and Mass Education: The Beginnings of a Study of Social Structure and Educational Policy.' Department of Economics, Harvard University, March, 1970. (Mimeo).

Bruton, H. J. 'The Import Substituting Strategy of Economic Development: A Survey of Findings.' *Pakistan Development Review* (1970), 10–21.

Cameron, J. 'The Integration of Education in Tanzania.' *Comparative Education Review*, XI, 1 (February 1967), 38–56.

Carvalho, V. N. 'The Control of Managing Agents in Tanzanian Parastatal Organizations with Special Reference to the NDC.' *East African Law Review*, Vol. 5, Nos. 1 and 2 (1972).

Chenery, Hollis and Alan Strout. 'Foreign Assistance and Economic Development.' *American Economic Review*, Vol. LVI, No. 4 (Sept. 1966).

Clark, Edmund. 'Socialist Development and Public Investment in Tanzania 1964–73.' Ph.D. Dissertation, Harvard University, 1974.

Cohen, Michael. 'The Myth of the Expanding Centre: Politics in the Ivory Coast.' *Journal of Modern African Studies*, 11, 2 (1973), 227–246.

Connell, J. 'The Evolution of Tanzanian Rural Development.' *Tropical*

Geographer, Vol. 38, (1974), 7–18.

Coulson, A. 'Blood Sucking Contracts.' University of Dar es Salaam, 1972. (Mimeo).

———. 'The Fertilizer Factory.' *Maji Maji*, No. 8 (1972), 26.

Court, D. 'The Social Function of Formal Schooling in Tanzania.' *African Review*, Vol. 3, No. 4 (1973), 577–594.

Dodd, William A. 'Girls' Education in Tanganyika.' *African Women*, 1, 1 (December 1954), 10–13.

Donnithorne, Audrey. 'China's Cellular Economy: Some Economic Trends Since the Cultural Revolution.' *China Quarterly*, No. 52 (October/December 1972), 605–619.

Dos Santos, Theotonio. 'The Concept of Social Classes.' *Science and Society*, Vol. 34, No. 2 (1972), 166–193.

Fernando, Henrique Cardoso. 'Dependency and Development in Latin America.' *New Left Review*, 74, (July–August 1972), 83–95.

Finucane, R. 'Hierarchy and Participation in Development: A Case Study of Tanzania.' *African Review*, Vol. 2, No. 4 (1972), 573–595.

Gintis, Herbert. 'New Working Class and Revolutionary Youth.' *Socialist Revolution*, Vol. 1, No. 3 (May/June 1970).

Gitelson, S. A. 'How are Development Projects Selected: The Case of UNDP in Uganda and Tanzania.' *African Review*, Vol. 2, No. 2 (1972).

———. 'Multilateral Aid.' *East African Journal*, Vol. 8, No. 2 (1971)

Grundy, Kenneth. 'The "Class Struggle" in Africa: An Examination of Conflicting Theories.' *Journal of Modern African Studies*, 2, 3 (1964), 379–393.

Gurley, John. 'Maoist Economics.' *Monthly Review*, (February 1971).

Halpern. A. M. 'The Foreign Policy Uses of the Chinese Revolutionary Model.' *China Quarterly*, No. 7 (1961), 1–16.

Hazari, Bharat. 'Import Intensity of Consumption in India.' *Indian Economic Review*, Vol. 11, No. 2 (October 1967).

Hirji, K. F. 'School Education and Underdevelopment in Tanzania.' *Maji Maji*, No. 12 (1973).

Hirschman, A. O. 'The Political Economy of Import-Substitution.' *Quarterly Journal of Economics*, Vol. LXXXII, No. 1 (February 1968).

Home, Angus. 'The Primary Commodities Boom.' *New Left Review*, 81, (September–October 1973), 90–92.

Hughes, G. 'Socialist Development in Africa.' *Monthly Review*, Vol. 22 (May 1970).

Inkeles, A. 'Participant Citizenship in Six Developing Nations.' *APSR*, (January 1970).

Kalecki, J. 'Foreign Aid and Economic Development.' *Social Sciences*, (May 1966).

Kariok, J. N. 'Socialism in Africa: The Tanzanian Experience.' *Civilizations*, Vols. 13–14, 1/2 (1973–4), 31–46.

Kelin, D. W. 'Peking's Diplomats in Africa.' *Current Scene*. Vol. 2, No. 36 (1 July, 1964).

Kitching, Gavin N. 'The Concept of Class and the Study of Africa.'
   African Review, 2, 3 (1972), 327–350.
Kjekshus, Helge. 'The Elected Elite: A Socio-Economic Profile of
   Candidates in Tanzania's Parliamentary Election 1970.' The
   Scandinavian Institute of African Studies, *Research Report No. 29*
   (1975).
Kriesel, H. C. 'Agricultural Marketing in Tanzania, Background
   Research and Policy Proposals.' Michigan State University, Dept. of
   Agricultural Economics, (June 1970).
Laclau, Ernesto. 'Capitalism and Feudalism in Latin America.' *New
   Left Review*, 67, (May–June 1971), 1938.
Langdon, Steve. 'The Political Economy of Dependence: Notes
   Towards Analysis of MNC in Kenya.' *Journal of East African
   Research Development*, Vol. 4, No. 2 (1974), 123–159.
———. 'MNC's, Taste Transfer and Underdevelopment: A Case Study
   from Kenya.' *Review of African Political Economy*, No. 2 (1975),
   12–35.
Lema, A. A. 'Education for Self-Reliance: A brief survey of self-reliant
   activities in some Tanzanian schools and colleges.' University of Dar
   es Salaam, Institute of Education, 1972.
Loxley, J. and Saul, J. 'Multinationals, Workers and Parastatals.'
   RAPE, 2 (1975), 54–88.
Manson, Allan. 'Educating Our Children in Ujamaa Villages:
   Education for Ujamaa Living.' *Mbioni*, IV, 11 (May 1968), 26–34.
Mapolu, H. 'The Organization and Participation of Workers in
   Tanzania.' *African Review*, Vol. 2, No. 3 (1972), 381–415.
Mbilinyi, J. J. 'Attitudes, Expectations and the Decision to Educate in
   Rural Tanzania.' Dar es Salaam BRALUP Research Paper No. 3/1,
   (November 1973). (Mimeo.)
———. 'Education, Stratification and Sexism in Tanzania.' *African
   Review*, III, 2 (1973), 327–340.
———. 'The Problem of Unequal Access to Primary Education in
   Tanzania,' in Papers, Social Science Conference, 1973, University of
   Dar es Salaam. (Mimeo.)
McHenry, D. E. 'Tanzania: The Struggle for Development.' Ph.D.
   Dissertation, University of Dar es Salaam, 1971.
Mckinnon, Ronald. 'Foreign Exchange Constraints in Economic
   Development and Efficient Aid Allocation.' *Economic Journal*, Vol.
   LXXIV, (June 1964).
Mihyo, Pascal. 'The Workers Revolution in Tanzania.' *Maji Maji*, No.
   17 (August 1974).
Mmapachu, J. V. 'Operation Planned Villages in Rural Tanzania: A
   Revolutionary Strategy for Development.' *African Review*, Vol. 16,
   No. 1 (1976), 1–16.
Mramba, Basil and Mwansasu, Bismarck. 'Management for Socialist
   Development in Tanzania: The Case of the NDC in Tanzania.'
   African Review, Vol. 1, No. 3 (January 1972).
Muhl, G. Von der. 'Social Experiences and Political Socialization: A

Study of Tanzania Secondary Students.' *Comparative Political Studies*, (July 1970).

Nellis, J. 'A Note on the Policy-Programme Dichotomy.' *Rural Africana*, No. 4 (Winter 1968).

Newman, J. L. 'Hazards, Adjustments and Innovation in Mainland Tanzania.' *Rural Africana*, 19 (1973), 4–19.

Niblock, T. C. 'Aid and Foreign Policy in Tanzania 1961–1968.' Ph.D. Dissertation, University of Sussex, 1971.

Nsari, K. 'Tanzania: Neocolonialism and the Struggle for National Liberation.' *Review of African Political Economy*, No. 4 (1975), 109–18.

Nwabachili, C. C. 'Contradictions in Education in Tanzania.' Working Group 2/8 General No. 78, University of Dar es Salaam, Sociology Department, 1973. (Mimeo.)

Nyerere, J. K. 'Progress Comes with Production.' *African Review*, Vol. 3, No. 4 (1973), 519–540.

O'Brien, P. 'A Critique of Latin American Theories of Dependence.' Institute of Latin American Studies, University of Glasgow, March 1973. (Mimeo.)

Packard, P. C. 'Corporate Structure and Socialist Development in Tanzania.' Dar es Salaam, 1971. (Mimeo.)

Penrose, Edith. 'Some Problems of Policy in the Management of the Parastatal Sector in Tanzania: A Comment.' *African Review*, Vol. 1, No. 3 (January 1972).

Poulantzas, Nicos. 'On Social Classes.' *New Left Review*, No. 78 (March–April 1973), 27–54.

Prabhat, Patnaik. 'On the Political Economy of Underdevelopment.' *Economic and Political Weekly*, (February 1973).

Pratt, R. C. 'Foreign Policy Issues and the Emergence of Socialism in Tanzania 1961–68.' *International Journal*, (Summer 1975), 445–70.

Prewitt, K.; Muhl, G. Von der and Court, D. 'School Experiences and Political Socialization: A Study of Tanzanian Secondary School Students.' *Comparative Political Studies*, Vol. 3, No. 2 (July 1970), 203–225.

Pye, L. W. 'The Concept of Political Development.' *The Annals of the American Academy of Political and Social Science*, Vol. 358, (March 1965).

Paikes, P. K. 'Ujamaa and Rural Socialism' *Review of African Political Economy*, No. 3 (May–October 1975), 35–52.

———. 'Village Planning for Ujamaa.' *Taamuli*, Vol. 3, No. 1 (1972), 3–26.

Ransom, David. 'The Berkeley Mafia and the Indonesian Massacre.' *Rampart*, (October 1970).

Romnicianu, M. 'Management Agreements: Are They Really Necessary.' *Jenga*, No. 9 (1971), 28–31.

Rosberg, Carl. 'National Identity in African States.' *African Review*, Vol. 1, No. 1 (March 1971).

Rweyemamu, J. 'International Trade and Developing Countries.'

Uchumi, Vol. 1, No. 1 (1972).

Scalapino, R. 'Sino-Soviet Competition in Africa.' *Foreign Affairs*, 42 (1964), 640–654.

Schatten, F. 'Peking's Growing Influence in Africa.' *Swiss Review of World Affairs*, (August 1960), 8–11.

Seers, Dudley. 'What Types of Government Should Be Refused What Types of Aid.' *Bulletin*, Vol. 4, Nos. 2/3 (June 1972), 6–15.

————. 'The Role of Industry in Development: Some Fallacies.' *Journal of Modern African Studies*, (December 1963)

Shivji, Issa. 'Capitalism Unlimited: Public Corporations in Partnership with Multinational Corporation.' *African Review*, Vol. 3, No. 3 (1973), 359–382.

Slawecki, L. M. S. 'The Two Chinas in Africa.' *Foreign Affairs*, 41 (1963), 398–409.

Temu, P. E. 'The Employment of Foreign Consultants in Tanzania: Its Values and Limitations.' *African Review*, Vol. 3, No. 1 (1973), 69–84.

Teng, Shou. 'The Cultural Revolution and the Chinese Political System.' *China Quarterly*, No. 38 (April–June 1969), 63–91.

Thornton, T. P. 'Peking, Moscow and Underdeveloped Areas.' *World Politics*, XIII, No. 3 (1973), 15–25.

Voglin, A. 'Africa in Peking and Foreign Policy.' *International Affairs*, No. 9 (September 1965), 26–32.

Warren, Bill. 'Imperialism and Capitalist Industrialization.' *New Left Review*, 81, (September-October 1973), 3–44.

Wienhold, H. 'On Socialist Transformation of Agriculture.' Seminar Paper. University of Dar es Salaam, 1972. (Mimeo.)

Williams, Gavin. 'There is no Theory of Petit-Bourgeoisie Politics.' *Review of African Political Economy*, No. 6 (May–August 1976), 84–89.

Wilson, D. 'China's Relations with Africa.' *Race*, Vol. 5, No. 4 (1964), 61–71.

Winckler, Edwin. 'Political Management of the Development Process: Assessing the Chinese Development Experience.' *China Quarterly*, 54 (1973).

Yudelman, M. 'Agricultural Development in Tanzania.' Seminar on Foreign Aid and Rural Development in Tanzania. Government of Tanzania, 1970.

Zalla, T. 'Dairy Development in Tanzania.' Economic Research Bureau, University of Dar es Salaam, 1972.

Documents – Government Publications, Reports and Newspaper Articles

Crittenden, Ann. 'Apolitical American Consultants: Third World Uses Firms' Expertise.' *New York Times*, September 14, 1975.

Daily News, Dar es Salaam, Friday, March 15, 1974.

The Economic Survey 1970–71. Dar es Salaam: Government Printer, 1971.

Hutchinson, R. 'How U.K. Firm Exploited Tanzania.' *Daily News*, Dar es Salaam, July 26 and 27, 1973.

International Bank for Reconstruction and Development. *Economic Development of Tanganyika*. Johns Hopkins, 1960.

McKinsey Report by Christopher Walker in *Business Observer*, August 9, 1970.

Pearson, L. B. 'Partners in Development.' *Report of the Commission on International Development*. London: Pall Mall, 1969.

Rubin, E. 'Manpower and Aid.' *Problems of Foreign Aid: A Conference Report*. IPA Study No. 3, University College, Dar es Salaam, 1965.

Survey of the High and Middle Level Manpower Requirements and Resources. Dar es Salaam, 1969.

Tanzania. National Scientific Research Council. *The Young Child Study: Tanzania*. Dar es Salaam: UNICEF, October 1973.

Tanzania Second Five-Year Plan for Economic and Social Development. July 1, 1969–June 30, 1974.

Tanzania. *Tanzanian Government Report*, 1969/70.

World Bank Report, April, 1977.

INDEX

Note: only the more significant references to persons, organizations and places have been entered; in the absence of any mention in an entry of a specific geographical location the country referred to is Tanzania. Page numbers followed by a small n indicate footnotes.